(1 DISC, 1 BOOK)

Cheap and Easy
Internet Access

—Windows—

LIMITED WARRANTY AND DISCLAIMER OF LIABILITY

Cheap and Easy
Internet Access

-Windows-

Bob LeVitus • *Jeff Evans*

AP PROFESSIONAL

Boston   San Diego   New York
London   Sydney   Tokyo   Toronto

AP PROFESSIONAL is a division of Academic Press, Inc.

AP PROFESSIONAL

An Imprint of ACADEMIC PRESS, INC.
A Division of HARCOURT BRACE & COMPANY

ORDERS (USA and Canada): 1-800-3131-APP or APP@ACAD.COM
AP Professional Orders: 6277 Sea Harbor Dr., Orlando, FL 32821-9816

Europe/Middle East/Africa: 0-11-44 (0) 181-300-3322
Orders: AP Professional 24-28 Oval Rd., London NW1 7DX

Japan/Korea: 03-3234-3911-5
Orders: Harcourt Brace Japan, Inc., Ichibancho Central Building 22-1, Ichibancho Chiyoda-Ku, Tokyo 102

Australia: 02-517-8999
Orders: Harcourt Brace & Co. Australia, Locked Bag 16, Marrickville, NSW 2204 Australia

Other International: (407) 345-3800
AP Professional Orders: 6277 Sea Harbor Dr., Orlando FL 32821-9816

Editorial: 1300 Boylston St., Chestnut Hill, MA 02167 (617)232-0500

Web: http://www.apnet.com/approfessional

United Kingdom Edition published by
ACADEMIC PRESS LIMITED
24–28 Oval Road, London NW1 7DX

LeVitus, Bob.
      Cheap and Easy Internet Access for Windows / Bob LeVitus, Jeff Evans.
            p.   cm.
      ISBN 0-12-445597-2 (alk. paper)
      1. Internet (Computer network)   2. Microsoft Windows (Computer file)   I. Evans, Jeff, 1955–
TK5105.875.I57L485   1996
384.3'3—dc20   96-17240
                                                                                                                          CIP

Printed in the United States of America
96 97 98 99 IP   9 8 7 6 5 4 3 2 1

Contents

Introduction

So what's with the title? Why this book? How could we be so presumptuous as to assume that there needed to be yet another Internet-related book?

Do you want the truth? We took a look around the bookshelves of our local Barnes & Noble (and Book People, and Borders, and B. Dalton, and BookStop, and so on) and decided it was our duty to single-handedly squash the trend among writers and publishers to crank out 750-1000 page Internet tomes and call them starter kits and tour guides (sorry Adam and Michael). We felt it was time for a no-nonsense book that gets you going without trying to explain everything about everything about the Internet. One that doesn't fill countless pages with screen shots of World Wide Web home pages you could care less about. And one that saves you time, money, and effort in the bargain. We like to think of Cheap & Easy Internet Access as a kind of "Steal This Book" (Abbie Hoffman's epic '60s anarchist cookbook) for the net-surfing set.

Who Cheap & Easy Is For

It's for the penny-pincher in all of us. If you're a student with limited Internet access, or if you're just finishing college and about to lose your free Internet account, or if you're a bargain hunter who doesn't want to pay a premium for customer support you never get anyway, or you're just plain cheap, you probably want some cheap and easy Internet access. Which makes Cheap & Easy Internet Access (the book) perfect for you.

We're going to take you beyond how to get on the Internet and how to find and use Internet surfboards like Netscape and Eudora. We'll do that, of course, but our plan is to turn you into a raging beast of an Internet power user, able to sniff out bargains and discounts, saving money and time every time you connect.

This book is for anyone who wants to learn to connect to the Internet cheaply and easily, from rank beginners to experienced power users. We've tried our best not to overwhelm you with complicated instructions and useless information about how to configure software or learn UNIX commands that no one needs or uses anymore. (You'll have plenty of opportunities to waste time and get useless information once you're connected. If that appeals to you, there are several Web sites that specialize in providing the latest in everything under the sun, such as Yahoo's "Computers and the Internet" site at **http://www.**

yahoo.com/Computers_and_Internet/Internet/. You name it, you can get to it from there.)

Another point worth noting: Cheap & Easy Internet Access doesn't limit itself to a single service provider like many other books. We're provider agnostic. Rather than recommend one over another, we cover many of the major national Internet providers such as UUNET, PSI, and Netcom, plus offerings from CompuServe, America Online, and Prodigy. We also cover how (and why and when) to consider a local Internet service provider (ISP) as well as opening the door to the whole Internet bulletin board system (BBS) scene.

Beware, though, there will be trade-offs from time to time. For example, we might recommend that you choose an Internet provider who is a little more expensive but who distributes a killer connectivity package. Please trust us. Cheaper isn't always better. Our goal in this book is to help you figure out which service is best for you, then how to use it effectively and efficiently.

How to Get the Most out of Cheap & Easy

The first thing you need to do is choose an Internet provider. We're going to show you in Chapter 1 how it all works and who the players are. You need to know what to look for, what questions to ask, and what answers to expect. You need to know when it's better to use a major online service like America Online (AOL), CompuServe, or

Prodigy and when it really does make more sense to use a local mom-and-pop Internet provider in your neighborhood. You'll learn that and more in Chapter 1.

Getting connected and configuring your PC to surf the Net can be a real drag if you don't know what you're doing. Chapter 2 will walk you through this process, step by step. Luckily, many Internet providers are starting to make what used to be a nightmare a real no-brainer by including pre-configured software in their package, so it's easier these days than it used to be. We're going to give a quick lesson in what hardware and software you need to get up and running.

You need to know how to set up and surf the World Wide Web with a browser such as Netscape or WinWeb. You need to know how to use your browser to do file transfers and read newsgroups. You need to know how to do Internet e-mail with a program like Eudora, and you may need Telnet to log into the Internic to search for a domain name. And all of that is in Chapter 2. But here's the big secret: Those few things are all you really need to surf the net like a pro. Everything else is for geeks. By the end of Chapter 2, all your essential Internet software should be up and running smoothly.

Of course, if you're a geek like us, you'll find lots of other cool stuff at our WWW site:

`http://www.cheapandeasy.com`

where you can always find the latest versions of WS_FTP, EWAN Telnet, Trumpet Newsreader, and everything else under the sun. But remember what we just told you: You don't really need 'em.

We are big fans of simplicity. Take it from us. We've been using the Net big time for almost 2 years now. The last thing you need to be doing is messing around with 20 different apps, all with their own subtle nuances that make them just a little bit better at doing a particular task such as a file transfer. Forget it. You'll never see the light of day or moon at night, let alone find the time to check out anything useful or entertaining on the Net. You'll be forever configuring and downloading the latest versions of everything. Relax. We're professionals. You can trust us. It's up to sick puppies like us to try everything and bang around on every piece of software and preference settings there is and then let you know what's best. We want you to have a life. We want you to have fun. We bear the pain so you don't have to. So the easy way is always going to be to follow our advice.

Chapter 3 tells you how to shop for the best deal. We'll show you some great sources for pricing information and teach you how to compare apples to apples. And in the best "Steal This Book" tradition, we'll tell you who to call to try to hustle free access, how to get a better deal, how increase the monthly base time allowance that most Internet providers offer without paying more, and much more. You'll also get some tips on how you can learn who is the best provider in your area. Finally, we'll teach you what questions to ask and what gimmicks to watch out for.

Speaking of fun. You're going to love Chapter 4: "Great Deals on the Net." We cruised around and found some fantastic sites for you to check out for incredibly great deals. You name it, you can get it wholesale on the Net. T-shirts, wine, flowers, hardware, software, shrubs, and vintage guitars—it's all out there. You just gotta know where to look. That's what Chapter 4 is all about—where to go if you're looking for deals.

Finally, you'll find some great appendices at the back of Cheap & Easy. OK, so there's a glossary as in everyones computer book, but the rest of our appendices—Internet Service Providers; FreeNets; Mailing Lists, Newsgroups WWW and FTP Sites; Internet BBSs; Zines, Rags, & Online Buys—are extremely useful and designed to make your life on the Internet easier.

Our Promise to You

We promise to make you self-sufficient. That's the name of the game. It takes a little time and patience to filter through all the hype, tools, and options and start using the Internet effectively, but that's what this book is all about. Stick with us and you'll soon be surfing with total impunity.

Cheap & Easy Internet Access is about trying stuff out, having fun, and learning to use the Net. It's also about doing it better, or cheaper, or easier. We promise all of that, plus where to get everything you'll ever need to surf the net (most of it is on the CD-ROM that comes with the book) and how to get connected to the Internet itself.

Thanks for deciding to buy our book and spend a little time with us—and for bearing with our jokes and irreverent style. At the end of the day we hope you'll be as wide-eyed and enthusiastic as we are about the Internet. And believe us, you're going to have a blast as soon as you get jacked in and pointed in the right direction.

So have at it. And while you're out there, don't forget to visit the Cheap & Easy WWW site at:

http://www.cheapandeasy.com

One last thing—please send us your feedback on this book and our Web site. We care. Here are our e-mail addresses:

Bob LeVitus: levitus@powercc.com

Jeff Evans: jevans@versa.com

chapter 1

Internet Service Providers (ISPs)

What Every PC Nethead Needs to Know about Who's Zoomin' Who

The first question we always get when we speak to user groups or friends about the Internet is: "Where do I start? I don't have a clue." Well settle in—this book's for you. It's not like you were born with the knowledge or can cognize it by reading your genetic code with some ancient technique of meditation or something. We tried that and all we got was a headache. The fact is, most people aren't on the Internet yet. Most aren't even online with a service like America Online, CompuServe, or Prodigy. Many don't have a modem, let alone know where to plug it in.

We've heard of studies indicating that only 1–2% of all computer users had access to the Internet. It's not like Internet access is ubiquitous or anything. Yet. It is the case, however, that about 30% of all people who have computers have a modem. And sooner or later some of them are going to figure out where to plug it in and how to turn it on. The point we're making is that while it may seem that everyone is "jacked in to the Internet" except you, that's hardly the case. Since it's only a matter of time, though, there's no time like now. So hang tough—you'll be jacked in soon.

A Brief Aside About Demographics and Statistics

By the way, if you ever want more information about the Internet's demographics or statistics, we're big fans of a couple of sites on the Net. The first is updated regularly by the Georgia Tech Research Corporation. Once we show you how to use your WWW software in Chapter 2 you can visit it at:

```
http://www.cc.gatech.edu/gvu/user_surveys/User_Surv
ey_Home.html
```

Hey! We're off to a good start. It's free. You can't beat that! And, other than the fact that that's a tough address to type, it was pretty easy, too. Think of this as the beginning of a beautiful tradition of cheap and easy. (We make it even easier—the CD-ROM that accompanies this book includes a special file called "cheesy.html" that you can use with Netscape to quickly get to every site mentioned in the book.)

There are a couple of other sites that publish Internet demographics—kind of. One we like a lot is by O'Reilly & Associates and Trish Information Services. You can find it at:

`http://www.ora.com/survey/`

What you get for free at this site is a succinct executive summary with some nice pie and bar charts. (The surveys themselves cost a boatload and are the kind of things advertising agencies and big corporate muckity-mucks salivate over.)

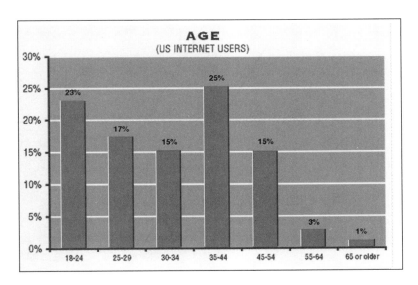

Figure 1.1: Average age of U.S. Internet users. Source, O'Reilly & Associates, 10/1/95.

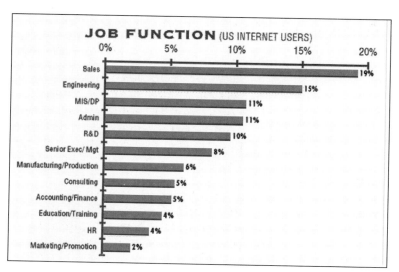

Figure 1.2: Job types of U.S. Internet users. Source, O'Reilly & Associates, 10/1/95.

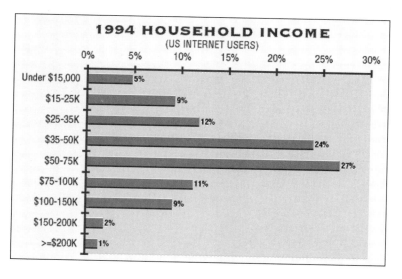

Figure 1.3: Income of U.S. Internet users. Source, O'Reilly & Associates, 10/1/95.

Where to Start

There are two paths to choose from when you decide to become a denizen of the Internet. One is get your connection from a commercial online service like AOL, CompuServe, or Prodigy. The other is to go with a straight Internet service provider (ISP) such as Netcom, PSI, or UUNet.

Let's take a look at what each of them has to offer. Keep in mind that a lot of what follows—especially pricing—will be out of date later this afternoon. That's why we provide phone numbers and e-mail addresses for the six services. If you're really serious about getting service as cheaply as possible, you need to contact each of the about-to-be-mentioned services for its current pricing (and software offerings and even, perhaps, support policies). Really. It changes almost daily.

Commercial Online Services

America Online

8619 Westwood Center Dr.
Vienna, VA 22182
800.827.6364
FAX 703.448.0760
info@aol.com
www.aol.com

America Online, Inc., based in Vienna, VA, is one of the nation's fastest-growing providers of online services, offering services such as e-mail, conferencing, software, and computer support to over 4 million members at affordable rates. For $9.95 per month for 5 hours of use ($2.95 per hour for each additional hour) and no setup fee America Online (AOL) is currently among the least expensive Internet solutions.

AOL offers 28.8Kbps maximum dial-up connectivity and 166 POPs (points of presence) nationwide. All cities offer connectivity at 14.4Kbps, with 9.6Kbps also available. AOL users have the option of connecting via TCP/IP only through SprintNet but not directly.

The standard suite of Internet tools is available on AOL, including Archie, FTP, Gopher, Telnet, and Usenet. The Usenet reader now accesses more than 20,000 groups. AOL offers the ability for users to download selected groups for offline reading, a feature absent in all other commercial online services. Search functions such as Veronica (gopher sites), Archie (FTP sites), and DejaNews (Usenet newsgroups) are straightforward and intuitive, enabling easy searching of other Internet resources. There are plenty of forums on which to discuss and find out more about the Internet.

AOL includes a basic but functional browser to access the World Wide Web. AOL's browser is currently HTML 2.0 compliant, with plans to support HTML 3.0 in the near future. It offers the standard browser functions such as back, forward, home, reload, images, stop, and the ability to build a list of favorite places. Currently, AOL members do not have the capability to store individually created Web pages on AOL's server.

AOL GROWING PAINS

AOL is well known for sporadic service to some customers. They are experiencing growing pains, with frequent "service too busy to complete that request" messages and occasional difficulty maintaining a connection. Bob connects via a 28.8 Global Village Platinum modem to seven different services including AOL. His AOL connection is easily the most troublesome.

That said, AOL is probably the least expensive way to get on the Internet. And though service can sometimes be spotty, when it's good, it's pretty good. Hopefully, it'll be better by the time you read this.

If you can make a reliable connection, AOL is a good choice. Its non-Internet (sometimes called "proprietary") content is broad and deep, its discussion boards are lively, its chat rooms are legendary, and its client software package—all free—is mostly intuitive. You can't beat it for $10 a month.

CompuServe Information Service

5000 Arlington Centre Blvd.
PO Box 20212
Columbus, OH 43220
800.848.8199
70006.101@ compuserve.com
www.compuserve.com

CompuServe Information Service, while being known for its online services before the Internet boomed, has regrettably less to offer than America Online or Prodigy in terms of customer service and Internet access. However, members can enjoy full, uncencored access to FTP, Telnet, Usenet, and the World Wide Web more at competitive prices. CompuServe offers either a basic rate of $9.95 per month for 5 hours of basic service or a better rate which includes unlimited services plus 20 hours of Internet use for $24.95 per month ($1.95 per hour thereafter) through the Internet Club.

CompuServe offers dial-up access speeds of 9.6Kbps, 14.4Kbps, and 28.8Kbps worldwide in addition to direct PPP access to the Internet. There are currently 420 POP (points of presence), but 14.4Kbps connectivity is available in only 300 cities and 16 cities offer 28.8Kpbs.

CompuServe's host of Internet tools include FTP, Gopher, Telnet, and e-mail as well as their own browser, NetLauncher (Mosaic based). NetLauncher allows members to set up hotlists or browse through the numerous stored pages. Other conveniences include the ability to scroll through documents as they load and to view the status of each document in a status bar at the bottom of the page. However, the user must launch a separate session to use the browser, therefore missing out on the integrated feel of AOL or Prodigy. CompuServe is rumored to be working on integration of their proprietary content and content on the Web, which could change things considerably. Before making any decision, ask about CIM 3.0, the client tool rumored to contain many new Internet features.

CompuServe's Web site (www.compuserve.com) has an Internet searching mechanism which allows the user to search by keyword over 50 different engines. Currently, CompuServe members do not have the capability to store individually created Web pages on CompuServe's server.

Prodigy

445 Hamilton Ave.
White Plains, NY 10601
914.448.8000
freetrial@ prodigy.com
www.prodigy. com

Prodigy offers its members competitive rates for relatively reliable access at $9.95 per month for 5 hours of use ($2.95 per hour thereafter). Also offered is Prodigy's new 30/30 plan, which costs $29.95 per month for 30 hours of usage and $1.00 per hour for Internet access. Additional hours are again $2.95 each. Both 9.6Kbps and 14.4Kbps access are available, with 28.8 making an appearance in 10 cities so far.

Prodigy leads the commercial online services in World Wide Web access with a Web browser, which remains an easily accessible, affordable onramp to the Internet. It is integrated into the service; however, the browser and the online service cannot be used simultaneously.

Prodigy's Internet access focuses on the World Wide Web, integrating Gopher and FTP into the browser instead of keeping them separate (as AOL and CompuServe do). Extensive assistance is available on the World Wide Web through tutorials and tours and links to popular search engines such as Lycos, Web Crawler, and Yahoo. Parental control features include alerts that go off when the browser leaves the predefined list of pages. As a valuable feature, Prodigy provides ready-made fill-in-the-blank templates for quick and easy creation of personal Web pages, which can be stored on its servers at no extra charge. This is definitely the easiest, cheapest way to put your (albeit limited) page on the Web.

National Internet Service Providers

NetCom Internet Services

3031 Tisch Way,
San Jose, CA 95128
800.353.5600
FAX 408.556.31853
info@netcom.com
www.netcom.com

NetCom Internet service is fully scalable, from simple dial-up access to high-speed dedicated data lines. A personal dial-up account for individuals includes full Internet services such as the WWW, FTP, Telnet, Usenet, and e-mail.

New users who are eager to get online but still need a little help doing so will find NetCom's approach most gratifying. The tools that NetCom distributes to accomplish that goal include NetCruiser, which is a graphical user interface intended to open the Internet to a new generation of computer users. Its simple point-and-click interface allows new users to roam the vast, worldwide Internet without knowing a single UNIX command.

NetCruiser is easy to install and allows users to connect to and cruise the Internet in a matter of minutes. NetCruiser includes tools that allow users to connect to Usenet news and to send and receive e-mail by simply clicking icons and selecting options from pull-down menus. NetCruiser also supports the two major Internet browsing tools, World Wide Web and Gopher, as well as Telnet for remote access and FTP for file transfer.

Best of all, NETCOM claims to deliver complete Internet access solutions for the lowest individual and commercial usage costs in the industry. So go ahead—make 'em live up to it!

NETCOM's extensive network around the United States includes over 200 POPs. Though some NetCom users complain about slow e-mail transmission rates and peak time inaccessibility, NetCom is a hard deal to beat.

InterRamp/PSI

510 Huntmar Park Dr.
Herndon, VA 22070
800.774.0852
800.450.4200
`interramp-info@psi.com`
`www.psi.net`

PSI brings the newbie as well as the seasoned Internet user flexible, high-speed access with AOL-esque ease of use. With plans to reach over 200 POPs, InterRamp provides a simple, inexpensive way to access the power of full TCP/IP access, 28.8Kbps dial-up speed, or ISDN using software that the user is free to choose. InterRamp provides native support of TCP/IP applications and software, unlike the commercial online services' limited Internet access.

PSI does have a service similar to the commercial online services—kind of—called "PipeLine USA" that offers competitive rates of service and connectivity at $19.95 per month for unlimited use. Alternatively, InterRamp's full-fledged TCP/IP service goes for $9.00 for 9 hours or $29.00 for 29 hours ($1.50 per hour thereafter). Go with the full-fledged TCP/IP service. We think it's a better deal and you'll get up the full-bore Internet learning curve faster.

InterRamp works with anything that will run over a TCP/IP connection including Finger, FTP, Gopher, IRC, PING, and Telnet. And InterRamps's free trial is really free: they provide a 7-day, no obligation account which expires at the end of the trial period with no strings attached if you don't dig it.

PSI provides basic but not spectacular tools to help the user take advantage of the latest Internet applications such as the World Wide Web, Gopher, and WAIS. In order to access these tools, PSI provides each user with a PPP dialup access to the Internet, an e-mail account, an unlimited Usenet account, and access to the InterRamp users home page.

AlterDial/UUNet

3060 Williams Dr.
Fairfax, VA 22031-4648
800.488.6384
703.206.5601
`info@uu.net`
`www.uu.net`

UUNet brings reliability and sound service to users who know what they want and are not intimidated by the technology requirements of setting up their own software. AlterDial offers excellent connectivity and a superb software package, NetManage's Internet Chameleon for Windows, which includes FTP, Gopher, e-mail, Usenet News, and WWW software.

New Internet users should be wary of jumping into an account with UUNet based on the lack of coddling the company provides to subscribers. The price structure is a bit higher than that of the competition, with a $25.00 setup fee and $30.00 per month for 25 hours ($2.00 per hour thereafter). The trade-off is reliability in connectivity: users have less use for customer service when the service is reliable. Every AlterDial POP provides 28.8Kbps and ISDN connectivity and will intervene in the users' efforts to establish ISDN with their phone company.

For businesses, UUNet's AlterNet is the way to go: they specialize in leased-line connections for businesses which require full-time access. AlterNet's direct TCP/IP access allows users to choose TCP and Net applications other than what's provided in the Internet Chameleon package.

Customer support again works best for the seasoned Internet user; however, basic connectivity customer service is available 24 hours per day.

Comparison Charts

Commercial Online Services

	America Online	CompuServe Information Service	Prodigy
Address	8619 Westwood Center Dr. Vienna, VA 22182	5000 Arlington Centre Blvd. PO Box 20212 Columbus, OH 43220	445 Hamilton Ave., White Plains, NY 10601
Phone	800.827.6364	800.848.8199	914.448.8000
Fax	703.448.0760	N/A	N/A
E-mail	info@aol.com	70006.101@compuserve.com	freetrial@prodigy.com
URL	www.aol.com	www.compuserve.com	www.prodigy.com
Tech support hours	24 hours, 7 days	7am-2am M-F, 12am-10pm Sa-Su	24 hours, 7 days
Max speed	28.8Kbps	28.8Kbps	28.8Kbps

	America Online	CompuServe Information Service	Prodigy
POP	166	420	325
ISDN	ø	ø	4
28.8Kbps	166	16 cities	10
14.4Kbps	All	300 cities	All
9.6Kbps	√	√	√
Dial-up	√	√	√
TCP/IP	ø	√	ø
800-number access	√	√	√
Software	America Online	NetLauncher	Prodigy
Standard TCP/IP stack	√	√	ø
Setup	None	None	None
Per month	$9.95	$9.95(basic)	$9.95
Hour limit	5	5	5
Per hour	$2.95	$2.95 (basic)	$2.95

National Internet Service Providers (ISPs)

	NetCom Internet Services	InterRamp/PSI	AlterDial/UUNet
Address	3031 Tisch Way San Jose, CA 95128	510 Huntmar Park Dr. Herndon, VA 22070	3060 Williams Dr. Fairfax, VA 22031-4648
Phone	800.353.6600	800.827.7482	800.488.6384
Fax	408.556.31853	800.450.4200	703.206.5601
E-mail	info@netcom.com	interramp-info@psi.com	info@uu.net
URL	www.netcom.com	www.psi.net	www.uu.net
Tech support hours	24 hours, 7 days	24 hours, 7 days	24 hours, 7 days
Max speed	28.8Kbps	28.8Kbps	28.8Kbps
Points of presence (est)	200	150	100
ISDN	6	150	All
28.8Kbps	All	75	All
14.4Kbps	All	150	All
9.6Kbps	All	150	All
Dial-up	√	√	√
TCP/IP	√	√	√
800-number access	√	ø	√
Software	NetCom NetCruiser	Internet Valet	Internet in a Box
Standard TCP/IP stack	√	√	√

	NetCom Internet Services	InterRamp/PSI	AlterDial/UUNet
Setup	$25	$9.00-$50.00`	$25
Monthly	$19.95	$29	$30
Hour limit	40	29	25
Per hour	$2	$1.5	$2

So What Do I Do Already?

On the surface, the basic difference between the commercial online service and the Internet over the last few years has been that the online services have had ease of use, abundant content, and local phone call access from almost anywhere in the world. Just under the surface is the fact that they are big private telecommunications networks that have poured tons of money into infrastructure that is now being short-circuited by the Internet itself.

Until Internet publishing via the World Wide Web came along, the Internet never pretended to be anything other than a big network of computers used by nerds. The Net was (and still is) a big, organic anarchy of networks linked together by the common protocols of the UNIX operating system on which it is based and has its origins. People, researchers, and companies sent files and e-mail across it and shared info with each other electronically. Content for public consumption was never much the issue until recently. But now it's a REALLY BIG DEAL. In other words, hypertext and the World Wide Web really upset the whole enchilada.

And so today the line between traditional online services and the Internet is becoming increasingly blurred. Local number access to the Internet is becoming the norm for ISPs (ISPs aren't stupid), while online services in turn are starting to convert their huge telecommunications network toward providing direct access to the Internet.

With the advent of the WWW as a vehicle for publishing content for public consumption and internal corporate use, the die is cast. You can see the truth of this in the fact that Microsoft and Apple basically decided to blow off Microsoft Network and E-World as private online systems and to make their services Internet based using the World Wide Web. And America Online, CompuServe, and Prodigy better figure out how to fit in and fully integrate the Internet with the best netsurfin' software available or they will disappear like dinosaurs.

The power of the press belongs to those who own the presses, and the Web gives that power to almost anyone with an interest. Many people who in the past have developed content for the private online systems and who have thousands and thousands of visitors to their online forums on CompuServe, AOL, and Prodigy are starting to think: "Hey, wait a minute. I can go buy Bob and Jeff's WebMaster Windows book, set up a Web site, and do this myself." It's like the desktop publishing revolution all over again.

But we digress from the point. That is, unless you have a specific need for some content that exists only on one of the commercial online services, there is no reason to do anything other than get a full-blown Internet account. Given the tremendous amount of cool stuff on the Internet, it's hard to believe that you won't be able to find almost anything you need there. Plus, an ISP lets you choose your own weapons, which means you can use better tools if you know of them; CompuServe, AOL, and Prodigy pretty much sentence you to the software they provide.

Things used to be worse. Much worse. In the old days, all service providers provided was a temporary password and a phone number. It took the Internet geeks a while to figure out that the average person doesn't care about or want to configure complicated software, much less figure out what we need and download it from somewhere. (Where's the logic there?) We want to get on with the work. Or fun. We're Power Users users, for gosh sake! But it's only recently that Internet providers have started to offer simple software installers that make life easy. All three of the afore-mentioned ISPs do. You just turn on your modem, double-click on a icon, and blammo, you're connected to the Internet and 20–30 million other people.

The bottom line: probably the only reason we can think of to go with a commercial online service as your Internet access provider is that none of the ISPs have a local access number where you live. Unless you really and truly want features like chat rooms (AOL), threaded message forums and surcharged databases (CompuServe), or the thrill of doing business with Sears and IBM (Prodigy), ISPs are the better way to connect to the Internet.

The BBS World

There's a whole other world of online systems that you may have heard of called bulletin board systems, or BBBs for short. Austin, Texas alone has over 200 of them.

A BBS is usually an online system with a few modem lines and content that is of specific interest to the subscriber. There are environmental ones, entertainment ones, PC user groups, etc. They tend to be very inexpensive at the cost of busy phone lines, little customer support, and limited content. But check them out sometime.

There are many excellent BBSs. There are some really good ones accessible directly from the Internet. We think the best ones are those that run on FirstClass software. They tend to have the best user interface and are the easiest to use and find your way around.

There are others. We like FirstClass.

There is a list of FirstClass systems and other BBSs accessible via the Internet in Appendix D. We've included some instructions to help you get started. The software you need to connect to a FirstClass system is included on the CD-ROM that came with Cheap & Easy.

We probably won't get to talk much more about BBSs, but we wanted you to have a glimpse into another fascinating microcosm of the Internet.

To Surf and Provide: The Internet Service Provider Story

We're not ever going into business as Internet providers—there is just not enough money in the world. But it's useful to know a little about what their business is all about and how it works, when it comes to choosing a service provider for your own account. So now that we've made the case for why you should use an ISP and not a commercial online service for your Internet connection, here's how to choose the right one for you.

Competition among all the Internet providers is a boon for the rest of us to enjoy. It means cheaper access and better service. The trick is to figure out what you need to know to pick the right one for you. There might be one in your area charging only $5 a month for unlimited access. Sounds great, but they may not be in business next month. Or you may spend hours and hours trying to get their modem to work with your modem. Or worse, constant busy signals. Some small, local Internet providers have stared raising their rates for these very reasons. Watch out for that when you shop. Ask about rate protection.

We're busy. If it were us we'd pay a little extra for the peace of mind of knowing that a big national Internet provider is more likely to be around longer. And provide some level of support for what they sell. But before you can intelligently choose an Internet provider, there are some questions you need to ask and answers you need to hear. Just because you see an Internet provider's ad plastered in every magazine and newspaper in town doesn't mean they're any good. In fact, beware of most Internet service companies that make a lot of marketing noise—especially a local or regional provider. They often lack the technical expertise to run the show. We guess they figure that's something they can always add after they get all those eager new customers.

Not.

Running an Internet service business is no small task. It requires a lot of UNIX and system administrator expertise to keep it up and running smoothly.

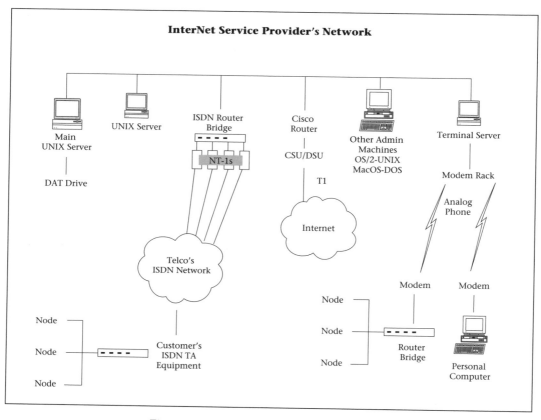

Figure 1.4: Internet site layout. Tomorrow's Technologies, Austin, TX, January 1996.

Top 10 Questions to Ask an ISP—OK, So It's Not Exactly 10

With the help of our friends who run an Internet training business called Learning Curve, we've put together the important questions to ask when choosing an Internet service provider (ISP). They've got great training programs for all levels of expertise, and after we teach you how to get you e-mail up and running you can send an e-mail to them at info@learningcurve.com for details.

Some of these questions will make more sense once you know what they mean by the time you finish Chapter 2. It's kind of a chicken-and-egg thing. You just have to trust us that these are the questions and answers you need to deal with.

Yeah, it's kind of a bummer that you can't start at the beginning of something and go step by step. But you need to get an Internet account before you can connect to an Internet account. And in order to connect smoothly to an Internet provider you need to have a provider whose setup lets that all happen smoothly.

Relax. It isn't a test. At least not for you…. We're going to give you the answers you should be listening for too.

Access Questions

1. Do you support SLIP, PPP, or both?

    You want both or PPP. PPP is better. We'll tell you why in Chapter 2.

2. What is the speed of your connection to the Internet (full T1, fractional T1, or ISDN)?

    Faster is better. Full T1 fastest, ISDN slowest.

3. Do you offer "full Internet access?"(That is, Internet e-mail and full access to Internet services including the Web.)

The answer to this needs to be an unequivocal yes.

4. What speed of modems do you have? 14.4Kbps? 28.8Kbps? Or a mix? If it's a mix, which ones am I more likely to hit, or do you have separate phone numbers for each speed? Is the cost different?

   You'll find that 28.8 is getting more common and indicates a provider who has the beans to afford better equipment and invest in the future. You should not pay extra for 28.8.

   (None of the above matters, of course, if you're using a 14.4 or slower modem. If so, we recommend strongly a 28.8, which we consider the bare minimum for enjoyable Web surfing.)

5. Does the account come with the ability to put my own WWW page on the Internet. If so, what are the limits?

   If you never plan to have your own Web page, of course, this question doesn't matter. But if you do, we suggest you buy our book WebMaster Windows (subtle plug, eh?), which teaches you everything you need to know to set up your own WWW site. One of the things you'll learn is that it sometimes makes more sense to park your pages at your provider's site. It's nice to know in advance that they can do it and what they charge.

6. Do you register domain names for personal users/business users?

   If you want a personal or business e-mail address like jevans@evans.com or bob@levitus.com instead of the one you get from your Internet provider (j7t8@mailpop.is.net or jeff@outer.net), you need domain name. It's easier to have your Internet provider apply for it than do it yourself. It's going to cost you $50–$200/year, depending on your

Internet provider, to register and keep your domain name active. It used to be free if you did it yourself. Not any more. Bummer, huh.

Support Questions:

7. Do you have a "no busy signals" policy?

    This means they have figured out the math of how many modems per user they need to keep customers satisfied. See what they'll promise.

8. Do you have tech support personnel versed in my platform (Windows)?

    If they are UNIX heads who have an attitude about beginners and only answer what you ask without pointing out everything else you need to know, find a different provider.

9. Is documentation included?

    Good documentation is a must even with everything you're going to learn in this book. And do all of us a favor and read it.

10. How is tech support available? (Telephone? E-mail?) During what hours?

    Telephone is best. If you can't make a connection, e-mail is a problem. Try to suss out if the tech support is going to be friendly. Ask for a referral and talk to someone else who uses them. Better still, call tech support yourself prior to making a commitment. See how long it takes them to answer. See if they can answer one of the above questions.

It's a real drag when your Internet provider's customer support staff have an attitude and you have a problem you need help with. Better you should try it before you buy.

Cost Questions

11. Do you have a monthly rate, or do you charge by the hour? If there is a monthly rate, what are the limits and the charges for overtime?

12. Are there any "prime time" charges?

13. Is there a "setup" fee? What do you get in return besides an account? What exactly is the "free" software you provide?

14. Is there a free evaluation period?

    The answers you get to the cost questions above will help you compare apples to apples.

Landed on the Beach and Bummin'

So, now that you have a notion of the lay of the land, pick an Internet service provider. Choose one with local number access. If you travel a lot, find one who has an 800 number or one with lots of local number access points all over the country. Believe us, you want to be able to jack into the Net when you are on the road or visiting your parents. As soon as they realize you are an "expert" you can forget about playing golf, going to the beach, or just hanging out at their place on a beautiful day in Florida. You'll be loading the Jeopardy and Wheel of Fortune games on a new Pentium laptop they had you pick out for them. You want to be able to visit the WWW site at **http://www.man-i-wish-had-one.com** and get some solace.

Seriously, shop around. Ask the questions. Pay attention to the answers. Start with one of the providers included with Cheap & Easy from the list in Appendix B that we struck a deal with for you. Or try one of your local service providers if you like. But go ahead. Be brave and crash right into this stuff. Get an account and get started. Take advantage of free trial periods. That's what they're for.

If you'd rather keep reading or if you're waiting for your modem to arrive, read on. In the next chapter we're going to cover how to get your hardware and software up and running so you can get connected.

Parting Advice on Modems: Faster Is Better

You have a modem already, right? If you don't, or you have an older, slower one, pick up the phone and call any decent mail-order place (pick up any computer magazine) and get yourself a 28.8 modem. Or check out the next chapter, which starts off with a list of great places you can nab a 28.8 modem for about $225.00.

"28.8" refers to the speed of the modem in baud, and 28.8 pretty much pushes the envelope as far as modems goes. If you want faster than that, you need ISDN, which requires special phone lines and adapters.

It's hard to even find a 14.4 modem anymore, not that you'd want one. You want 28.8 for the Net. It used to be you could just deal with hankering after more RAM or a bigger hard drive. These days you also need to hanker after a fast net connection. Speed is king. That old 300 or 2400 baud modem you have is history. Don't even think about it. Though it's possible, you'll hate using anything slower than 28.8 on the Web. And we're not being snobby, we're just saying the way it is. Slow modems suck on the Net. Order your fast new modem by midnight tonight and it will arrive tomorrow. (If you have a modem and network connection already, you can order a fast modem from an online vendor like Cyberian Outpost at **http://cybout. com**.) Hey, why schlepp all the way across town?

chapter

2

How to get WIRED!

Some Assembly Required—Batteries Not Included (and some of the parts are missing as well)

To get connected to the infinite and ever-expanding world of the Internet you need only a few things: a computer, a modem, a phone line, an account with an ISP, connection software, a list of all the configuration parameters, and the time to set it all up. Well, we guess that's more than a few, but don't despair. It looks worse than it really is. These days it's relatively easy to get a solid Internet connection up and running. Let's take a look at what you need to get started.

What You Need to Do It on Your Own

Hardware: Get the Lead Out

The most important part of accessing the Internet is your computer. Although you can use any computer that will run Windows (yes, this is one of those books), the only way to get satisfactory use out of the Internet is to have a good quality system. Our recommendations for an Internet-worthy system include: a 28.8 modem, 16550 serial ports, 16MB RAM, 486 DX2/66 CPU, 100+MB of free hard drive space, a 256-color (or better) monitor, and a mouse. It should be obvious that this short list does not constitute a complete computer system; these are only the components which will significantly speed up (or without them, slow down) your Internet activities. This list is a non-negotiable minimum for a machine used to access the Internet. If you compromise on any of these, your ability to access and enjoy the Internet may be severely hampered. In fact, don't even bother, you'll hate it.

We would love to show you how to install, set up, and configure every aspect of your computer, but that's not what this book is about. We want to talk about getting on the Internet and exploiting its resources at the least possible cost in time and money. So if you have trouble installing a hardware product, consult the store where you bought it, the manufacturer, or one of the many computer set up books on the market.

In the next few sections of this book, we'll take a closer look at each of our recommended/required minimum components.

Modems

Even if you own the most powerful computer in the universe and all the software ever written, you still can't use the Internet without a connection to it. Usually the connection takes place over telephone lines with a modem. A modem is a device which converts digital computer information into an analog signal, and transmits the signal to a receiving modem, which in turn decodes the analog signal back to digital, sending it to the computer to which it's attached. Due to the high volume of information that any Internet user will transfer to and from the Internet, a 28.8 v.34 modem is strongly recommended to save time. A 28.8 modem allows transfers up to 115200 bps—which is about the maximum a nondigital phone line can transmit with consistent accuracy. We also recommend external modems for two reasons. First, external modems are not susceptible to internal device interrupt request (IRQ) and I/O address conflicts, thus making installation much easier. Second, external modems have eight cute blinking lights which not only serve as cheap entertainment on rainy days but also inform you at a glance about the status of the connection and current transmission activities.

Serial Ports

The serial ports on your computer are the portals through which data is transmitted. Your external modem is connected to a serial port; internal modems have a serial port built into the hardware. Either way, the speed of the serial port used by the modem is significant. The 16500 UART serial ports are designed for high-speed data transmission and lend themselves nicely to modem communications. Any serial port that is slower than a 16550 will have noticeable negative effects on a modem's transmission speed. The easiest way to check your serial port's UART chip set is to run MSD.EXE (the Microsoft Diagnostic utility which is packaged with DOS and Windows). In MSD, selecting "COM Ports…" will display information about your serial ports. If you do not have a 16550 UART serial port, take a trip down to your local computer store and spend the $35 or so to get one.

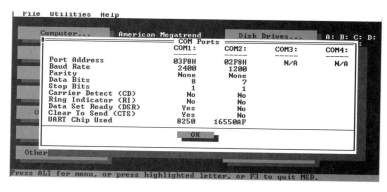

Figure 2.1: Microsoft Diagnostic utility—COM Port… display.

Faster than Lightning

You should also note that there are some newer, faster serial port chips in development and some are even already in stores. With speeds 2 to 10 times that of a 16550 UART, these new ports will be able to offer even faster data transmission but at a significantly greater price. If you can afford the faster ports—and can justify their purchase—you should take the plunge.

RAM

After a high-speed serial port, the next important feature of your computer is the memory or RAM. RAM is king. RAM is where the computer stores information before and after the CPU uses it. RAM is 10 to 1000 times faster than a hard drive, so by having enough memory you can reduce disk access and speed up your computer's response time. The Windows 95 operating system (by far the best PC platform for Internet access) recommends 8MB of RAM, but—as with all recommendations on software packages—double it to 16MB to get the performance you really want. Face it, you'll never have too much RAM. Buy as much as you can afford. Many of the Internet services, especially Web browsing, will be accelerated when you give your computer enough memory.

And don't just grab the first RAM you see advertised. There are different types of RAM. Just having a large amount of RAM doesn't do the trick; you also need to worry about RAM speed. RAM speed is measured in nanoseconds or ns. The lower the number, the faster the chip. For all 486 and Pentium desktops, 70ns RAM is sufficiently fast to keep up with your CPU. If you can afford faster memory, however, the expense will be well worth it.

When Parity Isn't Enough

Until 1995, the PC memory feature that was of utmost importance was parity. Parity is a error-checking method within the memory which checks the "oddness" or "evenness" of a segment of data on its way into and out of RAM. If the parity of the data segment of these two checks is not the same, the RAM requests the data to be resent from wherever it originally came from. This is a very nice feature for RAM chips and worked remarkable well throughout the 486 CPU line. However, with the introduction of the end-all-and-be-all Pentium processor, the virtue of the parity memory chip has had to be discarded—at least for now. The Pentium is not at present fully compatible with the parity check system and can cause more rereads or RAM parity errors than are actually occurring—thus slowing down your system. If you own a Pentium, be sure to get nonparity memory when you upgrade.

CPU

The brains—or at least the number cruncher—of your computer is the CPU. The 486 or 586 (usually called the Pentium) label on your CPU is simply the version number of the internal architecture. As technology progresses, new ways to allow a CPU to function faster are discovered or invented and are worked into the design of the next chip. The second number associated with a CPU is its clock rate, measured in megahertz (MHz). (See the sidebar, "What the Heck Is a MHz?") When you purchase a system, or even just a motherboard and CPU, getting clock multiplied chips will offer better overall system performance. We recommend at a minimum a 486 DX2/66 CPU—this is a 486 architecture chip with a math coprocessor (DX means it has a math coprocessor, SX means it doesn't) which operates at 66 MHz (clock doubled). Most upgradable motherboards in today's PCs can easily be upgraded to this chip without much hassle, and the faster your CPU, the faster your overall system performance will be. But before you rush out and buy a Pentium 133, make sure that your motherboard can handle the CPU's clock multiplier, the architecture, and the voltage settings. (Frying an $800 CPU on a motherboard without the proper voltage setting voids the warranty; i.e., you now have a real expensive paperweight.)

What the Heck Is a MHz?

MHz is the measurement of the clock rate of a CPU. To the user-on-the-street, what this actually means isn't important. However, knowing what to look for is important. Most motherboards (in the 486 and low- to midrange Pentium classes) operate at 33 MHz. CPUs can operate at much faster rates, from 33 to 150 MHz, one to five times as fast as a motherboard. Even though the CPU can process information fast, it still must speak slowly (33 MHz) when communicating information back to the motherboard. You may have heard the phrase "clock doubled" or "clock tripled"—this is just a fancy way of saying the CPU runs at two or three times the speed of the motherboard. BTW, this is a good thing.

Storage Space

You can never ever have enough hard drive storage space. Take our word for it: we've been on the Internet for years, and in that time we have collected a number of useful Internet tools which now take up over 150MB of hard drive space. These include six Web browsers with dozens of helper applications, news readers, e-mail clients, IRC software, FTP interfaces, three encoding/decoding utilities, and so on. And your Internet activity won't be limited to just the access software; you also will inevitably download an enormous amount of information. Even after our last delete-and-clean of our Internet download area, we still have over 800MB of movies, sounds, pictures, software, documents, demos, and other unnamed junk that we just can't live without. If you are an Internet beginner, a drive with 100MB of free space should be enough—until you contract the often terminal Internet disease "just-one-more-minute-itus." Soon you will find that the 9-gigabyte Seagate Barracuda is the only drive that will satisfy your storage needs. The best thing is to plan ahead and buy a large drive to add additional storage space for your Internet activities (and the rest of your computer tools). It's cheaper and easier than buying another drive later.

I Know I Downloaded It...

One of the problems we hear from new computer and Internet users is the inability to locate a file after they have created or downloaded it. Our usual answer to these type of questions is "Your file is right where you left it, all you need to do is find it." Great. Thanks a pantload. After the snide remarks subside, I then explain that in order to know where a file is, you need to organize your hard drive and software so files have a place to go and so they always go in their proper place. Basically, construct a "roadmap" of how you want your drive(s) to be laid out, then reinstall (yuck!) everything to match your plan. Stay with your roadmap and you'll always know which way is north.

As an example: One of our test machines has three drives: (two 420M IDE (C & D) and a 1.2G SCSI (E). Our operating system, Windows 95, and all hardware-specific drivers, utilities, and software are on the boot drive C. All other software and non-Internet data is stored on D. All Internet software and data and other volatile software (e.g., demos, betas, games) are stored on E. In addition, we have designed the directory tree to keep similar applications together (on drive D the DATA dir has all the Word and Excel documents we create and the UTILITY dir has all the small utility programs we use; drive E has a DL dir for Internet downloads—which is further divided into PICTURES, SOUNDS, TODO, and SOFTWARE, as well as an INTERNET dir for all the Internet client software). This may sound a bit anal-retentive, but the ease with which we are able to locate files has saved us a lot more time than it took to erase the drives and set up the organization.

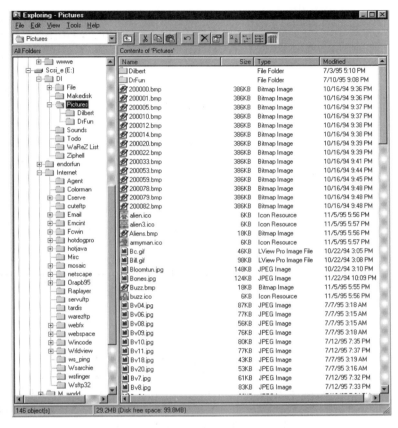

Figure 2.2: A sample drive with good organization.

Color Monitor

Your computer monitor is where most of your interaction with the Internet will take place. It's on the glass screen that you will see the fantastic graphics, animation, movies, and text that give the Internet its unique flavor and attraction. The standard color depth for images is 256 colors, so it should be fairly obvious that this should be the minimum color depth of your video card and monitor. When possible, 64K or 16.7M color depth is preferable. (However, take note that there are some Internet utilities which require 256-color mode and will not function at any other color depth, so be prepared to switch color depths on demand.)

How Do I Set My Color Depth?

A simple to ask but not always easy to answer question. If your computer is less than a year old you should have at least a 256-color video card already installed. Once you have the proper windows video driver software for your video card installed, you'll need to consult the video card's manuals for altering the color depth; usually this is done with a setup utility provided on the driver diskette. In Windows 95, once you have the proper drivers installed, you can use the Control Panel display's Settings tab to change the color depth of your display, but you will have to reboot for the changes to take effect. However, there is a wonderful utility called QuickRes that will allow on-the-fly alterations of your color depth and screen size right from your desktop—we highly recommend getting this. Its last known location was:

```
http://www.windows.microsoft.com/windows/software/
powertoy.htm
```

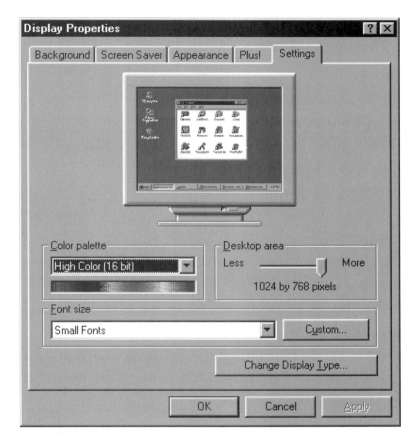

Figure 2.3: Settings tab of the display application of the Control Panel.

Mouse

A pointing device, whether a mouse, trackball, touchpad, light pen, magic finger, or direct neural interface, is an important element for achieving the enjoyable Internet surfing experience. Just make sure you have the proper drivers loaded; they usually come with instructions in the device package. (Yes, read the instructions.) As you might guess, it's difficult to point and click on a graphical interface without a mouse.

Software: More than Lingerie

Now that you have the hard(ware) part solved, we move on to the tantalizing world of software. What do you need to get connected to the Internet? An Internet connection package—it's just that simple. However, there are a few background issues you need to resolve first.

The Operating System

To get started on your journey through the Internet, you need the controlling software to make all that fancy computer equipment work. This type of software is called the operating system or OS. There are many varieties and versions available from DOS to OS/2, but the best OS for Internet access is Windows 95. We have tested and tried most of the operating systems for PCs, and Windows 95 has come out on top as the best for graphical Internet access. No other OS offers Windows 95's wide range of software, options, or robustness.

"But I just bought the Windows 3.11 upgrade—can't I use that?" Well, yes—you can settle for the out-of-date, sluggish, and non–Internet friendly environment of Windows 3.1 or 3.11, just as you can stick with homemade lye soap and potato sack shirts, if you like the rustic life. The Internet software listed in this book focuses on the 32-bit Windows

95 platform. Many of the utilities and add-ons listed have 16-bit Windows 3.1/3.11 versions which operate and function similarly to the 32-bit versions. So relax, both the Windows 3.1/3.11 and 95 users will be able to find valuable information on how to access the Internet in the materials in this book. But get with 95. It's '96 already anyway.

The Internet Connection Software

Once you have an operational computer, getting connected to the Internet is done with Internet connection software—duh. This is a software program that operates your modem to make a connection with your Internet service provider (ISP). Windows 95 has a built-in connection utility, but there are many third-party commercial products that you could try as well.

Getting TCP/IP Working

The Internet is a world-wide network—this means that many computers in many places are linked together in order to share information. But for the computers to communicate they need to speak a common language. The common language, called a protocol, of the Internet is TCP/IP. This is fairly complicated subject and the full inter-workings of TCP/IP are at best useless to the casual Internet surfer, so we won't bore you with all the details. However, there are a few tidbits which just may interest you. For instance: TCP/IP is the reason the Internet is so robust. It is a powerful networking protocol which is able to transmit data rapidly, route around slow or broken links, and handle synchronous transmission.

It should be clear that the way to work on the Internet is to have your computer on the Internet. This is a difficult problem, but it does have a reasonable solution. You need to have a direct connection to the Internet and a translation program to speak TCP/IP for you, since your PC's operating system isn't built on TCP/IP.

A direct connection to the Internet is established by using your modem as a network interface. This is done by using a dial-up utility with a communications protocol (PPP or SLIP) to open a pathway for TCP/IP packets to travel to and from your computer. Once the modem pathway is open you are on the Internet, but until you teach your computer to speak the local language it won't do you much good. That's where PPP or SLIP comes in.

What Are PPP and SLIP?

PPP stands for Point to Point Protocol, and SLIP stands for Serial Line Interface Protocol. That explains it, right? Basically, these are modem protocols used to establish a network connection to the Internet. Usually PPP is easier to set up and is a bit more stable, but not every ISP offers it.

To get your computer to speak TCP/IP, your connection software uses a networking interface called a TCP/IP stack. Mainly it is a collection of protocols, translators, and control processes which allows your computer to communicate with the rest of the Internet. You've probably even heard the name of the top layer of this stack—winsock.

Winsock

Winsock is the orange thing flapping on a pole at an airport that let's people jack into the Net. OK, OK. We couldn't resist the lame humor. Winsock in our context is a networking protocol standard which was developed by Microsoft and IBM. Winsock translates the operations of Internet utilities into standardized TCP/IP commands or data packets which it sends to the Internet's TCP/IP layer. These operations are performed almost instantly and in both directions at the same time, providing you with a seamless connection to the Internet right on your desktop. All the Windows utilities listed in this book are fully winsock compliant (and any that you should even consider using should be).

Warning Although the winsock protocol is a fully publicized and documented standard, this has not prevented software manufacturers from "adding" and "improving" upon the standard to add special functions to their particular implementation of the TCP/IP stack and winsock. Most connection software packages have a file named "winsock.dll" which the Internet utilities call upon to perform its magic. But be warned that some third-party connection packages are a bit too reckless with their alterations of the winsock.dll, which causes some utilities to function poorly or not at all. Unfortunately, the only way to find this out is to install the new stack and try it. (Remember to make a backup!)

Windows 95

With the unveiling of the long anticipated master operating system for PCs—Windows 95—all the problems of the world are now solved. Well, maybe not all of them. OK, none really, but at least it has built-in Internet connection software. Windows 95 was the first operating system to be fully Internet compatible right out of the box. (OS/2 WARP initially required the Internet add-on package, which was usually sold separately.) With Windows 95 you have a full TCP/IP stack which has both a 32-bit and 16-bit winsock, meaning you have the ability to run a wider variety of Internet utilities. This OS is so Internet friendly it even has built-in FTP and Telnet support. (We'll talk about that in the next chapter.) If you have Windows 95, the next sections will help you get connected to the Internet quickly and easily. If you don't have Windows 95, go buy it. If you don't want to buy it, then skip down to the "Commercial Packages" section, where Windows 3.1/3.11 packages are discussed.

Before you start on the installation, use the following list to collect the information you'll need about your ISP and your intended configuration.

- Your user name:

- Your password (you probably shouldn't write that down; just be sure to remember it):

- ISP telephone number:

- Your host name (usually your username):

- Your News or NNTP server:

- Your WWW server:

- Your POP account:

- Your SMTP server:

- The domain name:

- The IP subnet mask (most likely 255.255.255.0):

- The gateway IP address:

- The DNS address:

- Your IP address (this probably is a dynamically assigned number):

You won't use every one of these items in the Windows 95 dial-up networking configuration, but all this information will be useful at some point in your utility installation, setup, and configuration. It's best to get all this at one time, so you don't have to keep bugging your ISP.

GETTING IT ALL INSTALLED

Windows 95 has a wonderfully simple installation process that automatically configures itself around your hardware—that is, if it's on the hardware compatibility list. To make sure that you have all the right software pieces installed, let's take a little trip to the **Add/Remove Programs** application in the Control Panel. (To get there use the Start button, Settings…, then Control Panel.) Select the "Windows Setup" tab and make sure the Communications box is checked. Also, be sure the text box says "4 of 4 components" (see Figure 2.4). Click OK. You may be prompted for the Windows 95 CD (or floppies—yuck) if the components are not already on your hard drive.

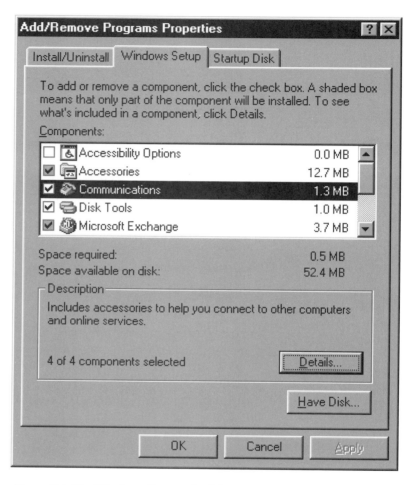

Figure 2.4: The Windows Setup tab of the Add/Remove Programs application of the Control Panel.

NETWORK CONFIGURATION

Now you need to set up your desktop for Internet communications. As we mentioned earlier, this involves establishing a direct network connection and installing a TCP/IP stack. Both of these actions can be performed from the

Network Control Panel application. Once the Control Panel is opened you need to add the Dial-Up Adapter and the TCP/IP protocol. If your computer is not attached to a LAN (local area network), you can safely remove any adapters and protocols listed. If you are not sure, leave them; they don't take up that much memory and it's easier than finding out later you really needed them. To add the Dial-Up Adapter:

1. Click the Add button.

2. Select Adapter.

3. Click Add.

4. Scroll down to find Microsoft.

5. Select Dial-Up Adapter.

6. Click OK.

To add the TCP/IP protocol:

1. Click the Add button.

2. Select Protocol.

3. Click Add.

4. Select Microsoft.

5. Select TCP/IP.

6. Click OK.

7. Next, select the Adapter.

8. Click Proprieties.

9. Select the Bindings tab.

10. Be sure the TCP/IP box is checked. Your Network applications screen should look similar to that in Figure 1-5. If so, click on OK to close Properties window, then click on OK to close the Network window.

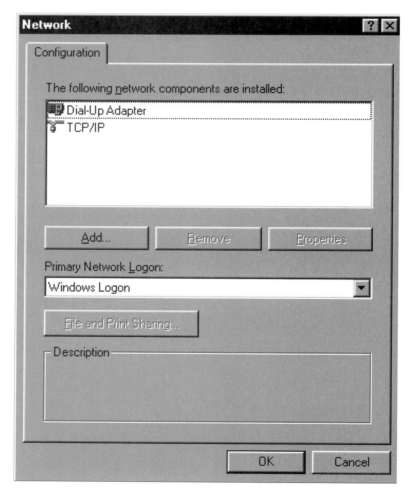

Figure 2.5: The Network application of the Control Panel.

TCP/IP CONFIGURATION

Now you need to grab that list of ISP information we asked you to get earlier. Get back into the Network application of the Control Panel. Select the TCP/IP Protocol and click on Properties. You should see a window similar to the one in Figure 1-6. Be sure to look at each tab to make sure the proper selections and information are present. The changes are listed here in order:

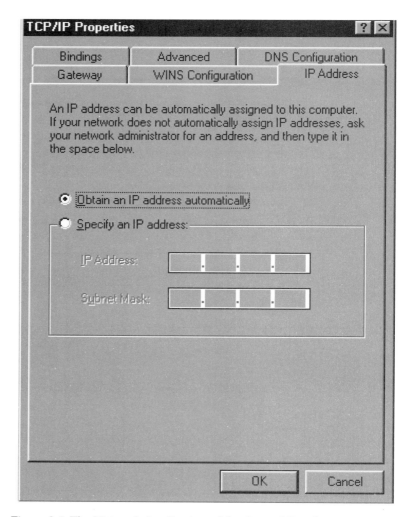

Figure 2.6: The Network Application of the Control Panel.

1. **IP Address:** Select the "Obtain an IP address automatically" option, unless you have a permanent IP assigned to you; then select specify and enter the number.

2. **WINS Configuration:** Select the "Disable WINS Resolution" option. You will not need this option as long as you are using your network capabilities for Internet access only.

3. **Gateway:** Type in the gateway IP address and click on Add.

4. **Bindings:** No changes needed from the default.

5. **Advanced:** No changes needed from the default.

6. **DNS Configuration:** This is the most important tab to fill in properly. First, select the Enable DNS option. Enter your user name in the Host box. Enter the domain name in the Domain box. In the DNS Server Search Order section, put in the DNS address and click on Add. In the Domain Suffix Search Order section, type in the base domain for your ISP.

When you're all done setting these options, click on the OK button at the bottom of the TCP/IP Properties window, then click on the OK button in the Network dialog box. You will be asked to reboot; select Yes.

CONFIGURE THE DIALER

Before you can set up the dialer to call your ISP, you need to make sure that your modem is configured properly. Go to the **Modems** application in Control Panel. If your modem is not already listed here, click on the Add button and follow the wizard to set up your modem.

Once your modem is properly configured, you need to configure a dialer to make the call to your ISP. Open the My Computer icon from the desktop and double-click on "Make New Connection." (If you happen to have done this before, you will need to double-click on "Dial-Up

Networking" first to get to the application.) Another setup wizard will appear to guide you through the process:

1. Give this connection type a name (the ISP name will work fine).

2. Select a modem.

3. Click on Configure.

4. Set the maximum speed to 115200 (leave the only connect at this speed box empty).

5. Got to the Options tab.

6. Check the box beside "Bring up terminal window after dialing."

7. Click OK.

8. Click Next.

9. Enter the phone number for your ISP (be sure to use the modem number and not the voice number). (If you have call waiting, add "*70," before the number to turn off call waiting when you dial your ISP.)

10. Click Finish.

You should see a new icon appear inside the Dial-Up Networking window. Right-click on this icon and select Properties. Click Server Type. Verify that PPP is listed in the top box and TCP/IP is checked at the bottom, then click on OK. Then click on OK to close the ISP Dial-Up window.

You have now finished configuring your dial-up Internet connection for Windows 95. You can leave the connection icon where it is or click on and drag a shortcut copy to the desktop for faster access. Go ahead and test it to make sure you didn't fumble. The first time you open the dialer it will have empty boxes for your name and password, so fill them in. On some ISP connection designs, Windows 95 will handle everything; on others, you will have to type your information into the pop-up box which appears and click on continue. Eventually, the dialog box in the center of your screen will say "Connected at ?? bps, Duration: 000:00:01." Go do a little happy dance; you are now connected to the Internet. Don't get too excited, though; you need some Internet utilities to actually do anything. Jump to the next chapter to get the scoop on obtaining Internet utilities.

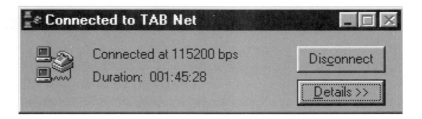

Figure 2.7: The Connected to Dialog Box.

Commercial Packages

You've probably gathered by now that we lean strongly toward the built-in connectivity of the Windows 95 OS. However, you may still want a bundled Internet utility/connectivity package, so we did our homework in order to review and comment on the more popular packages on the market. Some of these even work under Windows 95, but why you would want to use them instead is beyond us.

We did not cover every package on the market, so if you are serious about purchasing a Internet suite, you'll need to do a little research of your own. Take some time to look over the utilities and programs we mention in the next chapter. You just might find that everything you want is on the Internet waiting for you and all you need is a simple dial-up connection to get to it. (That's another reason why we like Windows 95 so much—it's a connection utility with standard FTP and Telnet utilities to boot—all you have to do is download and install the individual pieces to get the Internet Suite you really want.)

Instant InterRamp

Performance Systems International, Inc. (PSI)
510 Huntmar Park Drive
Herndon, VA 22070
800-82-PSI82; 703-904-4100
Direct sales: 703-709-0300
FAX: 703-904-4200
MSRP: $.99 with access purchase
Minimum RAM required: 4 MB
Disk storage required: 8 MB

PSI offers an easy-to-install no-nonsense Internet hookup for less than a dollar a day. The PSI connection software is a preconfigured NetManage Chameleon 4.5 Internet suite (see below). Thus, PSI has combined inexpensive access with a solid software package. The Internet services offered by PSI include: Web, gopher, FTP, e-mail, Usenet news-groups, and Telnet. PSI also offers disk space for hosting personal Web pages.

Figure 2.8: PSI's Web site at http://www.interramp.com

AfterDial

UUNet
3060 Williams Dr., 6th Fl.
Fairfax, VA 22031
800-4-UUNET-4; 703-206-5600; http://www.alter.net
FAX: 703-204-8001
MSRP: $25 startup fee plus access account
Minimum RAM required: 4 MB
Disk storage required: 8 MB

AfterDial is UUNet's inexpensive dial-up Internet service. UUNet offers two Internet suites preconfigured to their system: NetManage's Internet Chameleon and Spry's Internet-in-a-Box. UUNet's Internet services include: e-mail, Usenet newsgroups, Web, FTP, Telnet, and gopher.

Figure 2.9: UUNet's Web site at http://www.uu.net

NetCruiser/NetCruiserPLUS (V.2.0)

NETCOM On-Line Communications Services, Inc.
3031 Tisch Way, 2nd Fl.
San Jose, CA 95128
800-353-6600; 408-345-2600
Direct sales: 800-501-8649
FAX: 408-241-9145
MSRP: $40 and up
Minimum RAM required: 4MB
Disk storage required: 4MB

Offering e-mail, Web access, FTP, and Usenet newsgroups, NETCOM has a simple package. The software is easy to install - however, it is only compatible with the NETCOM's Internet service. If you want full Internet access, move on to something else.

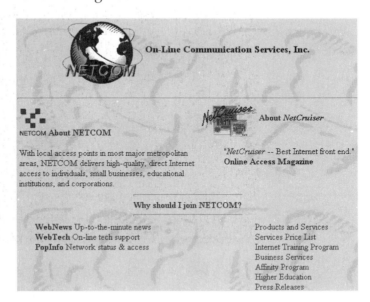

Figure 2.10: NETCOM's Web site at http://www.netcom.com.

Chameleon (V.4.6)

NetManage, Inc.
10725 N. De Anza Blvd.
Cupertino, CA 95014
408-973-7171
FAX: 408-257-6405
Tech support: 408-973-8181
MSRP: $125
Minimum RAM required: 6 MB

The NetManage Chameleon is an Internet suite package with the module approach to Internet applications. In the package are utilities for dial-up, mail, FTP, Usenet news, Web browsing, gopher, Telnet, talk (chat), ping, finger, whois, viewing graphics, and a sound player. Each of these utilities is functional and quite powerful. With a quick and easy installation, you'll be Internet savvy in a jiffy.

Figure 2.11: NetManage's Web site at http://www.netmanage.com.

Quarterdeck InternetSuite

Quarterdeck Corp.
150 Pico Blvd.
Santa Monica, CA 90405-1018
800-354-4757; 310-392-9851
Direct sales: 800-683-6696
FAX: 310-314-4219
Tech support: 310-392-9701
Tech support BBS: 310-314-3227
MSRP: $80
Minimum RAM required: 4MB
Disk storage required: 7–40MB

This package is built around the Quarterdeck Mosaic Web browser—a re-engineered copy of the Mosaic line of browsers. In addition, this package has utilities for dial-up, e-mail, Usenet news, FTP, and Telnet. Although it does not include all the utilities you can use on the Internet, it's not a bad starting point.

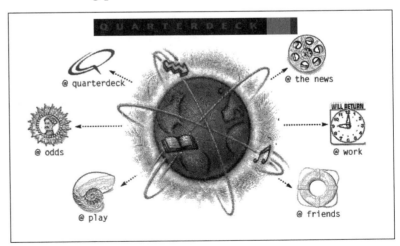

Figure 2.12: Quarterdeck's Web site at http://www.qdeck.com.

Internet Office (V.4.0)

CompuServe, Inc. (Internet Division)
316 Occidental Ave., S, Ste. 200
Seattle, WA 98104
800-SPRY-NET; 206-447-0300
FAX: 206-447-9008
Tech support: 206-447-0958
Tech support BBS: 206-447-9060
MSRP: $499
Minimum RAM required: 4MB
Disk storage required: 4MB

Designed more for the business user, this package offers
Spry Mosaic as its Web browser with other utilities for dial-
up, e-mail, Usenet news, FTP, and Telnet. This is another
good startup package for the novice, as it is easy to install
and use.

Figure 2.13: CompuServe's Web site at http://www.compuserve.com.

Where to Turn for Help?

Help! The cry for mercy and relief is often screamed in vain, especially when you don't have this handy list we have so generously compiled for you. But before you rush off, consider what you need to know or do before you seek help.

- Make sure you have a real problem: Check to see that the "problem" is repeatable. Once you make that determination, write down the steps you need to make the problem occur.

- Know your system: A technical support representative will need information about your computer—its hardware components as well as setup and configuration.

- Know your enemy: The person you speak with on- or offline may not be the designer or programmer of the software which is causing you problems, so they are not responsible for the problem. They are there to help solve the problem. Don't take your wrath out on them. Try to make that person a partner instead of an enemy.

Now that a few ground rules have been laid regarding technical support, all you need to do is get some!

Online

The best Internet help is often available on the Internet. If your problem deals specifically with getting an initial connection, you should skip to the Offline section. If you are not familiar with any of the online services listed here, consult the next chapter, where we introduce each service and list some of the top utilities used to access them.

Web Sites

The World Wide Web is the largest collection of information available to anyone with an Internet connection. There is so much information that locating what you need can sometimes be a difficult process. The key to finding relevant information the Web is using search engines efficiently.

A search engine is a Web site that is designed to collect data about the information available on the Web and store it in a database. We show you some examples of search engines, such as Yahoo and AltaVista, in Chapter 4. Check 'em out. They make the whole thing work much easier than trying to find something out on your own.

When you access a search engine, you provide a query string for which to search this stored database and the background programs return matches. Each search engine on the Web (there are over 50) uses a different method to gather and search information. You should always use more than one engine when researching a topic. Here are a few points to keep in mind as you look for information:

- Be as specific as possible when providing search strings.

- Be sure to spell everything correctly and use proper capitalization.

- Try synonyms, related words, and even alternate the form of the words.

Some Internet-savvy software developers have created Web sites with good technical support information, and they may even list the URL in their documentation or readme files on the diskettes or in the archives. Take a look through the materials available; you may save time by jumping straight to their site instead of searching world-wide for it.

E-mail

E-mail does not have the most reassuring form of online technical support, mainly because you have to wait until support staff reads your message and responds. Requesting information by e-mail can be very time-consuming and frustrating, especially if you have an emergency or are extremely impatient. We highly recommend looking for a Web site, Usenet postings, or even asking someone on IRC (see below) before seeking help by e-mail.

Once you decide e-mail is the way for you, you'll hit a significant roadblock: finding out the technical support e-mail address. Unless it is listed in the materials that came with the software, you probably will have better luck giving them a call and asking for the URL instead of rooting around on the Net for it. On the other hand, if you are going to call them anyway, why not go ahead and talk with them on the phone?

Usenet

Usenet postings often can get your answers immediately, especially if others have encountered similar problems and have posted the information for all to see. To look for technical support information on Usenet, you'll need to locate one or more relevant newsgroups and then find and read their frequently asked questions (FAQs). Once you are familiar with the topics of a group and the etiquette for postings, you can search through the thousands of message headers looking for a keyword or phrase. (Most Usenet utilities provide a FIND function to look for keywords in the header and sometimes even the message body.) If your search proves successful, great; but if you don't find anything relevant, you may need to post a request.

Always be sure you are complying with the guidelines of a newsgroup's FAQ limitations before attempting to post. Improper postings can result in bad karma, e-mail floods, flaming, and even quivering in small animals. Post a short direct message requesting help or information, give it a focused heading with good keywords, and indicate the preferred means of contact—either by a follow-up Usenet posting or by e-mail. Now wait; you'll need to check your e-mail or the newsgroup periodically to see if anyone was kind enough to answer your plea.

IRC

IRC (Internet Relay Chat) provides one of the quickest and most enjoyable methods of getting help and information, but the reliability of the information you get can be highly questionable. On IRC you can "chat" with people from all over the world, in any age group and with many levels of computer knowledge. Take time to look for a channel which is close to the subject you need help with. Then join the channel and read the conversations. If your request falls in line with the tone of the current channel environment, ask your question. Be prepared to be ignored or given false information. You'll need to use common sense and caution when following information gained via IRC. There are no truth restrictions on IRC, so anyone can mislead you about anything. But don't let this discourage you; many people enjoy providing solid information and relevant help to others. With luck, you will encounter such a entity.

Offline

Getting help offline for a computer-related problem is similar to getting help about any other type of service or product—you either make a call, go to a place of business, read a book, or talk to a friend.

Tech Support

Tech support is often given a bad rap; however, this is not necessarily the fault of the technician who handles your call. Here are a few things to keep in mind when contacting technical support by phone:

- Speak clearly and be polite.

- Answer all questions as specifically and directly as possible—it is OK to say, "I don't know."

- Be prepared to be put on hold for as long as it takes.

- Write down the solution or information given to you.

You can usually find technical support numbers in the product's documentation. Other places to search are computer magazines or books with vendor glossaries. You can also try calling local computer stores or national information (1-900-555-1212) to ask for a number, if you know the company name.

Local Computer Sales and Repair

Most local computer software stores and computer hardware repair centers have well-trained staff members who may be able to help you. But since computer repair and sales are their business, they may not want to give free help over the phone. Take a walk through your yellow pages for computer retail and service/repair shops near you.

Books

There are hundreds of great books about troubleshooting and repairing computers. Many are focused on a single computer platform or product, which makes their content highly relevant. If you don't already have a few good general computer reference or repair books handy, it's a good idea to see what your bookstore carries. With the wide variety of software and hardware available today, it is difficult to recommend a single title that encompasses all the materials we discuss in this book. Speak with one of the salespersons at your bookstore and ask if they have materials which relate to your system and products.

Geeks, Dweebs, the Kid Down the Street, and Other Experts

The Internet is a breeding ground for "geeks." Almost anyone associated with computers, communications, and high-end business has to have contact with and knowledge of the Internet. You probably know a few of these people: they are in your office, down the street, or the kid in your upstairs bedroom. Never underestimate the fortitude of a young genius who spends all day in front of the game box. He may already know the solution to your problem and can fix it before you can blink. They have something weird going on in their genetic code.

If all these support avenues fail, you have one other option—give up and go hit the beach. You're hosed.

chapter 3

Surf's Up!

To Catch the Wave, You'll Need a Good Board

By this point, you should have an operational Internet dial-up connection. However, to get any surfing done, you need a surfboard—or less metaphorically, you need an Internet service utility. And what is an Internet service utility? Well, it's a software application that gives you access to one (or more) of the Internet services. And, you may well ask, what are the Internet services? They are such things as the Web, e-mail, FTP, and Usenet—with variations and unique offerings appearing regularly. In this chapter, we're going to give you a brief overview of each of the major Internet services and recommend some of the best utilities available. We even help you get the utilities installed, configured, and fully operational.

One of the great things about the Internet is that there are hundreds of service utilities just waiting for you to retrieve and use. Some of the utilities, especially Web browsers, can manage more than one service. You'll have to pick and choose the tools that work best for you. You can have as many as you want; the only limit is your hard drive space.

There is, however, one catch: in order to download anything, you have to have one utility to start out with. (Yes, it's the chicken-and-egg problem all over again). With any luck at all, your ISP's connection software has not left you high and dry. We highly recommend starting off with a Web browser. If you are a Windows 95 user, there is a built-in FTP utility that can be used to retrieve a Web browser. If you don't have either of these FTP or Web utilities on hand, get in touch with your ISP. They can provide you with a service utility to start out with.

A Few Internet Basics

There is a little bit of necessary background information before the rest of this chapter will do you any good or even make much sense. So bear with us for a bit while we get you up to speed.

URLs

You should already be familiar with the basic concept of the Internet—that it is a worldwide network of computers. Everything is out on the Internet (at least in theory), and to get access to any of it you need to know where it is. Everything on the Internet has a Uniform Resource Locator, or URL. Just as a postal package must have a name, number, street, city, state, zip, and sometimes a country, a file on the Internet must have a URL. Let's take a look at an important URL and what it means:

These two lines need to be in monospaced font.

```
http://www.w3.org:80/hypertext/WWW/Addressi
ng/Addressing.html#top
```

```
|-1-|---2--|-3|--------4-------|----5---|-6-|
```

There are six pieces to this URL:

1. protocol/data type
   This will be the name of the protocol or service types used to access the data. Possible syntax for this part:

   - ftp:// FTP or file resource

   - gopher:/ gopher resource

   - http:// hypertext http resource; i.e., a Web document

   - mailto:// causes a compatible browser to launch an e-mail utility

   - news:// Usenet newsgroup

- telnet:// causes a compatible browser to launch a telnet utility

- WAIS:// a WAIS resource, which is usually spawned off to a helper application

- file:/// indicates a local file with syntax: file:///<drive name>|/<path>/<filename>

2. domain name
   The domain name of the host computer.

3. port address
   In most cases, port addresses are automatically selected by the protocol/data type being used. However, when a port is specifically listed it is wise to include it.

4. directory path
   The directory path, document tree, or symbolic pathway.

5. object name
   This is the actual name of the file, object, or resource.

6. spot
   This indicates a specific internal anchor within a Web document. It allows direct linkage to a point within a long document.

A URL is the standard method for indicating the location of an Internet file, document, or resource. You need to be familiar with URL structure, because you will have to parse the address manually for some of the service utilities.

Most Web browsers can handle all of the URL types we just listed, which means you can cut and paste a full URL into the browser to load the document or resource. However, many Internet service utilities are not able to use a fully qualified URL; you will have to input portions of the URL into the utility as they are needed. For example, an FTP utility cannot use the URL ftp://ftp.netscape.com/2.0 /windows/n32e20.exe. Instead, you first have to connect to the site ftp.netscape.com, change directories until you reach /2.0/windows/, then select and retrieve the file "n32e20.exe." This is called manual parsing of a URL. You will need to perform this type of operation with most of the Internet service utilities. We all hope that the authors of these utilities will incorporate automatic URL parsing soon. It will make life way easier. If you hate the idea of figuring out this stuff, just use your Web browser. It can do it all.

Network Load

"Network load" is the term used to describe the condition of a network (or a portion of it) when it is working at full or near full capacity. Network load results in local (if not overall) slower performance and response time. The Internet is a mind-bogglingly huge network with uncountable connections and routes through which to direct information. As a whole, the Internet is able to handle just about any amount of use and abuse thrown at it. But individual computers and subsections of the Internet can experience network load when too many users try to access the same resources. When this occurs, communication can become slow or completely interrupted. In fact, so much network load can be placed on some systems that it causes them to disconnect themselves from the Internet altogether or "fail"—obviously this is not a good thing. You will encounter Internet network load during your surfing—it's a fact, so prepare yourself for it.

Just as Panama City Beach, New Orleans, and Colorado get overcrowded at especially popular times of the year (spring break, Mardi Gras, and winter), so, too, an Internet site can be so popular that it becomes too busy to let you in. When this occurs you will experience: 1) extremely long transmission times, 2) interrupted and canceled transmissions, 3) service time-outs, 4) messages about the current load, or 5) no information or access to a site whatsoever. When you encounter network load, you have a few options in dealing with it: 1) wait and try again later, 2) look for an alternate site or mirror, 3) give up. Usually, you will encounter network load only around extremely popular sites or locations where new software has just been released (e.g., Netscape and Microsoft).

Mirrors

Many Internet FTP sites which experience a high level of network load are often mirrored. To mirror a site is to dynamically copy the contents of one system to another, creating an exact duplicate of the original. Most mirrors are automatically updated on a daily or weekly basis. Often, when you try to gain access to an FTP site which is too busy to grant entry, the system's mirror sites will be listed. Simply use one of the mirror domain names or IP address to gain access to the files located elsewhere on the Internet.

Internet Service Utilities

In the next somewhat long-winded sections, you'll find:

- Listings of our favorite service utilities for each of the significant service types

- Installation/configuration instructions

- Hints and tips about how to use the utility

- Why we think the utility is worth taking up space on your hard drive

General Installation Instructions

The file that you retrieve from the Internet can have any name the company chooses to give it. Where possible we list the most current version and filename, but this is subject to change. Whatever the filename is, we will refer to the main file as the "original file" in all the discussions about its installation and setup.

Many of the files you will be retrieving are self-extracting executable files. This means that when you run, open, or execute them they automatically uncompress their contents, usually creating multiple files. For this reason, you should always transfer the original file into an empty directory before running it (for example, create a directory named "TEMP" or "ZIPHELL"). This will save you many headaches and make postinstallation clean up easier.

Some files will also automatically start their own install/setup program after uncompressing themselves; many companies are incorporating this feature into their latest releases of software. If in the installation instructions for a utility we state that you have to execute the install/setup program, but the self-extracting archive does it on its own, don't be alarmed, be happy. This is evidence that the software company is making their software easier to use—an end devoutly to be wished.

We try to list the exact file name you will need to run in order to start the setup process. However, as new versions of these utilities appear, the name of the install program may change. Usually the name of the install/setup file is "SETUP.EXE," "SETUP.BAT," "INSTALL.EXE," or "INSTALL.BAT." If you do not see one of these filenames, look for a readme, .txt, or .doc file which may contain instructions on installation and setup.

Another popular file type for the software you will download is .zip. This is a type of compressed archive which was created using the PKZip 2.04g compression utility. In order to open and extract these types of files, you will need either the pkz204g.exe file or one of the Windows Zip utilities such as WinZip. (Please see the section WinZip for location and operation.)

Once you have successfully installed a utility, you should move the original file to a storage directory or diskette and delete any extracted or temporary files and directories which remain in the "TEMP" directory. If the installation was unsuccessful, delete all the files (including the original file) from the "TEMP" directory and try retrieving the original file again. You may have experienced an error during the initial downloading.

The World Wide Web

The World Wide Web is the most versatile, powerful, and popular Internet service. It is a standardized method of accessing and transmitting Internet resources with a wonderful, colorful, and easy-to-use GUI (graphic user interface). This interface, called a Web browser, has the ability (or at least the potential) to handle every type of resource on the Internet, either through built-in support or through some of the helper applications we're going to describe shortly.

How to Use the Web

Web browsers can access the information on the Internet by using URLs (as we discussed earlier). Web browsers are designed to parse a URL automatically, retrieve the information, and display it for you. Usually you can cut and paste a URL into the "open location" window of the browser to access whatever is there.

The browsers listed here will load their company's home page the first time they are used. Often there is a 'getting started' page or hotlist of cool sites to visit. Just in case you don't find what you want on the preloaded home page, take a look at the section in which we discuss search engines.

Web Browsers

Since a Web browser is one of the most important tools you will use to access the Internet, we have listed both the standard Web (HTTP) URL and an FTP URL. This should allow you to access these full-featured browsers, even if you are limited to an FTP utility.

Netscape

Netscape is by far the most popular Web browser on the Internet. Designed by Netscape Communications Corporation, this beauty is available as a commercial off-the-shelf product as well as downloadable shareware. There are multiple versions available, including Windows 3.1/3.11, Windows 95, Mac, and UNIX.

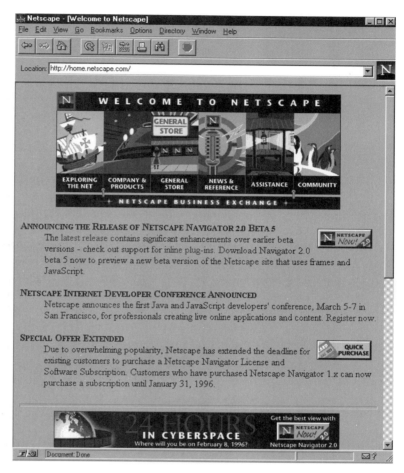

Figure 3.1: Netscape Navigator 2.0.

WHERE TO FIND IT

You can obtain the browser from the Netscape Web site if you have any other Web browser: http://home.netscape.com/comprod/mirror/index.html. If you have only an FTP utility, you can retrieve Netscape from ftp.netscape.com or one of the mirrors. The Netscape software sites are high-traffic areas. If the site is too busy, it will give you a list of alternate sites where the software can be found. Your best time to grab the software is between the hours of 11 PM and 7 AM.

VERSION

The current commercial and shareware versions of Netscape is 2.0 (filename: n32e20.exe or n16e20.exe).

FEATURES

Netscape has hundreds of built-in features, not to mention its numerous configurations with add-ons, plug-ins, and helper applications. Instead of listing them all (which is done at: http://home.netscape. com/comprod/products/navigator/version_2.0/datasheet.html), we have included just a few highlights.

Netscape 2.0 has an advanced bookmark utility, support for multiple simultaneous Windows, streaming audio and video support, intelligent e-mail capabilities, Usenet threading and posting, security, drag and drop compatibility, and Java support and is able to send and receive files.

WHY WE LIKE IT

Netscape is easy to use, simple to master, and looks nice without sacrificing speed, features, or compatibility. Why anyone would even consider using any other browser is a mystery we may never solve. Everything we can think of or would want in a browser, Netscape has and does it with style. Some of our favorite features are spawned FTP sessions, context-sensitive right-click on pop-up menus, fast page display, and file upload capabilities.

WHAT WE DON'T LIKE

We found it hard to name anything about the Netscape Navigator we are displeased with. However, as we didn't want to give you the idea it was perfect, we came up with a few things we think are missing. Netscape does not have a lifetime history file, only a current session history file. An old version of Netscape did have a lifetime history file, but obviously that wasn't a hereditary feature. This makes locating that one page you saw last week impossible unless you added it to your bookmark list (which you didn't since you didn't think it was that important at the time). Netscape also has opted not to include any local help files, not even operational basics. If you want help you have to go online and access their Web site's database of help files. You can purchase the commercial or "GOLD" version to get a printed manual (and don't forget the shiny box!), but we prefer having something useful in that little Help menu item other than site links.

HOW TO INSTALL

Netscape's installation is easy: execute the original file. On some versions the installation program will start automatically. If it doesn't execute the "SETUP.EXE" file. Follow the prompts.

HOW TO UNINSTALL

You will probably never want to or need to uninstall Netscape, but just in case we will give you a few hints. Windows 95 users can uninstall Netscape by using the Control Panel application Add/Remove Programs. Select the Netscape listing and click on the Add/Remove button. You should have no problem following the prompts from there.

If you are a Windows 3.1/3.11 user, you can delete the desktop icon and the "NETSCAPE" directory to remove the software. However, this does not remove all the files and alterations from your system. Netscape fails to offer an uninstall guide for the 16-bit version. The remaining alterations should not affect your system's performance.

SETUP/CONFIGURATION

The setup and configuration interface has changed from version to version of Netscape; however, most of the same options are available, they're just in a different location. The instructions here are specifically for the Windows 95 32-bit 2.0 Beta 5 version. If you have another version at hand, it may differ slightly from our example.

1. Run/execute the browser.

2. The first time you use the browser, you will be asked to read the license agreement. Do so, then click on Accept.

3. Resize the browser window to your personal preference.

4. Select Options General Preferences from the menu bar.

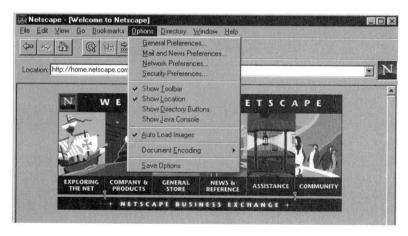

Figure 3.2: Netscape n32e20b5 Menu Bar.

5. On the **Appearance** tab select:
   Toolbar: Pictures
   Startup: Browser, Blank page
   Link Styles: (deselect) Underline, Expire After 1 Days.

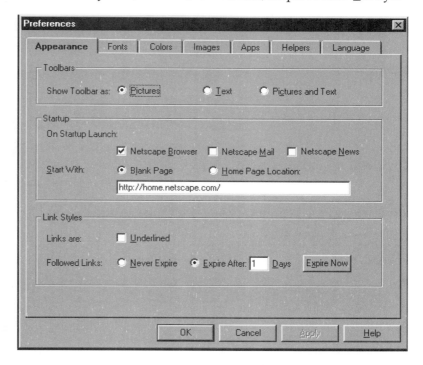

Figure 3.3: Netscape n32e20b5 Options General Preferences, Appearance Tab.

6. You do not need to make any changes to the **Fonts** or **Colors** tabs.

7. Select the **Images** tab. Be sure Automatic and While Loading are selected.

8. Select the **Apps** tab. Fill in the pathnames by using the Browse buttons for each of these apps that are already

installed on your system. For Windows 95, your Telnet path should be similar to "C:\WIN95\Telnet.exe." We highly recommend listing a good text editor for the View Source app—this will allow you to view and edit HTML documents right from the browser. Be sure to fill in a path for the Temporary directory; Netscape will use this often (this is not the same as the cache directory).

9. The **Helpers** and **Language** tabs do not need any changes.

10. Click OK.

11. Open the Options Mail and News Preferences.

12. The **Appearance** tab needs no changes.

13. Select the **Composition** tab.

14. In the boxes labeled "By default, e-mail a copy of outgoing message to:" place your e-mail address.

15. Select the **Servers** tab.

16. Fill in the correct domain names or IP numbers for your SMTP and POP servers.

17. If you plan on using Netscape as your e-mail utility, you should fill out the rest of the Mail section according to your preferences.

18. Fill in the correct domain name or IP number for your NNTP server.

19. Select the **Identity** tab.

20. Fill in the information about yourself.

21. If you have already created a signature file, add its pathname with the Browse button. (The signature file will be attached to all outgoing e-mail or newsgroup messages.)

22. If you are using Netscape as an e-mail and/or news-reader, you can configure the **Organization** tag to your preferences.

23. Click OK.

24. If you want a larger memory or disk cache, change the settings under the Options Network Preferences **Cache** tab.

25. No changes are needed in the Options Security Preferences.

26. Deselect the Show Directory Buttons line from the Options pull-down menu.

27. Verify that Auto Load Images is selected on the Options pull-down menu.

28. Select Save Options from the Options pull-down menu.

HOW TO USE IT

Getting started: Netscape is a graphical Web browser that allows you to select hyperlinks on screen using a pointing device to jump anywhere and everywhere on the Web. But you do have to start somewhere—click on File Open Location from the menu bar. In the pop-up box type: "http://www.yahoo.com." (See Search Engines for detailed instructions on the use of Yahoo!) Now you are surfing!

Bookmarks: Bookmarks, sometimes called a hotlist, are stored URLs listed in a pull-down menu. Bookmarks allow you to save the address of a page to which you want to return in the future. Simply click on Bookmarks, and choose Add Bookmark to add the currently open page to your list. Do that now to add Yahoo! to your bookmarks. Now every time you want to revisit Yahoo!, just click on Bookmark and select the name Yahoo! on the menu. If you need to edit or remove a bookmark, click on Bookmarks, and choose Go To Bookmarks; there is a Help file there if you need instructions.

HINTS AND TIPS

Go Home: To get to the Netscape home page, just double-click on the "N" icon in the upper right corner beside the location box.

More Menus: Try right-clicking over the browser, you should get a context-based pop-up menu. You can use these menus to "steal" images, download pages, open new browser windows, navigate, and even add bookmarks.

Mail and Print: From the File menu, you can e-mail a page and its URL to anyone or you can print it, including graphics to your local printer.

On Screen Text Selection: One great feature Netscape has adopted is allowing you to highlight or select text within the display window and copy it (<CTRL-C>) into the Windows clipboard (from which you can paste it into any other application, usually with <CTRL-V>).

STOP!: The small stop sign icon has two useful purposes. First, as long as a page is being loaded, it will remain red. Second, when the icon is red, you can click on it to halt the loading, which will allow the browser to display information it has already received.

Images: Images are vastly huge; often the graphics of a page are 100 to 10,000 times the size of the HTML code used to lay out the page. You can speed up the display of the textual portion of a page by turning off the Auto Load Images in the Option pull-down menu. If you need to see the images, such as imagemaps or navigation icons, click on the Load Images button or right-click on an image and select Load this Image. (The Load Images button is the one with the arrow pointing at an empty graphic icon, right below the Bookmark menu item.)

Internet Explorer

Microsoft's entry into the Internet browser race has made a good first showing. Not to be outdone by Netscape, Microsoft has added their own proprietary HTML tags as well as support for most of the popular Netscape extensions. With eyes on controlling the Web as they do the desktop, Microsoft is sure to build power and versatility into their "end-all-be-all" Web browser. Currently the Internet Explorer is available only for Windows 95; versions for Windows 3.1/3.11 and NT Server are on the drawing board.

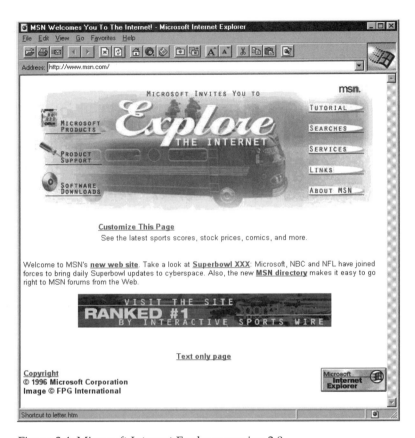

Figure 3.4: Microsoft Internet Explorer version 2.0.

WHERE TO FIND IT

Online: You can obtain Internet Explorer from the Microsoft Web site: http://www.microsoft.com/windows/ie/iexplorer.htm. You will need a Web browser to access this page. If you have only an FTP utility, you can retrieve Internet Explorer from ftp.microsoft.com in directory /Softlib/MSLFILES/. Take note that this is a heavily used host and getting connected may be impossible during peak hours.

Offline: The Internet Explorer is one of the programs included in the Microsoft Plus! for Windows 95 package. If you choose this route, be sure to read the packaging carefully; you don't want to end up with anything earlier than version 2.0.

VERSION

The current commercial and shareware version is 2.0 (filename msie20.exe or msie20dl.exe). However, as of January 20, 1996, the Plus! package still included only version 1.0. (But hey, you can always use it to get the new one online!)

FEATURES

The Microsoft Internet Explorer is a full-featured Web browser, complying with the current standards of HTML and HTTP. With support for most of the HTML 3.0 proposed standards (tables, figures, and math), multimedia (sound, video, VRML), Usenet, and FTP there is little you will be unable to accomplish with this puppy.

For all the information about Internet Explorer that is fit to publish (and even some that's not) see http://www. microsoft.com/windows/ie/ieinfo.htm.

WHY WE LIKE IT

The Internet Explorer was designed by the same people who brought us Windows 95, so it has the best "seamless" integration and takes advantage of the multitasking 32-bit OS. (This is not to say that other don't, but the award always goes to the homeboy). One of the nifty features that we haven't seen elsewhere is drag-and-drop to and from the browser and the desktop.

WHAT WE DON'T LIKE

We don't like Microsoft's reckless renaming of standard Internet concepts, especially those related to the Web. In Milord Gates' crusade to rule not only the desktop but everything it comes in contact with, Microsoft has gone too far in redefining terms. One of the most annoying examples of this is calling hypertext links "shortcuts". (A shortcut is a faster way to get somewhere, a hypertext link is the direct path to the resource—anyone not working for Microsoft can see the difference.)

HOW TO INSTALL

If you downloaded the file from the Microsoft site, simply execute the original file and follow the prompts.

If you have the Plus! Pack, you'll have to follow the instructions that came with the box, banal as that may seem.

The standard installation of the Explorer will add an icon to your desktop. However, if you want to add it to your Start menu, you will need to use the taskbar's Properties command. (You can get this pop-up menu by right-clicking over an empty area of the taskbar. Select the Start Menu Programs tab and click on Add. You should be able to follow the prompts to add the Explorer to your Start menu. (If you want to delete the desktop Explorer icon, you will need to drag it into the recycle bin.)

HOW TO UNINSTALL

Since Internet Explorer is a native Windows 95 utility and uses an installation wizard, it can be uninstalled by using the Control Panel application Add/Remove Programs. Select the Internet Explorer listing and click on the Add/Remove button. You should have no problem following the prompts from there.

SETUP/CONFIGURATION

To configure the Internet Explorer, open the browser.

1. Resize the browser to your personal preference.

2. First load a Web site which we will set as the default page in step 7. The default page will load first each time the browser is started. Use the File Open command and type in "http://www.yahoo.com" or any other URL.

3. Select the View Options command from the menu bar.

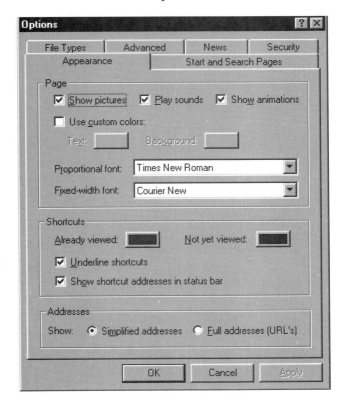

Figure 3.5: Microsoft Internet Explorer Options window.

4. Select the **Appearance** tab.

5. Deselect the Underline shortcuts.

6. Select Full addresses (URLs).

7. Select the **Start and Search Pages** tab.

8. Click the Use Current button to set the currently loaded Web site as the default start page. If you need to set the start page to a site other than the currently loaded page, click on OK, load your desired start page, then return to this tab page.

9. No changes are needed on the **File Types** tab.

10. Select the **Advanced** tab.

11. Set the number of global history addresses to save; set a reasonable number between 50 and 500.

12. Be sure the once per session option is selected for page updates.

13. Set the cache slide bar to read 5% of disk.

14. Select the **News** tab.

15. If you would like to view Usenet newsgroups with Internet Explorer, you will need to check the top box to activate this tab page. If you do so, you will need to fill in all the information about your NNTP news server.

16. Select the **Security** tab.

17. Set the security features to the level you desire; our recommendation is to set the security feature to low or

off to prevent superfluous pop-up windows warning you of form field data transmission. (This gets annoying real fast, especially when using search engines!)

18. Click OK.

Your options are automatically saved once you exit the Options window.

HOW TO USE IT

Getting started: Internet Explorer will load the start page you defined in the configuration steps—or the default Microsoft IE home page—when the browser is opened. Once the page loads, you are ready to surf! You can load new pages by clicking on hyperlinks or using the File Open command and typing in a URL.

Bookmarks: Microsoft has once again renamed a standard concept: the Internet Explorer bookmark list is called Favorites. Under this menu you can add the current page to the list or jump to the master bookmark/favorite folder to edit or delete saved locations.

HINTS AND TIPS

Go Home: To get to the Microsoft Internet Explorer home page, all you need to do is hit the home icon on the button bar. However, if in configuring Explorer you changed the start page, you will need to click on the Use Default button the View Options **Start and Search Pages** tab to reset the start page. A third way to get home is by accessing the main Microsoft Web site at http:/www. microsoft.com and following the Internet Explorer links.

More Menus: Right-click on any part of the browser display window to get a context sensitive pop-up menu. You can add pages to your list of favorites, view the source, save a links target to disk, grab an image, and even set an image as your desktop wallpaper.

Mail and Print: From the File menu, you can send a document anywhere using the Microsoft Exchange (if you have that Windows 95 feature fully configured) or print to a local printer.

STOP!: The stop button is the page with the red "X" on it. (You'd think they could make something this simple easy to recognize, but, no, Microsoft has to be different.)

Images: One feature that Microsoft got right is displaying all the textual portion of a page before starting to retrieve the graphics or other resources imbedded in a Web document. However, if you still want to turn off the auto-load function, go back to the View Options **Appearance** tab. From this tab page you can turn off the automatic loading of images, sounds, and animations.

HotJava

HotJava is the Java-based Web browser from Sun Microsystems, Inc. HotJava's central function is to display and play Java applications, and it is thus a great browser for Java programmers. Unfortunately, this central function caused Sun to be nearsighted in the development of other features. This is a great browser for viewing Java applications, but it's on the lousy side for everyday surfing. HotJava is not the only browser that is Java enabled; you can add Java plug-ins to Netscape (and soon a few others). So unless you're a Java programmer, you are probably better off going elsewhere for your coffee.

Pay attention to what you read about Java. It has the potential to significantly alter the way information is exchanged via the Internet. It's still early days, but Netscape and others are working closely with Sun to integrate Java with the WWW.

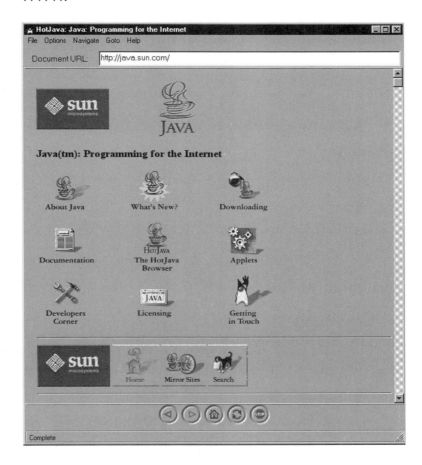

Figure 3.6: HotJava, the Sun Microsystem Java browser.

WHERE TO FIND IT

HotJava can be found at the Sun Microsystem HotJava Web site at http://java.sun.com/. Select Downloading to access the software retrieval page. The software can also be obtained via anonymous FTP at java.sun.com in directory /pub.

VERSION

As of January 1996, the HotJava browser is in version 1.0Alpha3 for Windows NT and Windows 95 with the file-name "hotjava-alpha3-win32-x86.exe." (There is a UNIX version as well, but this is a Windows book—so just forget we said anything.)

FEATURES

HotJava has some extremely powerful features, which unfortunately most casual users will never appreciate: built-in Java applet support, security, multithreading, full mailto, FTP, and Telnet support. One nice display feature that is missing on many other popular browsers is the delayed image and applet loading. HotJava places status icons inside image areas while the images are being loaded.

WHY WE LIKE IT

There are a few things we really like about Hotw things we really like about HotJava. First, it has a great status bar which displays bytes remaining and percentage completed of a loading page. Second, it has an extensive resident help archive accessed from the default start-up page. Third, there's a nifty progress monitor window that can be dragged anywhere on your screen—giving you a progress bar for every item linked to the currently loading page with color-coded type listings.

WHAT WE DON'T LIKE

Sun fails to incorporate some of the standard features you expect to find in a Web browser, such as the ability to select text in the display window and right-click on pop-up menus. The browser has a nice clean layout, but it is little awkward to use with the control buttons at the bottom of the display instead of at the top.

HOW TO INSTALL

Execute the original file; it will expand itself creating a directory "hotjava" with a directory tree underneath. Once the extraction has completed—and it will take a while—you can move the "hotjava" directory and all of its contents to your "Internet" directory—that is, if you took our advice about organizing your hard drives. The extraction process does not add HotJava to your Start menu or your desktop; you'll have to do these by hand or always run it from the Start Run command. To add an icon to your desktop, right-click on any stop on your desktop. select New Shortcut, and follow the prompts. To add an icon to the Start menu, right-click on an empty area of the Taskbar, select Properties, select the Start Menu Programs tab, click on Add…, and follow the prompts.

HOW TO UNINSTALL

Uninstallation of HotJava is fairly simple. First, remove any icons or shortcuts you created on the desktop or in the Start menu. Then delete the "hotjava" directory and all of its subdirectories.

SETUP/CONFIGURATION

HotJava does not offer many configuration options. All of them fit into two windows—Properties and Security—which are located in the Options pull-down menu.

1. Open the HotJava browser.

2. Resize the browser window to your personal preference.

3. Select Options Properties.

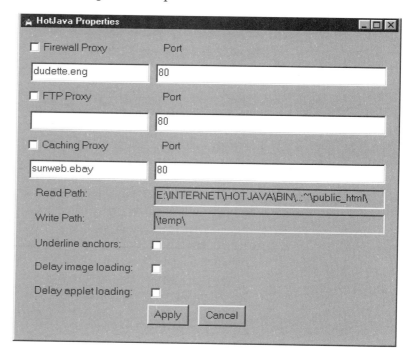

Figure 3.7: HotJava Options Properties window.

4. The proxy options listed here will not be of use to the common dial-up Internet user. If you do need a proxy for any of the functions listed, fill in the required information.

5. If you want to underline links, delay image, or applet loading, mark the appropriate boxes.

6. Click Apply.

7. Select Options Security.

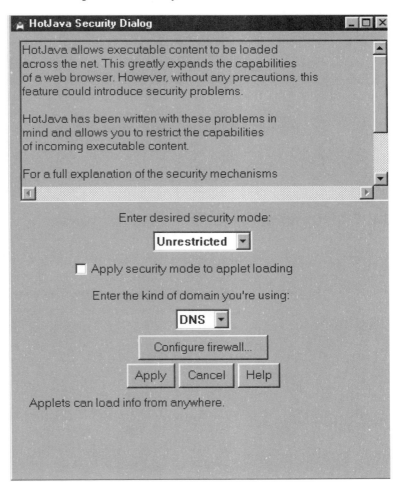

Figure 3.8: HotJava Options Security window.

8. From this window, you can alter the security mode, alter your domain type, and configure the use of a fire-wall. You should not need to make any changes here.

9. Click Apply.

HOW TO USE IT

Getting started: HotJava will automatically load its resident information pages each time the browser is opened. You can use these pages to start your Internet surfing or open other sites by selecting File Open and typing in a URL (e.g.., http://www.yahoo.com).

Bookmarks: HotJava calls it a Hotlist, but it works the same as every other browser's bookmarks. Use the "Navigate, Add Current to Hotlist" or "Goto, Add Current" command to save a page's address. You can edit the list with the Navigate Show Hotlist command—and while you are there click on the "In Goto Menu" box to have your hotlist displayed under the Goto menu item. There is one trick in using the Hotlist window: to exit the window without changing to another page, you have to click on the close button (the "X" in the upper right corner).

HINTS AND TIPS

Go Home: To get to the Sun home page, return to the default start page: select Navigate Home and scroll down to the bottom. There you will find two linked images, one to Sun's site and one to HotJava's.

History: Under the Navigate menu command is a Show History selection. Here a current session history list is kept.

STOP!: To stop a page from loading you can click on the stop sign icon in the button bar at the bottom of the screen.

Images and applets: If you selected the delay image or applet boxes in the Option Properties window, you will have to click on inside the empty image/applet box to load that image/applet.

Oracle PowerBrowser

Oracle, the leader in database development technology, has developed a Web browser specifically to access and interface with advanced Web-based client/server applications. Oracle has also included a Web page wizard to help you build HTML documents and other server features to get your own Web site up and running. (We won't be going into detail about these two features here, but there are volumes of information online. Just get the browser and read all about it.)

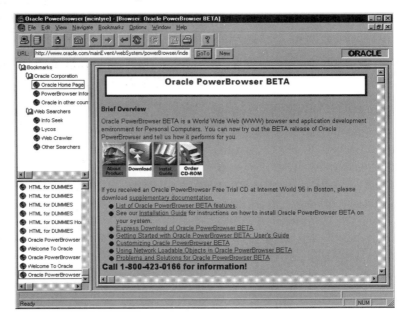

Figure 3.9: Oracle PowerBrowser BETA.

WHERE TO FIND IT

The Oracle PowerBrowser is available on the Oracle Web site. The PowerBrowser front page is at http://www.oracle.com/PowerBrowser/. Click on the Download icon, fill out the registration form, and grab the file. We were not able to locate an anonymous FTP site, so you will have to have another browser to get to this one.

VERSION

As of January 1996, the PowerBrowser is still in its original beta version. It is available in Windows 3.1/3.11 16-bit and Windows 95 32-bit versions, with filenames of "orapb.exe," and "orapb95.exe," respectively.

FEATURES

The Oracle PowerBrowser is fully standards compliant but also supports tables, frames, and backgrounds. It has nested bookmark folders, full e-mail and newsgroup support, and a lifetime history list.

WHY WE LIKE IT

We like the PowerBrowser for its great bookmark and history functions—easy to use with limitless storage ability (at least as long as the hard drive holds out). Another interesting feature of the browser is the use of windowing to organize multiple pages, which can be arranged in the main display area one at the time, tiled, or cascaded—similarly to most high-end word processors. However, unless you have a large monitor, viewing more than one page in the display area is difficult.

WHAT WE DON'T LIKE

The PowerBrowser does not support displayed text selection, which we feel is a must for any avid surfer. Oracle did provide right-click on pop-up menus but forgot to put any worthwhile commands in them. All you can do is add a link to the hotlist and open other document windows. There are no resident FTP capabilities—a definite oversight—and the display of the text of a page is delayed while the images are loaded. The windowing feature is nice, but it is impossible to view more than two pages and still be able to do anything with them—cute but fairly useless unless you stick with cascading. The layout of the browser is a little confusing as well; the default screen layout contains the hotlist, the history list, and the main view window—way too much information at one time. You can resize the hotlist/history areas, but reducing their size makes them unreadable. Unfortunately, there is no way to turn them off, you just have to shrink their display area until you can't see them anymore.

HOW TO INSTALL

Execute the original file. Click on the Install button and follow the prompts. Once completed, click on OK on the completion screen

HOW TO UNINSTALL

To remove the PowerBrowser from your system, remove the Oracle Browser folder from the Start menu, then delete the "orapb95" directory and all its contents.

SETUP/CONFIGURATION

The Oracle PowerBrower configuration options should be changed as follows:

1. Open the browser.

2. Resize the browser window to your personal preference.

3. Select Options Preferences.

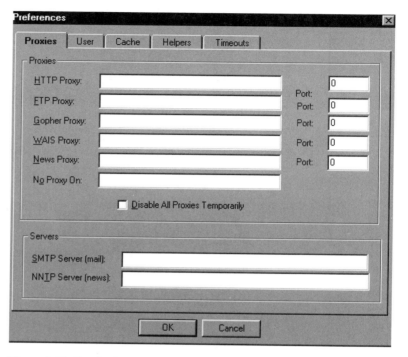

Figure 3.10: Oracle PowerBrowser Option Preferences window.

4. On the **Proxies** tab, enter the domain names or IP addresses for your SMTP e-mail server and your NNTP news server.

5. Select the **User** tab.

6. Enter your personal information.

7. You can leave the remaining options as they are, unless you want to alter the look and performance of the browser.

8. Select the **Cache** tab.

9. Here you can alter the size of the cache, set the page reload time, disable the cache, and clear the cache.

10. You should not need to change anything on the **Helpers** and **Timeout** tab pages.

11. Click OK.

12. Select the Options Save Options to save the changes you just made.

HOW TO USE IT

Getting started: Oracle has conveniently listed a few of the popular search engines in the hotlist. You can click on one of these to get your surfing under way. Or if you prefer to start off somewhere else, type a URL in the URL box above the display area (or click on File Load from URL for the long way around)—remember to press <ENTER> to get things rolling.

Bookmarks: To add a bookmark, you need to select one of the top level subfolders (or create a new one with the Bookmarks Add Folder), then select the Bookmarks Add Bookmark. Notice in the bookmark window (in the upper left corner of the Oracle window) that your new bookmark appears under the subfolder group currently selected or active. This may be a bit confusing at first, but you can always delete and try again.

HINTS AND TIPS

Go Home: Getting to the Oracle Web site (http://www.oracle.com/) is just a bookmark click on away—unless you deleted the Oracle Corporation bookmark folder.

Mail and Print: From the File menu, you can send a page to someone by e-mail or to your local printer.

Images: You can turn off automatic menu loading on the Options Preferences **User** tab page. Once off, the only way to view images is to turn them back on and reload.

Mosaic

Mosaic was the original graphical browser for the World Wide Web developed by NCSA. Over the last three years, it has continued to develop and adapt to changes in the Web landscape (mainly caused by Netscape). Today, Mosaic is still a solid Web browser which has been cloned by over a dozen companies. No list of graphical Web browsers would be complete without a look at one of the direct descendants of the first-generation Mosaic.

Figure 3.11: NCSA's Mosaic version 2.0.0.

WHERE TO FIND IT

The latest version of Mosaic can be obtained from the NCSA Mosaic home page at http://www.ncsa.uiuc. edu/SDG/Software/WinMosaic/Home Page.html, or via anonymous FTP at ftp.ncsa.uiuc.edu in the directory /Mosaic/Windows/ Win95/ (Windows NT version is in WinNT/ and Windows 3.1/3.11 version is in Win31x/).

VERSION

In January 1996, Mosaic is in version 2.0.0 for Windows 95/NT/3.1/3.11. The version filenames are all "mosaic20.exe," so you will need to be careful about which directory you retrieve the file from. The installation instructions below are for the Windows 95 version.

FEATURES

Along with being fully standards compliant, Mosaic has not been left behind in the race to have more features than a Swiss Army knife. Mosaic's long list of features (which can be viewed at http://www.ncsa.uiuc.edu/SDG/ Software/WinMosaic/Features.htm) includes: e-mail, newsgroup and FTP support, hotlist management, auto-surfing, and right-click on pop-up menus.

WHY WE LIKE IT

Mosaic is a solid well-featured browser—while it can't do everything, it does what it does very well. The right-click on menus are detailed and context sensitive. For example, some of the commands in the pop-up menu are page header and anchor information, saving a background image, and on-the-fly font alterations. There is both local and online help; just select one from the Help command.

WHAT WE DON'T LIKE

As with Netscape, we have to be picky to list our dislikes of the Mosaic browser. Mosaic does not have a lifetime history list and does not yet have security support. Mosaic also handles FTP transfers internally instead of spawning a separate process, so you cannot continue surfing while downloading a file.

HOW TO INSTALL

If you are a Windows 3.1/3.11 user, you must have Win32 with OLE installed in order to use Mosaic. Please visit the Mosaic home page for information about downloading and installing the latest version of Win32.

Execute the original file. Open the Control Panel from the Start Settings menu, and run the Add/Remove Programs application. Click Install, Next, then Browse. Locate the setup.exe file created by the unpacking of the original file. Click Open, then Finish. Follow the prompts.

HOW TO UNINSTALL

Removing NCSA Mosaic is as simple as its installation. Return to the Control Panel Add/Remove Programs application. Select the Mosaic program listing, click on Remove, and follow the prompts.

SETUP/CONFIGURATION

Mosaic has far too many options. You can take your own sweet time altering anything and everything about the browser, but we are going to show you just how to make the essential features operational.

1. Run/execute the browser.

2. Resize the browser window to your personal preference.

3. Select Options Preferences.

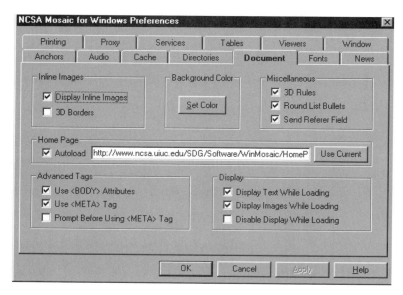

Figure 3.12: NCSA Mosaic 2.0.0 Options Preferences window.

4. Select the **Document** tab. (It should already be the default selection.)

5. The only option you may need to change here is whether or not to load the Mosaic home page each time Mosaic is opened.

6. Select the **Directories** tab.

7. Change the default download directory to something other than the default c:\win95\temp. (Use d:\dl if you followed our hard drive organization suggestions.)

8. Select the **News** tab.

9. Type in your NNTP server domain name or IP address.

10. Select the method of news article layout from the display options box.

11. You can use the Subscription button to subscribe to newsgroups that you want to read using Mosaic.

12. Select the **Services** tab.

13. Enter your name, e-mail address, and SMTP mail server domain name or IP address.

14. Use the Browse button to select the correct Telnet application.

15. Click OK to close the Preferences window.

Your changes are automatically saved once you exit the Preferences window.

HOW TO USE IT

Getting started: Unless you altered the autoload page option, the Mosaic home page will load when you open Mosaic. You can use this as a starting point or enter another URL with the File Open command, click on the open folder on the button bar, or clicking inside the URL list box just below the button bar.

Bookmarks: Mosaic has a great hotlist management utility, which you should take a little time to become familiar with. Basically, select Navigate Add Current to Hotlist or click on the burning page icon to add a page to the hotlist menu. To access a saved page address, click on the Hotlists command, drag your mouse around until you find the one you want, and click on it. To edit hotlist entries, select Navigate Advanced Hotlist Manager.

HINTS AND TIPS

Go Home: If you have altered the start page, you can still access the Mosaic home page from the Hotlist or from the Help Online Resources.

More Menus: Mosaic had the right idea when it added right click on pop-up menus. Try clicking over different areas of a page—images, links, headings, e-mail addresses, etc.— and you'll see dozens of commands you never even thought existed before.

Mail and Print: Mosaic has mail and print. Just click on the File menu command to get to them.

On Screen Text Selection: Netscape is not the only browser to have this feature. Just click on and drag to select any text on the display screen, then <CTRL-C> to copy it into Windows clipboard.

STOP!: To interrupt loading click on the stop hand sign button, click on the animated Mosaic icon, or select Navigate Stop Transfer.

Images: On the **Document** tab of the Option Preferences window, you can turn off the Display Inline Images to prevent the automatic loading of graphics. To load graphics again, you will need to turn this option back on.

E-mail

E-mail stands for electronic mail, and it is just what its name says—messages that are transmitted by an electronic medium, i.e., computers. E-mail is the single most important activity on the Internet. More people use e-mail than any other service by an almost two-to-one margin. Instantaneous, worldwide, free communication; no other means of interaction—telephone, radio, television, or postal service—provides an easier to use, more powerful, or more universal method for communicating with each other. E-mail can transmit not only written messages but any electronic resource, including audio, video, fax, and entire software packages

How Does E-mail Work?

E-mail works by using the TCP/IP network of the Internet to move messages from the author to the recipient. An e-mail message consists of a header, the message body, and any attachments. The header contains information about the origin of the message, the address of the destination mailbox, a time stamp, and routing information. The header is used like the address on an envelope to guide the message to the correct destination. The message body is simply the written text of the message. Attachments are binary files of any type which are "attached" to the message so that they are transmitted along with the rest of the e-mail message.

An e-mail mailbox is simply a directory on a host computer. This directory is where e-mail addressed to you is deposited and stored until you transfer it from the ISP's server to your local machine. You have to have an e-mail utility to retrieve the messages from the server, read the messages, and send out your own messages.

There are actually two e-mail protocol types which are very important, POP and SMTP. POP stands for Post Office Protocol. POP is the Internet protocol used to control how a message is transmitted from your incoming mailbox on the ISP mail server to your desktop computer. SMTP stands for Simple Mail Transfer Protocol. This protocol is what is used to transmit e-mail from your e-mail utility, across the Internet, and into the destination mailbox. You must have an e-mail service utility which is fully compliant with both of these protocols in order to transmit and receive e-mail on the Internet. Both of the utilities we suggest here are fully compliant with all current Internet e-mail standards.

What is a signature?

A signature is a short message which is attached to the end of an e-mail message. Generally your signature should contain your name, your e-mail address, Web site URL, and other contact information such as phone, fax, or mailing address. Many people also like to include business information, funny quotations, and ASCII art (pictures made with keyboard characters). There are no rules or requirements, unless defined by your e-mail utility, about the content or length of a signature. However, good netiquette suggests that a signature file of 4 lines is exceptional and up to 10 lines is tolerated. If you do use a signature, keep the information specific, easy to read, and up-to-date.

E-mail Utilities

Having a reliable e-mail utility is very important. It doesn't take long to accumulate hundreds of important messages. The two utilities we recommend are both solid products with which you are sure to be pleased.

Eudora

Eudora is one of the most popular e-mail utilities. It is available in both a full-featured commercial version and a free Internet light version. Eudora is also available for the Macintosh.

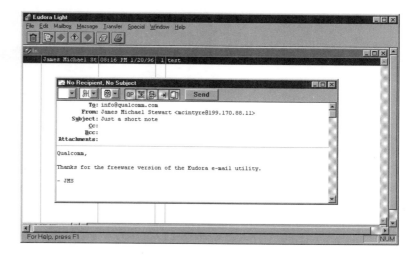

Figure 3.13: Qualcomm Eudora Light Freeware version 1.5.2.

WHERE TO FIND IT

Eudora Light Freeware version is available from the Qualcomm Web page at http://www.qualcomm. com/ ProdTech/quest/ or by anonymous FTP at ftp.qualcomm.com in the directory /Eudora/windows/light/.

Figure 3.14: Qualcomm's Eudora Web page.

VERSION

The current version, as of January 1996, is 1.5.2 with a file-name of "eudor152.exe." This is a 16-bit Windows version that functions under Windows 3.1/3.11 and Windows 95. Our installation instructions below focus on Windows 95.

FEATURES

Eudora is fully POP and SMTP compliant, with offline reading and writing of messages, find and sort utilities, attachments, hierarchical message filing, and MIME support, and is fully compatible with UNIX mail files. For a complete list of features see http://www.qualcomm.com/ ProdTech /quest/eudora.html.

WHY WE LIKE IT

Eudora is a time-tested utility which has survived and improved under the abuse of its users. Eudora includes almost any type of e-mail function you will ever need. However, the commercial version packs some extra features that the freeware version lacks, such as message filters and spell checking. If you like the product, spend the cash for the full version.

WHAT WE DON'T LIKE

We don't like it for two reasons. First, the freeware version lacks the ability to spell-check messages. Second, it is a bit cumbersome for the beginning user. If this is your first e-mail utility, take the time to download and read the manual. (Look for it on the Web page or the FTP site.)

HOW TO INSTALL

Execute the original file. Create a directory to store the Eudora program files (such as d:\internet\eudora), then copy the files extracted from the original file into that new directory. Add Eudora to the desktop (right-click on desktop, select New Shortcut) or Start menu (right-click on empty area of task bar, select Properties, Start Menu Programs tab, Add button). Be sure to point either of these shortcuts to the main program "eudora.exe."

HOW TO UNINSTALL

NOTE If you uninstall Eudora, you will lose all e-mail stored by Eudora. To remove Eudora from your system, delete the desktop or Start menu Eudora item, then delete the "eudora" directory and all its contents.

SETUP/CONFIGURATION

The first time you run Eudora, you will configure it in order to send and receive e-mail.

1. Open Eudora.

2. The Settings window will appear.

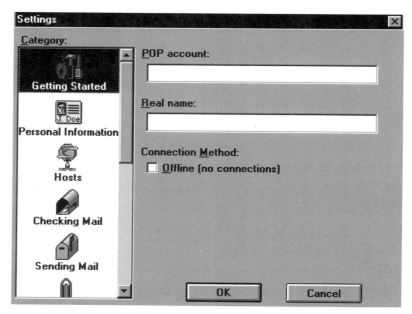

Figure 3.15: Eudora's Settings window.

3. Select the Getting Started category.

4. Enter your e-mail address in the first box and your full name in the second.

5. Select the Hosts category.

6. Enter the domain name or IP address of your SMTP e-mail server.

7. Select the Checking Mail category.

8. Enter a number in the Check mail every ? minutes box; 10 to 15 should be appropriate.

9. Check the save password box. This will store your access password so that you will not have to enter it every time you check mail.

10. Click the OK button to close and save the settings.

HOW TO USE IT

The basics of Eudora can be learned without too much headache. However, the more advanced features such as nicknames, attachments, and signatures will involve you reading through the manual (which you will need to download from the Qualcomm FTP site listed earlier).

To send an e-mail message: Click the new message icon button or select Message New Message from the menu bar. Enter the address to which you want to send e-mail on the To: line. Type in a brief subject in the Subject: line. Type your message in the main body area below the line. Once you are finished, click on the send button.

To retrieve e-mail: You can either wait for the timer setting to automatically retrieve your e-mail or select File Check Mail to do it manually. If you have messages waiting, Eudora will transfer them to your desktop and display the heading information in the "IN" window (if it's not already open, select Window indow In from the menu bar).

HINTS AND TIPS

We're going to give you one big tip. Pop for the $89.00 suggested retail price and go buy Eudora Pro, the commercial version of Eudora, from your favorite PC software mail order catalog. You can also do the electronic commerce thing and order it right off the Net with your credit card at the Qualcomm WWW site. The Interent address is:

`http://www.qualcomm.com/quest/`

We're not just copping out on the Hints and Tips section for Eudora. It's the one and only hint and tip worth giving.

Here's why.

The commercial version of Eudora has a killer feature that lets you set up "filters" that automatically sort your mail for you into mailboxes. Believe us. When you get up to speed and start subscribing to mailing lists on the Internet, your mailbox is going to get packed and unmanageable pronto.

E-mail is one of the big deals on the Net. It's something you're going to be doing a lot of. Count on it. Nab the commercial version of Eudora and you'll make your life a whole lot easier, Jack.

E-mail Connection

E-mail Connection is distributed by ConnectSoft. This e-mail utility is fast, easy to use, and fully functional. While E-mail Connection doesn't have every possible feature, we found its overall abilities very suitable for high-volume e-mail handling. We highly recommend this utility. There are two versions of this software: the full version and the Internet version. Both versions are completely functional and operational; however, the Internet version supports only Internet POP/SMTP mail, while the full version supports many other mail standards such as AccessCard, cc:Mail, and Lotus Notes. As long as you are using it for Internet mail, the Internet version will be all you'll need.

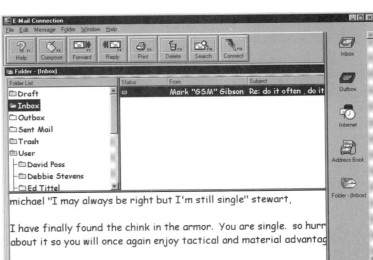

Figure 3.16: ConnectSoft's E-mail Connection Internet version.

WHERE TO FIND IT

You can retrieve the E-mail Connection from the ConnectSoft Web site at: http://www.connectsoft.com/. You will need to click on the Software Lotto ticket, then click on the link in the sentence which reads "To obtain the Internet Edition using your Web browser, click on here." Or you can obtain the file by anonymous FTP from ftp.connectsoft.com in the directory /pub/emc25/.

VERSION

E-mail Connection Internet version 2.5.03 is the latest release as of January 1996. The filename is "emcsetup.exe" and will operate on both Windows 3.1/3.11 and Windows 95.

FEATURES

E-mail Connection is a fully featured standards-compliant e-mail utility. This utility has a spell checker, offline reading and writing of messages, find and sort utilities, attachments, hierarchical message filing, MIME support, advanced e-mail/address/phone manager, and message filtering.

WHY WE LIKE IT

E-mail Connection is powerful, easy to use, and full of great features. It handles attachments exceptionally well: unlike many e-mail utilities which always crash on BinHexed files, this one doesn't even blink. It also has fully customizable layout, trash options, and scheduling.

WHAT WE DON'T LIKE

There are only a few quirks we would like removed or features we think need to be added. If you choose to move a message from the inbox to a new user folder, you have to create the folder first; there is no way to create a new folder from the move message window. Even with the automatic add addresses to the address book feature turned off, some addresses still slip in uninvited. One feature that we would like added is BCC or Blind Carbon Copy; currently only the CC address method is available.

HOW TO INSTALL

Execute the original file. Follow the prompts.

HOW TO UNINSTALL

NOTE If you uninstall E-mail Connection, you will lose all e-mail stored by E-mail Connection. To remove E-mail Connection from your system, delete the Start menu E-mail Connection item, then delete the 'emcint' directory and all its contents.

SETUP/CONFIGURATION

The first time you run E-mail Connection, you will need to configure it in order to send and receive Internet e-mail.

1. Open E-mail Connection.

2. Read and accept the license agreement.

3. The New User Information dialog box will appear.

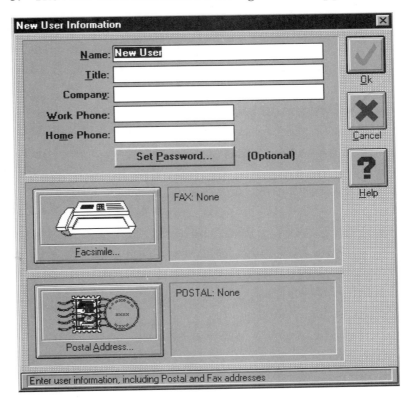

Figure 3.18: E-mail Connection's New User Information dialog box.

4. Input your personal information.

5. Click OK.

6. Input your correct address.

7. Click OK.

8. Click OK again.

9. Once the main program loads, the Internet Mail Setup window appears.

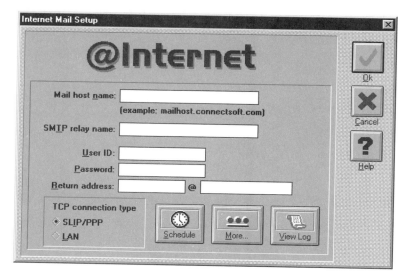

Figure 3.19: E-mail Connection's Internet Mail Setup window.

10. Input your POP mail server domain name or IP address in the first box.

11. Input your SMTP mail server domain name or IP address in the second box. (If your POP and SMTP servers are the same, you will not need to change the second box.)

12. Input your user login name, password, and standard e-mail address.

13. Click Schedule.

14. In the Begin box type "12:01am."

15. In the End box type "11:59pm."

16. In the Connect every box, type the number of minutes you want between automatic mail connections; 10 to 20 minutes should be appropriate.

17. Check Sunday and Saturday, so that all the days are selected.

18. Deselect the two Notify lines at the bottom.

19. Click OK.

20. The click on OK again.

21. Select File Preferences from the menu bar.

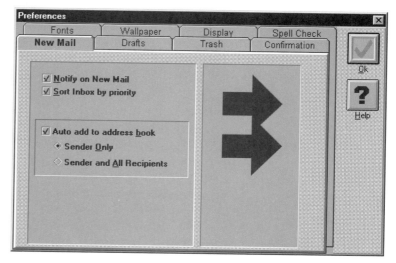

Figure 3.20: E-mail Connection's Preferences window.

22. Select the **New Mail** tab.

23. Deselect the Auto add to address book.

24. Select the **Drafts** tab.

25. Click the Signature button.

26. Type in your signature. You can always return here to update or alter it.

27. Click OK.

28. Select the Trash tab.

29. Select the Delete messages older than line and enter the number 3 in the box below it. This setting will remove deleted messages from a storage bin called "trash" once they are three days old—giving you a little time to recover deleted messages.

30. Select the Empty Trash after each use.

31. Select the **Confirmation** tab.

32. Deselect each of the Send, Forward, and Reply boxes.

33. Deselect the Delete Confirmation box.

34. No changes are needed on the **Fonts, Wallpaper**, or **Display** tabs. You may alter these to your own preferences.

35. Select the **Spell Check** tab.

36. Deselect the Automatic spell check.

37. Select Always suggest; deselect the two Ignore lines.

38. Click OK to save these changes.

HOW TO USE IT

With most Internet utilities, getting used to the operation of a program will greatly increase your productivity. With this in mind, E-mail Connection has made a valiant effort to make e-mail handling easy.

Send a message: Click the Compose button. Type in the destination e-mail address (or add it from the Address button if it is already in the Address book), click on the arrow button beside the To: box to "enter" the address. Type out your message body. Click the Send button to put the message in the Outbox. You will either need to wait until the timer settings automatically access the mail server or click on the Connect button to force a connection now.

Retrieve e-mail: E-mail is automatically retrieved based on the timer setting, or you can click on the Connect button to check for mail at any time.

Add to the Address Book: Click on the Address Book icon the left of the application window. Then click on Add, select the type of entry, and then input all the information. Once finished, click on OK. You can close the Address book window or switch windows with the Windows pull-down menu.

Attachments: Adding an attachment to a file is as simple as pressing the Attachment button while composing a message and selecting the file to add. Saving incoming attachments can be done from the Message Attachment command or by double-clicking on an attachment's icon.

HINTS AND TIPS

Multiple view options: You can read an e-mail message by selecting its title line with a single click on—which shows the message body in the lower display area, or a double-click on,—which opens a new message window with the body displayed as well as any attachments.

Message icons: In the message title display window, small icons are used to indicate the status of a message. A single closed envelope indicates an unread message (or at least that the message has not been opened by double-clicking). Multiple envelopes indicate that the message was sent to more than one recipient. An open envelope indicates that the message has been read. A paper clip beside the envelope indicates that the message has an attachment. A pencil pointing at a piece of paper indicates that a message is in draft form or still being written.

Outbox: When you click on the Send button the message is placed in the Outbox, where it waits for the next Internet mail server connection. You can open and alter any e-mail message sitting in the Outbox. Just double-click on its title line and edit it; then click on Send to put it back in the Outbox.

User Folders: User folders are subdirectories where you can sort and store e-mail. You can create new folders using the Folder Create User Folder command.

Moving Messages: You can move a message from one folder, such as the Inbox, to another, such as a User folder, with the Message Move command or by click on drag-and-drop from the title window to the folder window.

FTP

FTP stands for File Transfer Protocol. FTP is used to transfer files of any type from one Internet machine to another. The Internet has thousands of sites with innumerable files, and to get to them, you need an FTP utility. When you access a site, you will be asked to supply a username and a password to gain access to the system. If you have a valid account on the machine, you can enter your personal username and password. If you do not have a valid account, you must try to gain access using anonymous FTP. Anonymous FTP is FTP which offers public access to selected files and directories. To gain access to an anonymous FTP site, you first instruct your FTP utility to access the site by inputting the domain name or IP address. When prompted for your username enter "anonymous" or "guest," then when prompted for a password enter your correct e-mail address in the form: username@domainname. If the site is not full and you did not enter a false e-mail address, you will be given access to all the public file areas.

WS_FTP

WS_FTP is a Windows-based FTP utility which hides all of the FTP command lines and allows you to perform complex FTP activities with an easy-to-use interface. WS_FTP is by far the best FTP utility for Windows; it even comes in both a 16-bit version for Windows 3.1/3.11 and a 32-bit version for Windows 95.

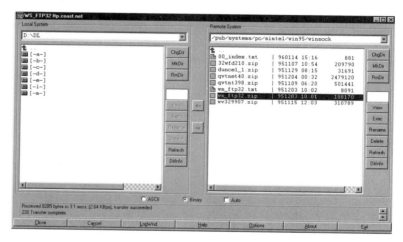

Figure 3.21: WS_FTP32 version 951130 main window.

WHERE TO FIND IT

WS_FTP can be obtained via anonymous FTP (remember you can use a Web browser with FTP support). The 16-bit Windows 3.1/3.11 version is at ftp://ftp.coast.net/SimTel/win3/winsock/ws_ftp.zip, and the 32-bit Windows 95 version is at ftp://ftp.coast.net/SimTel/win95/winsock/ws_ftp32 .zip.

VERSION

WS-FTP 32-bit Windows 95 is in version 951130 as of January 1996. The 16-bit Windows 3.1/3.11 is in version 951112.

FEATURES

WS_FTP has full FTP support, including ASCII and binary file transfers, and is compatible with all major file system types, directory structure transport, and all standard file/directory commands (i.e., rename, move, delete, mkdir, and view). WS_FTP has many display, notification, action, and function configuration options.

WHY WE LIKE IT

We like WS_FTP because it is a robust and fast FTP utility. With hundreds of control options this utility is simple and elegant to operate. One great feature that Web authors will appreciate is its ability to transfer a complete directory tree from your desktop to a remote FTP site.

WHAT WE DON'T LIKE

The only disappointing aspect of WS_FTP is its initial connection activity. We have noticed that once a connection is tried and fails, the WS_FTP software usually has to be closed and restarted before it will be able to connect to anywhere else. However, this may be a glitch in how winsock deals with interrupted connections and WS_FTP just happens to be in the wrong place at the wrong time.

HOW TO INSTALL

Create a destination directory, such as "d:\internet\ws_ftp" and extract the contents of the original file into this directory. Add WS_FTP to the desktop (right-click on desktop, select New Shortcut) or Start menu (right-click on empty area of task bar, select Properties, Start Menu

Programs tab, Add button). Be sure to point either of these shortcuts to the main program "ws_ftp32.exe" or "ws_ftp.exe."

HOW TO UNINSTALL

Remove WS_FTP from the desktop or Start menu, then delete the "d:\internet\ws_ftp" directory.

SETUP/CONFIGURATION

WS_FTP requires no special setup or configuration changes. However, if you want to fully customize the operation and display of the utility, you will need to consult the Help file (click on the Help button). WS_FTP has over 20 preset FTP sites for you to explore.

HOW TO USE IT

Every time WS_FTP is opened, the Session Profile box will appear over the main window. You can use the Profile pulldown listing to select one of the session settings, or add your own.

To add a new Session Profile, click on the New button below the Profile Name box. Enter a title or name of the new profile. Fill in the host name with a domain name or IP address. If you are adding an anonymous FTP site, click on the Anonymous Login box and change the Password from "guest" to your e-mail address. If you are adding an FTP site where you have a valid account, input your User Id (username) and Password. Be sure to select Save Password and Auto Save Config before leaving this window for the first time. To activate this profile, click on OK.

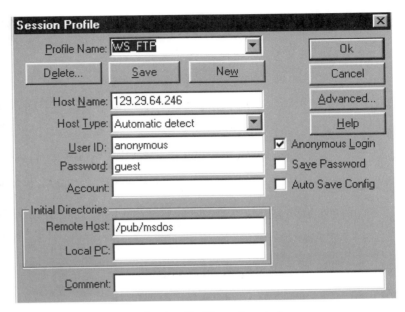

Figure 3.22: WS_FTP32 Session Profile main window.

Once you access a site, you can search through the directory structure of the remote FTP site just as you do with the Windows Explorer or File Manager. When you locate a file you want to retrieve, highlight it and click on the arrow pointing toward your drive.

After you have completed the session, click on Close to end the session or Exit to completely exit the WS_FTP utility. To start a new FTP session, click on Connect and the Session Profile box will reappear.

HINTS AND TIPS

Saving directories: Often you will transfer files to a specific directory on your local computer and maybe even visit the same directory on the remote FTP site. To save the open directory path of both the local drive and the remote

FTP site for the current session, click on Options Save Directory Names.

Multiple Files: Multiple Files: You can transmit multiple files by selecting more than one file before clicking the transfer arrows. To select a range, click on the first filename and then hold down <SHIFT> while you click on the second file name. To select multiple single names, click on the first filename, then hold down <CTRL> and click on each of the other filenames. Once you have selected multiple files by either method, release the hold key and click on the transfer arrow.

Directory Trees: To transfer a directory, simply select the parent directory and click on the transfer arrow. You will be prompted to verify that you want to transfer the directory structures.

Transfer status bar: By default, WS_FTP displays a small window with information about the currently transmitting file with a percentage bar showing its progress. If you are transmitting only a few files, this is a nice option. If you are transmitting many small files, this option will not allow you to use any other application productively while the transfer is in progress. Each time a new status bar window is created, Windows will make that new window active, thus deactivating whatever application you were just using. To turn this feature off, select Options, Session Options. Deselect the Show Transfer Dialog box and click on Save (for this session only), or click on Save as Default (to make this change for all future sessions).

Help File: There are many, many more options available to you and all of them are listed in the Help file. Be sure to look through the documentation about the options before changing anything else in the options menus.

Windows 95 FTP

Windows 95 has built-in resident command-line FTP. With Windows 95 you have a fully compatible FTP utility that can be used to retrieve other files such as WS_FTP or a Web browser. We are including instructions for the Windows 95 FTP utility, since it may be the only Internet service utility you have on hand to get yourself started. As we mentioned before, you have to have a utility to get a utility—and FTP is the best place to start.

WHERE TO FIND IT

The resident FTP utility is installed with Windows 95 if you also installed the Dial-Up Networking option. (See Windows 95 in Chapter 2.)

VERSION

The version of the FTP utility is dependent on the release version of Windows 95. Any full or upgrade release of the Windows 95 operating system has a fully functional and operational FTP utility.

FEATURES

Windows 95 FTP is a no-frills solid command-line FTP utility that is fully compatible with the Internet FTP standards.

WHY WE LIKE IT

It's free, it works, it doesn't need any configuration, it provides an alternative method of file retrieval.

WHAT WE DON'T LIKE

It's a command-line interface, which means you have to type in the FTP commands and there are no pretty display layouts.

HOW TO INSTALL

Select the Dial-Up Networking option under Communications when installing Windows 9.5/. (See Windows 95 in Chapter 2.)

HOW TO UNINSTALL

Microsoft has provided no instructions for uninstalling the FTP utility.

SETUP/CONFIGURATION

There are no setup or configuration options available.

HOW TO USE IT

To open the FTP utility, select the Run command from the Start menu. Type "ftp" in the box and click on OK. FTP will open a window and provide you with an "ftp>" prompt.

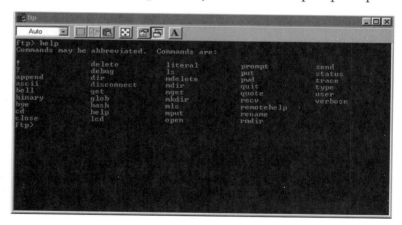

Figure 3.23: Windows 95 FTP session showing the Help information.

In order to use FTP you will need to be familiar with a few of the commands:

bin: Sets the file transfer type to binary.

cd: Changes the working directory on the remote computer.

close: Ends the FTP session with the remote server; does not exit FTP.

del: Deletes files on remote computers.

dir: Displays a list of a remote directory's files and subdirectories.

get: Copies a remote file to the local computer.

hash: Toggles hash-mark (#) printing for each 2048-byte data block transferred. By default, hash-mark printing is off.

lcd: Changes the working directory on the local computer.

open: Opens a connection to a remote FTP server; you will be prompted for the domain name or IP address.

pwd: Displays the current directory on the remote computer.

quit: Terminate FTP session and exit.

In order to demonstrate how to use FTP to retrieve a file, we have included an actual FTP session in which we obtained the WS_FTP utility. Please note that during an FTP session you will see numbers followed by a dash, "250-", at the beginning of each line; these are UNIX message type designators and can be completely ignored. Places where you input information have been underlined. Our additional comments are in brackets "[]" and in italics.

```
ftp> open ftp.coast.net

Connected to ftp.coast.net.

220 oak.oakland.edu FTP server (Version wu-
2.4(9) Wed May 3 15:02:49 EDT 1995) ready.

Name (ftp.coast.net:mcintyre): anonymous

331 Guest login ok, send your complete
e-mail address as password.

Password: [you must enter your password but
it will not appear on the screen]

230-

230-     Welcome to

230-     THE OAK SOFTWARE REPOSITORY

230-     A service of Oakland University,
Rochester Michigan

230-

[Welcome message removed]

230 Guest login ok, access restrictions
apply.

Remote system type is UNIX.

Using binary mode to transfer files.

ftp> cd SimTel

250-The files in this directory tree are a
mirror of SimTel, the Coast to

250-Coast Software Repository (tm). Please
read README.COPYRIGHT for

250-information distribution rights.

250-
```

[Directory message removed]

250 CWD command successful.

ftp> cd win95

250-This Windows 95 collection is a mirror of SimTel, the Coast to Coast

250-Software Repository (tm). Questions about or comments on this

250-collection should be sent to cctarch@SimTel.Coast.NET.

250-

[Directory message removed]

250 CWD command successful.

ftp> cd winsock

250 CWD command successful.

ftp> pwd [use this to make sure you are in the right directory]

257 "/pub2/simtel-win95/winsock" is current directory.

ftp> lcd d:\dl [This changes your local destination directory]

Local directory now D:\DL

ftp> dir ws*

200 PORT command successful.

150 Opening ASCII mode data connection for /bin/ls.

###
###
###

```
##############################################
##############
```

-rw-r—r— 1 djgruber system 8091 Dec 3 04:02 ws_ftp32.txt

-rw-r—r— 1 djgruber system 188170 Dec 3 04:01 ws_ftp32.zip

226 Transfer complete.

ftp> bin [Sets the transfer mode to binary - very important]

200 Type set to I.

ftp> hash [Turns on the hash marks to show progress]

Hash mark printing on (1024 bytes/hash mark).

ftp> get ws_ftp32.zip

local: ws_ftp32.zip remote: ws_ftp32.zip

200 PORT command successful.

150 Opening BINARY mode data connection for ws_ftp32.zip (188170 bytes).

226 Transfer complete.

188170 bytes received in 41 seconds (4.5 Kbytes/s)

ftp> quit

221 Goodbye.

Following this example you should be able to retrieve any publicly available file from any anonymous FTP site on the Internet.

HINTS AND TIPS

Case Sensitive: All filenames and many of the commands are case sensitive. Always type commands in lowercase and always check the exact spelling and case use of a filename (using the dir command).

Multiple files: You can retrieve multiple files at one time by using the "prompt" command to turn off confirmation prompts and "mget" to get more than one file. For example, if you wanted to get both the .txt and the .zip file, you would type "prompt" and then "mget ws_ftp*." Both files would be retrieved, one at a time.

Binary vs. ASCII: It is very important to turn on binary transfer mode when retrieving files that are not text only (i.e., ASCII). This ensures that the integrity of binary files will be maintained.

Usenet

Usenet is a worldwide hierarchical message system, where anyone can read and post articles. Usenet is organized into named group—called newsgroups—organized by topic and focus, with varying degrees of content control from strict moderation to free-form conversation. Almost every newsgroup has a FAQ (frequently asked questions), which is a document containing the focus, purpose, posting limitations, and rules for the specific newsgroup. We strongly suggest (even insist) that you locate and read the FAQ for a newsgroup before you even think about posting. This will save you headaches, frustration, and long lectures or even flaming. Take our word for it—when in doubt about the rules of a newsgroup, DON'T.

Here are two very popular newsreaders or Usenet utilities. We prefer to use Forte's FreeAgent and suggest you give it a try.

WinVN

WinVN (short for Windows Visual Newsreader) started out as a Macintosh utility and has been adapted to the Windows platform. (Since this adaptation, the Macintosh version has fallen behind as more development effort was directed toward the Windows version.) WinVN is available for Windows 3.1/3.11, Windows 95, and Windows NT platforms. Our installation example focuses on the Windows 95 version.

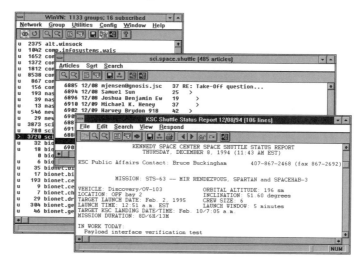

Figure 3.24: WinVN's Main, Group, and Message windows.

WHERE TO FIND IT

WinVN can be obtained from the WinVN web site at http://www.ksc.nasa.gov/software/winvn/winvn.html, or from anonymous FTP at ftp.coast.net in directory /SimTel/win3/winsock for Windows 3.1/3.11 or /SimTel/win95/winsock for Windows 95.

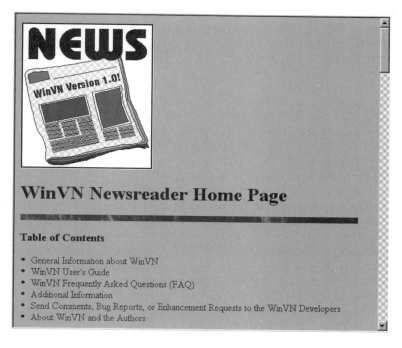

Figure 3.25: WinVN home page.

VERSION

As of January 1996, the current version of WinVN is 0.99-7. The filenames are Windows 3.1/3.11: "wv16_99_07.zip"; Windows 95 and NT: "winvn_99_07_intel.zip."

FEATURES

WinVN is a fully Internet Usenet-compliant newsreader. It supports binary decoding/encoding, article threading, and follow-up postings. WinVN also offers a wide range of customizable features that are fully explained in the Help file.

WHY WE LIKE IT

WinVN is an easy-to-use newsreader that is packaged with many Internet suites. It works without needing heavy configuration changes. WinVN is nice for a new user, but anyone who is serious about newsreading needs to find a more powerful utility with better server interaction abilities (such as FreeAgent).

WHAT WE DON'T LIKE

WinVN is not our favorite newsreader for a many reasons. First, offline newsreading is difficult to manage. Second, it does not support multiple simultaneous article retrieval. Third, we really don't like the multiple pop-up windows that appear every time you execute a new command or request another article: it is common to have a dozen or more windows open when trying to read through an article thread.

HOW TO INSTALL

Create a destination directory, such as "d:\internet\ winvn," and extract the contents of the original file into this directory. Add WinVN to the desktop (right-click on desktop, select New Shortcut) or to the Start menu (right-click on empty area of task bar, select Properties, Start Menu Programs tab, Add button). Be sure to point either of these shortcuts to the main program "winvn.exe."

HOW TO UNINSTALL

To uninstall, remove WinVN from the desktop or Start menu; then delete the "d:\internet\winvn" directory and all its contents.

SETUP/CONFIGURATION

Please read the "readme.txt" file before attempting installation. It contains last-minute instructions you need to review before continuing with our configuration suggestions.

1. The first time you run WinVN you will be prompted for a destination directory for the winvn.ini file. Choose the same directory as the main WinVN program, i.e., d:\internet\winvn. Once selected, click on Open, and then Yes to verify creation of the file.

2. Next, you will be prompted for the directory for the newsrc file. Place this in the same d:\internet\winvn directory. This file is where the names of all the newsgroups and related information will be stored. Once selected, click on Open, and then Yes to verify creation of the file.

3. The Communications Options window will appear.

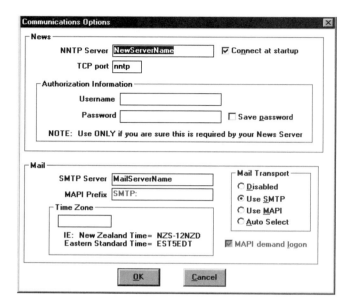

Figure 3.26: WinVN Communications Options window.

4. Input your NNTP news server domain name or IP address.

5. If your news server requires login validation, type in your username, and password and check the Save password box.

6. Input your SMTP e-mail server domain name or IP address.

7. Click OK.

8. Next the Personal Information window will appear.

9. Type in your name, e-mail address, and organization name (if any).

10. Click OK.

11. WinVN will contact your news server and before downloading the large newsgroup information file it will ask for confirmation. Click Yes.

12. After it has completed retrieving the newsgroup information file, the New Newsgroups window will appear.

13. Follow the on-screen instructions to subscribe to any of the new newsgroups. Once you have finished, click on OK.

WinVN has numerous configuration, appearance, and control options. Please read through the Help file to learn how to fully customize WinVN.

HOW TO USE IT

WinVN has many functions, and basic newsreading can be easily accomplished. Here are a few basic command procedures you'll need to be familiar with:

Subscribing: To "subscribe" to a newsgroup means that you are telling the news reader that you are interested in tracking, selecting, and viewing articles in that group. Non- or unsubscribed groups are completely ignored by the newsreader. To subscribe, single-click on one or more newsgroup names in the main window, then select the Group Subscribe Selected Group command. Your subscribed groups will move to the top of the newsgroups listing and turn from blue to black in color, indicating their status. Unsubscribing is the same as subscribing, by selecting the Unsubscribe command.

Opening a newsgroup: Double-clicking on a newsgroup name will open a new group window, retrieve all new headers, and display the headers in default sort method. If more than 300 articles are available, you will be asked to confirm the number of articles retrieved.

Reading a message: Double-clicking on an article's header in a group window will open a new message window, retrieve the message, and display it for you to read.

Posting new messages: You can post a new message by selecting the Respond Followup Article command from a message window or the Articles New Article command from a group window.

HINTS AND TIPS

Read the Help file; most of the higher functions of news-reading are fully explained through tutorfile; most of the higher functions of newsreading are fully explained through tutorials. You can learn how to download binaries, post binaries, track threads, search for keywords, and much more.

FreeAgent

FreeAgent is the premier newsreading product of Forte. This newsreader is available in a commercial version (Agent) and a freeware version (FreeAgent) for both Windows 3.1/3.11 and Windows 95. FreeAgent is the most advanced, powerful, and featured newsreader available anywhere.

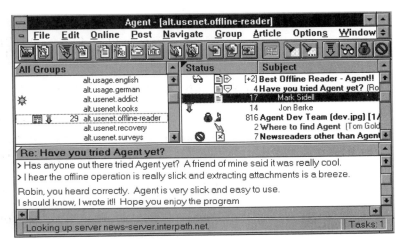

Figure 3.27: FreeAgent.

WHERE TO FIND IT

You can download FreeAgent from the Forte home page at http://www.forteinc.com/forte/. You will need to select Internet Products, then scroll down to select FreeAgent, and click on "download a free copy" to reach the instructions about how to download. Or you can use anonymous FTP at papa.indstate.edu in the directory /winsock-l/news/.

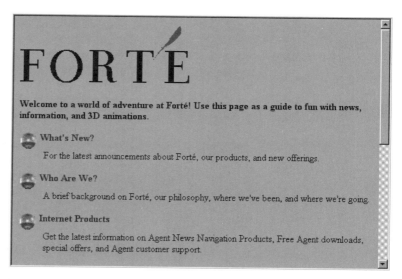

Figure 3.28: Forte's Web page.

VERSION

As of January 1996, FreeAgent is in version 1.0 with a file-name of "fagent10.zip."

FEATURES

The list of features for FreeAgent is long, but some of the highlights are fully Internet Usenet NNTP compliant, offline/online operation, internal multitasking, configurable interface, full attachment/binary capabilities, and a local article database.

WHY WE LIKE IT

FreeAgent is the best newsreader available, and it is free. We have been using FreeAgent for over a year and have never run into any Usenet activity that it couldn't handle. Our favorite aspect of this newsreader is its ability to read other messages while binaries are being downloaded.

FreeAgent also has wonderful pop-up menus and an easy-to-use and configure interface.

WHAT WE DON'T LIKE

To list our grievances with FreeAgent we have to get picky. The current freeware version is only a 16-bit application; the commercial version is available in both 16-bit and 32-bit versions. The freeware version does not come with a spell checker, kill lists, or an address book. But these features and many, many more are available in the commercial version, so if you get hooked, buy it!

HOW TO INSTALL

Create a destination directory, such as "d:\internet\freeagnt," and extract the contents of the original file into this directory. Add FreeAgent to the desktop (right-click on desktop, select New Shortcut) or Start menu (right-click on empty area of task bar, select Properties, Start Menu Programs tab, Add button). Be sure to point either of these shortcuts to the main program "agent.exe."

HOW TO UNINSTALL

To uninstall, remove FreeAgent from the desktop or Start menu, then delete the "d:\internet\freeagnt" directory and all its contents.

SETUP/CONFIGURATION

FreeAgent will request of all the mandatory configurations needed for interaction with your news server the first time you run the program.

1. Open FreeAgent. You will need to read and accept the license agreement. Click Accept.

2. In the FreeAgent Setup window, input your NNTP news server domain name or IP address, your SMTP

e-mail server domain name or IP address, your e-mail address, and your name.

3. Adjust the Time Zone window to your local time zone.

4. Click OK.

5. Next, you will be prompted to allow FreeAgent to contact your news server and retrieve the current newsgroups information file. Click Yes.

After FreeAgent has retrieved the list, all you have left to do is learn how to read and post.

HOW TO USE IT

All of FreeAgent's functions are easy to learn and easy to use. You'll find complete details, tutorials, and instructions in the Help file. Here are a few simple routines you will use to read and post messages.

Subscribing: To "subscribe" to a newsgroup means that you are telling the news reader that you are interested in tracking, selecting, and viewing articles in that group. Non- or unsubscribed groups are completely ignored by the newsreader. To subscribe, right-click on one or more newsgroup names in the groups window; a pop-up menu will appear. Drag the highlight to the Subscribe command and click on. All subscribed groups will have a small newspaper icon beside them. Unsubscribing is the same action as subscribing.

Opening a newsgroup: Double-clicking on a newsgroup name will open a window asking how many articles to retrieve. Make a selection and the retrieved headers will be displayed in the subject window.

Reading a message: Double-clicking on an article's header retrieves the message and displays it for you to read.

Posting new messages: You can post a new message by selecting the Post New Article command from the menu bar. Be sure to have the group or article you want to post to or after selected before using the New Article command.

HINTS AND TIPS

Read the Help file. Most of file. Most of the higher functions of newsreading are fully explained with tutorials in the Help file. You can learn how to download binaries, post binaries, track threads, search for keywords, and much more. But since this is our favorite newsreader, we will give you a few good pointers to get you started.

Learn the shortcuts: Most of the commands of FreeAgent have keyboard shortcuts; these will save you time and mouse attrition. Most of the shortcuts are listed next to the commands in the pull-down menus.

Binaries: Binaries are easy to download: just select one of the headers in the Subject window, and type <CTRL-B>. Before you spend too much time downloading binaries, take a look at the attachment Options available to you in the Group Properties and Options Preferences windows.

Status Icons: The status icons in the Subject window are there to keep you informed. To find out what each icon means, open the Help file and click on each of the icons in the picture of Agent.

Configure: Automatic body retrieval, hard drive optimization, new article notification, and much more are just waiting for you. Read the Help file to find out all the possibilities this snappy little newsreader offers.

Other Utilities

The list of Internet service utilities gets longer almost daily. You can accomplish 90% of all Internet-related activities with a Web browser, an e-mail utility, an FTP utility, and a newsreader. But if you want to stretch yourself to grab a hold of the remaining 10%, we haven't left you completely in the dark. Here are the best supportive utilities which handle online—and some offline—services that you may be interested in.

In this section, we list Web or FTP sites to obtain the utilities. We have listed utilities which are easy to install and provide adequate installation, configuration, and operation instructions. You will need to execute or unzip the original file to locate the utility-specific instructions. Often these are contained in files with extensions .txt, .doc, or .hlp, usually with a filename similar to "readme.txt."

IRC

IRC or Internet Relay Chat is a worldwide gathering place for conversing with other people. It's like having a computer-based conference call with many people located all over the globe. Meet new friends, look for help, ask about world events, even transfer files in over 2,000 channels. This little service will steal sleep from you; it's highly addictive.

MIRC

This is one of the best IRC utilities for Windows 3.1/3.11/95, derived from the current version of the UNIX-based IRC II system. The mIRC Web site is http://sunsite.nijenrode.nl/software/mirc/index.html, and its FTP site is ftp://ftp.demon.co.uk/pub/ibmpc/win3/winsock /apps/mirc/mirc392.zip. The January 6, 1996 release was version 3.92 with the filename "mirc392.zip."

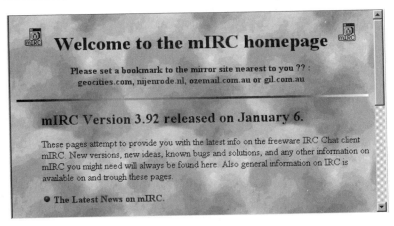

Figure 3.29: mIRC home page.

Telnet

Telnet is a Internet utility which allows you to control and operate on a remote system. Windows 95 has a built in Telnet utility, which is accessed by typing "telnet" in the Start Run command window. Many Internet suites have a Telnet application, and some freeware Telnet applications are also available (however, none of them are worth mentioning here). If you would like to try them out for yourself, use "telnet" as a keyword at the shareware library at http://www.shareware.com or http://vsl.cnet.com.

Archie

Archie is an information-gathering utility designed to create an indexed directory listing for all anonymous FTP sites on the Internet. Archie uses a filename query string to search an Archie server's database to obtain the location of a file. Using an Archie utility may help in locating a file on the Internet if you happen to know part of the filename.

WS_ARCHIE: The only Windows 3.1/3.11/95 Archie utility we have had any success with is WS_ARCHIE. One of its best features is that it interacts with WS_FTP for automatic retrieval of located files. You can find it at the following FTP site: ftp://ftp.coast.net/SimTel/win3/winsock/wsarch08.zip.

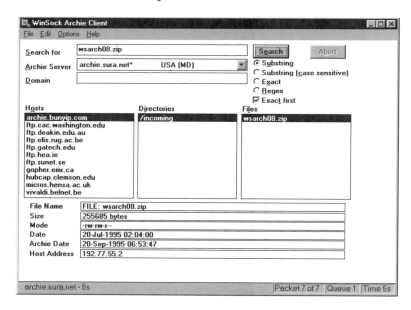

Figure 3.30: WS_ARCHIE Window with Archie Search Results.

Finger, Whois, and Ping

These three utilities are hard to come by and most of their usefulness is lost outside of a UNIX Telnet session. (We recommend using the UNIX command versions in a Telnet session if you have access to a shell account—ask your ISP about that one.) We have not found any utilities we like that add these functions to Windows. However, if you want to search through them on your own, use "finger," "whois," and "ping" as keywords at the shareware library at http://www.shareware.com or http://vsl.cnet.com.

Offline and Other Utilities

The Internet has many, many more services to offer to those who want to explore, and during your exploration you are certain to run across file types, archive methods, and a host of other weird items that you will need help with. Here are the rest of the utilities in our Internet toolbox that we think you should take a look at.

WinZip: The stylish Windows interface to the standard in compression archival software, PKZip. If you transfer files, download files, or even deal with e-mail attachments, you cannot live without WinZip. There are both 16-bit Windows 3.1/3.11 and 32-bit Windows 95 versions. Visit the WinZip Web site at http://www.winzip.com/.

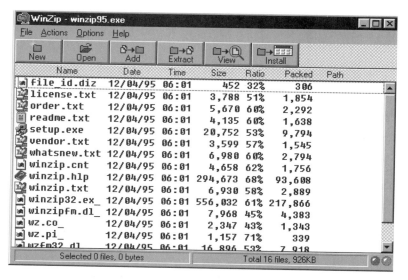

Figure 3.31: WinZip95 with Open winzip95.exe Archive.

PKZip: You'll need the main PKZip archive software in order to avoid possible pitfalls with WinZip (some of WinZip's higher functions require the original PKZip software). The newest version of PKZip as of January 1996 is 2.04g with the filename "pkz204g.exe." This version has been the standard since 1993; be very cautious of "new" versions of this software. They may be Trojan horses for viruses.

XFERPRO: This is a nice utility to help you decode and encode using one of the four common Internet encoding techniques: UUencoding, XXencoding, BinHex, and MIME. Simple, elegant, and fast. This small wonder is a Swiss Army knife. One FTP site containing this utility is ftp://ftp. coast.net/SimTel/win3/encode/xferp110.zip.

StuffIt Expander: This is another good decode utility; it supports StuffIt (.sit), Zip (.zip), Arj (.arj), Arc (.arc), gzip (.gz, .z), uuencode (.uu, .uue), and BinHex (.hqx), StuffIt, Zip, and Arj self-extracting archives (.exe, .sea); and Macintosh files in MacBinary (.bin) format. You can retrieve this utility from the Aladdin System's Web site at http://www.aladdinsys.com/ under shareware/freeware products.

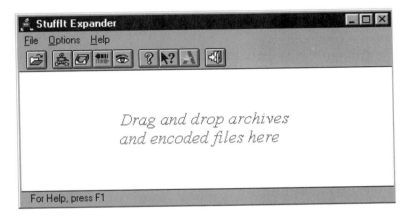

Figure 3.32: Stuffit Expander.

Pushing the Envelope

Browsing the World Wide Web has always brought you text and even some graphics. But now full interactive multimedia is available for those with the right browser, a configured helper application, and enough bandwidth. To spice up your Web surfing, take a look at our list of recommended helper applications.

Many of the listed plug-ins, add-ons, and helpers listed here require Netscape Navigator 2.0 on the Windows 95 platform. We have focused on this browser and platform;

you will need to consult the Web or FTP sites listed to obtain information for other browsers and platforms.

This is a very short list of helper applications and we have highlighted only a few of our favorites. To check out other helper applications, you can use a search engine with keywords "helper applications," "plug-ins," and "addons," or visit one of these sites:

`http://home.netscape.com/comprod/products/navigator/version_2.0/plugins/index.html`

`http://www2.netscape.com/assist/helper_apps/windowhelper.html`

`http://charlotte.acns.nwu.edu/internet/helper/`

`http://wwwhost.cc.utexas.edu/learn/use/helper.html`

`http://www.ncsa.uiuc.edu/SDG/Software/WinMosaic/viewers.htm`

RealAudio

In the past, the only sounds available on the Internet were common audio files, like .wav and .au, which the browser passed on to a sound player. However, a new sound technology has surfaced: RealAudio. RealAudio provides live and on-demand real-time audio over 14.4Kbps or faster connections to the Internet. If you have a 28.8 modem and a Pentium class CPU, you can use the 2.0 version of the player to hear FM mono quality voice and music. Visit the RealAudio site at http://www.realaudio.com/.

Figure 3.33: RealAudio's Web page.

There are three sites you must visit after you get your RealAudio plug-in installed:

C | Net Radio at http://www. cnet.com/Content/Radio/index.html for daily Internet- and computer-related news and information

Net.Radio at http://www.netradio.net for live 24-hour-a-day Internet radio (rock and classical channels)

1-800-MUSIC-NOW Online at http://www.1800music now.mci.com for "You Click, You Listen, You Like, You Buy."

StreamWorks

StreamWorks is an Internet delivery technique developed by Xing Technology Corporation for live and on-demand audio and video. For complete information and to obtain this excellent plug-in, visit the Xing Web site at http://www.xingtech.com/.

Figure 3.34: Xing's StreamWorks Web page.

Adobe's "Amber" Acrobat

The "Amber" version of the Acrobat Reader lets you view, navigate, and print Portable Document Format (PDF) files right in your Navigator window. PDF files are extremely compact, platform independent, and easy to create. They offer design control, print-ready documents, and an endless array of authoring applications. Many companies are now using the PDF technology to distribute documentation, product information, and other layout-dependent materials. Visit the Adobe Amber Web site at:

`http://www.adobe.com/Amber/Index.html`.

One of the best resources on the Net for tax information is the newly updated IRS Web site. You can download PDF files of all the latest tax forms, instruction sheets, and related documentation. Visit the IRS online at http://www.irs.ustreas.gov/prod/cover.html.

Figure 3.35: The IRS's Web site.

Shockwave

The Shockwave plug-in lets you interact with Macromedia Director presentations right in a Netscape Navigator window. Animation, click onable buttons, links to URLs, digital video movies, sound, and more can be integrated within a presentation to deliver a rich multimedia experience. Full interactive multimedia applications created by Director—the industry standard multimedia authoring tools, used to create CD-ROMs—is now available on the Internet. For more information and to get the plug-in, visit http://www.macromedia.com/Tools/Shockwave/sdc/Plugin/index.htm.

Figure 3.36: The Macromedia main home page.

Java

Java is a programming language developed by Sun Microsystems to allow client-side execution of applications. Small programs written in Java, called applets, can be quickly transmitted over the Internet and viewed/executed in a Java-compatible browser. Video, sound, interaction, and other special effects are some of the features this revolutionary programming tool can provide. Go for a test drive of the Java Beta plug-in available at http://java.sun.com.

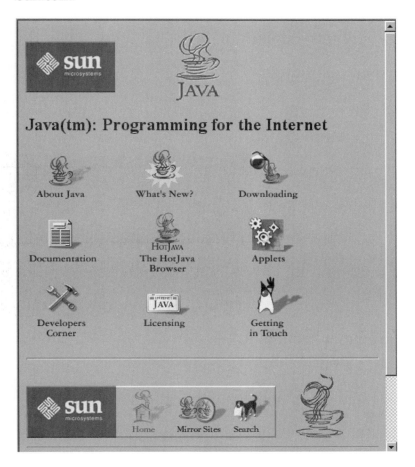

Figure 3.37: Java Web page.

VRML

Virtual Reality Modeling Language is another new tool on the Web scene. VRML allows the creation of three-dimensional worlds that you can travel or walk through using your Web browser. VRML is still in its infancy and it has a long way to go, but the view is amazing even now. For various information regarding VRML, please visit the VRML Web site at http://www.vrml.org/. For one of the popular plug-ins currently available visit http://www.chaco.com for VR Scout VRML; http://www.paper-inc.com for WebFX; or http://www.vream.com for WIRL Virtual Reality Browser.

Figure 3.38: VRML logo.

QuickTime VR

QuickTime VR plug-in allows your Web browser to display the virtual reality worlds created using QuickTime movies. The plug-in is still in beta testing; however, it works great. You can find complete information and installation instructions at the QuickTime VR Web site at http://qtvr.quick-time.apple.com/. If you are running Windows 95, get the newest release of the 32-bit QuickTime Player from http://quicktime.apple.com/.

Figure 3.39: QuickTime VR Web site graphic.

On Your Own

You should now have a solid foundation of utilities and additional software on which to build your Internet experience. However, we didn't want to let you go without giving you a little more information about what is out there.

Tricks of the Trade

The single most important thing you need to keep up with the Internet and all the rapidly changing, expanding, and emerging technologies is simply to be online. There is no substitute. As hard as we tried to include all the most recent information, this book is already out of date. Completely new software and new versions of the utilities we mentioned are already available. The only way to keep up is to stay acquainted with the hot spots on the Internet and visit them often. Here is a list of the Web sites we visit on a daily basis just to check up on what's new:

C | Net Online: http://www.cnet.com

HotWiReD: http://www.hotwired.com

ZD Net: http://www.zdnet.com

Netscape: http://www.netscape.com

Microsoft: http://www.microsoft.com

Search Engines

Search engines are tools to help you locate information the Internet. There are dozens of search engines, but there are only half a dozen that are really worth taking the time to learn how to use. Each search engine has its own tips, hints, and instructions on how to use its capabilities to the fullest. Take the time to read through the materials the authors placed there for you.

Each of these search engines is designed to access and locate Internet information in different ways.

Yahoo! http://www.yahoo.com

Excite! http://www.excite.com

OpenText http://www.opentext.com

Lycos http://www.lycos.com

InfoSeek http://www.infoseek.com

WebCrawler http://www.webcrawler.com

Betas, Demos, and Other Beasts

Many new and exotic software applications are available on the Internet for you to download and use. However, there are some significant variations between a full commercial application and the beasts lurking on the Internet disguised as software products. Let's take a brief look at the types of animals which are waiting to wreak havoc on your desktop.

Betas: Betas are pre–final release versions of a software product. Usually betas are distributed to a limited testing group for "real world" stress tests to determine if there are any remaining bugs, glitches, or mistakes in the product's coding. However, with a worldwide audience willing to try anything, software companies are now posting betas on the Internet for anyone to download, hoping to get feedback and testing information for free. When downloading a beta for your personal testing and use, you need to be aware that not every company releases a "safe" version. It is not uncommon for betas to alter startup-files, change other application settings, replace applications, corrupt data files, and freeze your system. Always make a backup of your hard drives before installing a beta.

Demos: Demos are small or crippled versions of a software product, often distributed to tease users into purchasing a full commercial product. When retrieving a demo, understand that many of the features you are really interested in may not be active or available in the demo version of the software. There is also another type of demo which you may have encountered—the time-dependent demo. This type of demo is fully functional for a certain length of time or until a specific date, after which it becomes inoperable.

Viruses: "Virus" is one of the few true cuss words on the Internet. Virus protection is a high priority with most computer owners worldwide, both on and off the Internet. But being on the Internet does open your system up to more ways of catching a computer virus. In our years of experience on the Internet, we have encountered only a few viruses on our systems. But just because we have been lucky does not mean we can get lazy about keeping our current virus defenses up. Always check downloaded materials for viruses before using or even before unarchiving them, and run a regular systemwide virus scan on each of your hard drives. If you need information on the latest virus software, perform a search using "virus" as a keyword, or visit the McAffee Web site at http://www.mcafee.com/.

Trojan Horses: Like the well-known Trojan horse of Greek mythology, there are many false-front software packages appearing on the Internet. Be cautious when retrieving files from nonpublic or unfamiliar sites, especially when the product is not from a well-known company. You may find that you have been misled into downloading something useless or damaging to your system. Consider every file you retrieve from the Internet as a virus-infected file; don't do anything until you have thoroughly checked and cleaned the file with an up-to-date virus scanner.

Shareware/Freeware: Most of the software to which you have legal access on the Internet is free for the taking. However, there are different categories in the area of "free" that you need to be aware of. Shareware is software which is freely distributed to anyone who wants to try it. If you decide to continue using the software, you are asked to pay a small registration fee, usually less than $45. For this fee you are often entitled to free upgrades, a printed manual, and even technical support. Freeware is software which has no registration fee and no guarantee of technical support or future upgrades. Often the authors simply want to know your opinion of their work and will ask for an e-mail or a postcard (often called postcardware). If you find yourself using a shareware or freeware product consistently, be sure to contact the authors to give feedback, to register, or even to give them a little cash for their efforts. Remember, without them that nifty little software would not exist.

Copyrighted Software: No matter what your personal opinion is about copyrighting computer software, having an unlicensed—and often unpaid for—copy of a software product is illegal in the United States. Even with the strict law enforcement in the United States, there are still hundreds of places to find and download illegal copies of commercial software. Be smart enough to avoid these areas, and when you want to test a commercial product, contact the manufacturer or your local software store—there just might be a demo.

Coming Up!

Well, that should be plenty to get you in way over your head! Don't get overwhelmed by all this. The main thing is to have fun learning your way around. You can get purposeful later. Remember our advice from the get-go.

Try stuff. Experiment. You won't break anything. The best way to learn and get comfortable is to bang around. Read the documentation that comes with everything. We've given you enough to get started, now go have some fun.

In the next chapter we're going to show you some cool places to go on the Net. We've been surfing for a couple of years and know where some great beaches are. Come on. Let's go.

chapter 4

Deals, Steals, and Shopping Wheels

And Oh Yeah—Where to Find Everything You've Always Wanted to Know about Everything There Is to Know about Everything That Is...

So now you have everything all set up and ready to rock. It's time to let you in on the best places to go on the Net. Instead of just turning the fire hose on and letting you drown in the sea of information that is the Internet, we're going to pour you a refreshing drink of nectar and turn you on to some of the best places to go.

The Internet can make you feel completely overwhelmed. A little over a year ago you could easily visit every new site in just a few hours of surfing on a Saturday afternoon. Not anymore. We've heard of estimates that over 10,000 new WWW sites are added every week. In the early days it was fun just to see what everyone was doing with a new site. Nowadays it's more important to know where to go quickly to get what you want—whether it's for fun or for serious research or work.

Yahoo—The Mother of all Sites

Fortunately, the nerds of the Net have been doing their part and there are some great "table of contents" sites and killer search engines that bring a good measure of orderliness to an extremely dynamic and ever-evolving scene. Let's start with a couple of the best sites on the Net for beginners. These are places that you can go with Netscape and have some fun getting comfortable cruising the Net.

We agree with just about everybody out there that the mother of all sites on the Internet is Yahoo at:

`http://www.yahoo.com`

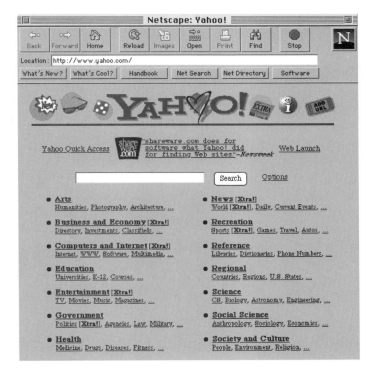

Figure 4.1: Yahoo home page.

The Yahoo WWW site was started by a couple of Stanford students, David Filo and Jerry Yang. Their brilliant idea was to build a software "robot" that runs around the Net and categorizes WWW sites based on content. Then they did the Tom Sawyer thing and made it possible for Webmasters (the geeks who build WWW sites) to go to Yahoo and register their own site. With all the people visiting the site, someone there got the bright idea to sell some "banner" space on the Yahoo Web pages to advertisers like IBM, MCI, and others. Pretty soon these guys hit it big and attracted the attention of investors, and now they have one of the most successful commercial sites on the Net. They've done a tasteful job of it, actually.

Yahoo's search page alone gets about 3 million hits a month. So you know that when they charge $20,000 per million hits for an ad, those guys (Filo and Yang) are on their way to the beach. In France. Way to go, guys!

Yahoo has a great search engine that lets you type in keywords and get back a list of links to sites on the Net that match. You can get really sophisticated with search techniques and quickly narrow in on what you're after.

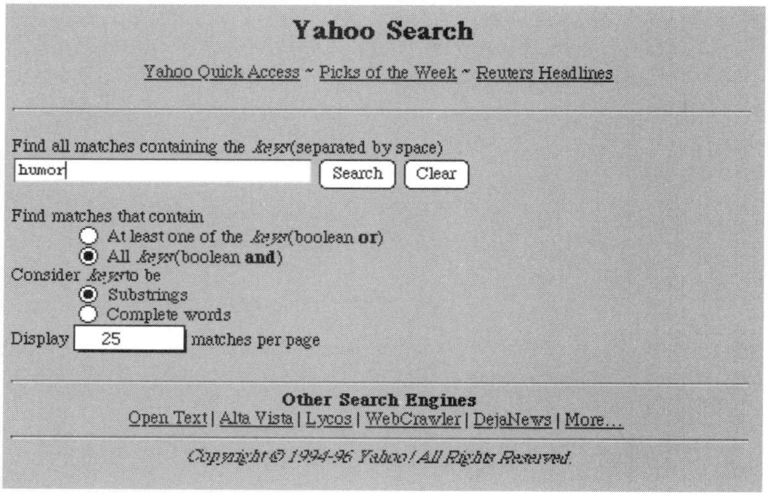

Figure 4.2: Yahoo search engine.

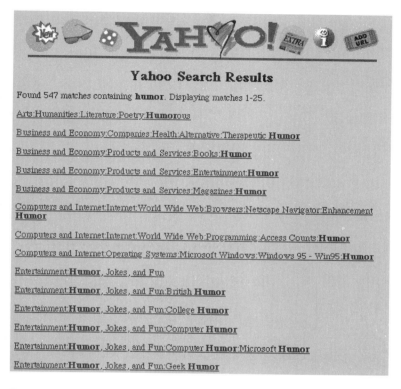

Figure 4.3: Yahoo search results.

There's even a navigation bar (commonly referred to by the big kahuna net surfers as a "nav bar") at the bottom of a Yahoo search result that points you in the direction of other Internet search engines such as Lycos and AltaVista.

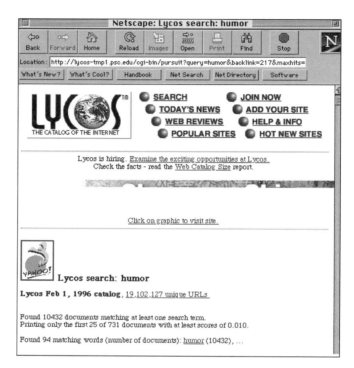

Figure 4.4: Yahoo links to additional WWW site search engines.

We visit Yahoo almost every day for something or other. So do a boatload of people. Yahoo is a great site to go to for Reuters news, for instance. You can get to it off any Yahoo page right from the news icon on the nav bar at the top of the page.

Figure 4.5: Yahoo nav bar.

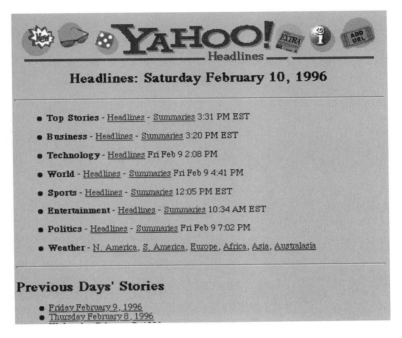

Figure 4.6: Reuters news feed from Yahoo.

With over 100,000 hits a day Yahoo is by far one of the most active sites on the Net. So check it out. Start there. We'd also like to point you to another great "table of contents" site, and that's the Galaxy WWW site at:

`http://galaxy.tradewave.com`

OK, the Galaxy site is based in Austin. So we're partial. It's another great site and definitely one worth checking out. With about 60,000 visits a day, it's another of the more popular sites on the Net.

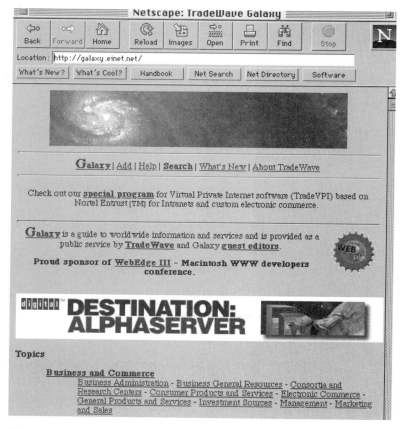

Figure 4.7: Galaxy WWW site home page.

Most Visited WWW Sites

Here's a list of 10 of the most visited WWW sites on the Internet and their URLs. Check 'em out and see why they are so popular.

CMP Tech Web
http://techweb.cmp.com/

C | Net
http://www.cnet.com

ESPN
http://espnet.sportszone.com/index.text.html

GNN
http://gnn.com

Hot Wired
http://www.hotwired.com/

InfoSeek
http://www.infoseek.com/

Netscape
http://home.netscape.com

Pathfinder
http://www.pathfinder.com

TimesFax
http://nytimesfax.com/cgi-bin/tmp/login

Ziff-Davis/ZD Net
http://www.zdnet.com

Source: *Information Week,* February 1996.

URLs and Domain Name Voodoo Whodo

We're going to pause here for a moment before we surf off to the other most excellent sites in this chapter. But first, there are a couple of mundane things you may be curious about. Like domain names. (If not, feel free to skip ahead.)

By now you're probably wondering what the ending ".com" in the address of a WWW site stands for. In fact, what does all the info in an Internet address mean? Maybe you don't care—and you definitely don't need to get too mental about this part of your life. If you care, it has to do with how the Internet is organized by what are referred to as domain names and "schemes."

Someone is scheming. They're trying to make our life more complicated.

The "http://" at the beginning of an Internet address means it's a Web site. The ".com" stands for "commercial." Here are some other common "dot" codes:

- .edu = educational

- .org = nonprofit organization

- .net = Internet providers

- .gov = government

- .mil = millionaires (just kidding: it's military)

(Pronounced "dot edu," "dot org," "dot net," and so on.)

The Net and the Web in particular use URLs to make surfing around easy. URL stands for Uniform Resource Locator. (It's not Uniform Resource Location or Uniform Record Locator. It's Uniform Resource Locator. We've heard and seen all these and worse.)

The Web uses URLs to find files on servers. If you want to cruise to other sites or nab software files off the Net, you need to know how to use URLs.

A URL "address" has the following defined format:

`scheme://host.domain [:port]/path/filename`

Yum. It's that UNIX stuff, back to haunt us. You need to understand it, at least a little, if you're going to surf. And since links are what it's all about, take a deep breath and dive in.

Here's what that gobbledygook means.

The scheme can be one of the following:

- **`file://`**
  a file on your local system or on an anonymous FTP server

- **`http://`**
  a file on a WWW server

- **`ftp://`**
  a file on an anonymous FTP server

- **`gopher://`**
  a file on a gopher server

- **`WAIS://`**
  a file on a WAIS server

183

- **news://**
  Usenet newsgroup

- **telnet://**
  a connection to a Telnet-based service

The *host.domain* part refers to the machine name (if any) and domain name of the server you want to link to.

The *[:port]* part of the URL syntax is usually not included when you create a link. (The default port for WWW servers is 80, by the way.) But it's part of the official spec, so we had to tell you about it. Unless you see it indicated in the URL of a place you want to link to, leave it out.

The *path/filename* is everything after the domain name (and port if any). It shows what directories or folders you have to nest your way down through to get to the file you want to link to. Sometimes all you'll want to link to is the "home page" of a WWW server, or the top-level directory of an FTP site for instance. In that case you don't have to concern yourself with the path and filename.

Now Blow All That Confusing Stuff Off

Aren't you confused by all this? We were at first. That's why we recommend you just start at Yahoo and cruise from there by clicking on hypertext links. Just be glad you don't have to surf the Net typing in UNIX commands using a command line WWW browser like Lynx. You have know idea how ugly that can get.

Let's march on now, to a bunch of other great sites...

ISP Comparison Shopping

Here's a catch-22 for you: The best place for extensive information on current Internet service provider pricing is on the Internet itself. Like we said, catch-22. Hey we just promised to get you started and point you in the right directions. Now that you're jacked in it's time to really nail down who you want to be with for the rest of your Internet connectivity life. We gave you some guidelines. Now it's time for you to do research.

By the way—there's a great article available on the Net on choosing an Internet service provider. It covers a lot of what we've talked about in earlier chapters—and then some. It was written by Rick Adams, the president of UUNet Technologies, one of the best Internet providers going. You can read it by pointing your Web browser to the following URL:

`http://web.cnam.fr/Network/Internet-access/how_to_select.html`

There are a couple of great sites to go to that have extensive listings of Internet service providers worldwide. Here are the URLs:

`http://www.celestin.com/pocia/index.html`

`http://thelist.com`

The list WWW site is particularly useful since it has a searchable database of ISPs. The POCIA list is included in Appendix B of this book.

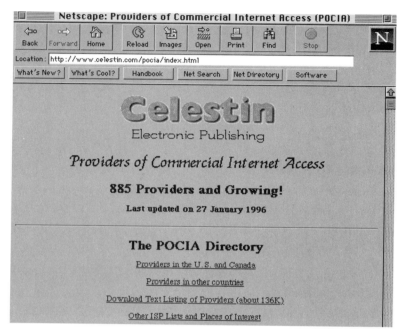

Figure 4.8: Celestin WWW site—POCIA list.

Figure 4.9: The list WWW site home page.

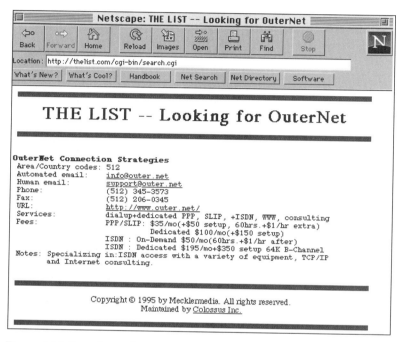

Figure 4.10: Search results on the list WWW site.

So Come On—Where's the Free Access?

Fair enough. We kind of suggest that free Internet access might exist somewhere out there in cyberspace. Well, you can find it. We have.

The thing is you often get scammed by something like a deal: the Internet access is free but you pay big long-distance charges or some gimmick to a company that is in the long-distance business and doing a little Internet on the side.

There is one thing to check out. It's called Free-Net and the "gotcha" (see below) is a good one. Here's the deal: Free-Nets help create access to the Internet and the info-super-bahn-way to a community at large. That means libraries, schools, rec centers, housing projects, hospitals, public buildings, etc.

Besides offering Internet access, the 100+ Free-Nets that are out in there worldwide (mostly in the United States and in varying degrees of development) create content. They often work closely with community groups to get the group's information repurposed and put up online on a WWW site or bulletin board system.

Here's a picture of the Austin Free-Net's home page. (We do go on and on about Austin, don't we. We live here and we love it.)

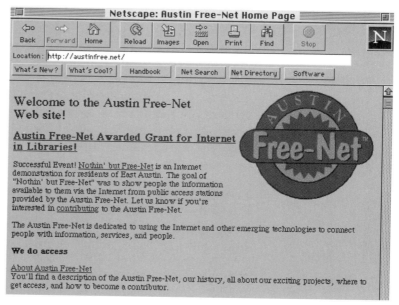

Figure 4.11: The Austin Free-Net home page.

So Free-Nets are a good thing. Anything that helps connect people with people helps everyone in the long run. On all levels. Big time. That's what the Free-Nets are all about.

If you want to hear the doctrine from the source go to the Free-Net home base at the National Public Telecomputing Network (NPTN) WWW site. The URL is:

`http://www.nptn.org/`

Yeah, yeah. We know. Stop the social commentary already. Get to the point.

OK, OK. Here's the gotcha: Our experience is that you can usually get a free Internet account from a Free-Net just by volunteering. Call one and find out. Helping out a few hours here and there for something worthwhile is a good deal.

Yeah, that's not exactly free. But what is? That's as close as you're going to get (to free) on the Net, unless you're a student, of course.

You can also try this angle with a commercial provider by the way. Especially a smaller one that is new in the business. Jeff has often gotten free access from different providers by bringing them new accounts with little effort. They're hungry for the business and you just tell your friends or colleagues and bring them along online with you.

Simple. Works too. Try it.

Before we leave the subject, here are the URLs and brief descriptions for a few more good Free-Net and community computing WWW sites and resources to check out. Most of the Free-Nets are moving to a WWW-based way of organizing community info. A couple are still Telnet sites (that means they're ugly menu-driven UNIX bulletin board systems, basically—an old, complicated, and almost extinct technology and way of organizing content).

FreeNet Newsflash
```
http://www.freenet.vancouver.bc.ca/vrfa/
newsflash/
```
Free-Net news and accomplishments.

Beyond our Borders
http://www.freenet.hamilton.on.ca/Beyond.html
A list of remote Free-Net sites all over the place.

About the Vancouver Regional FreeNet Association
```
http://freenet.vancouver.bc.ca/vrfa/
```

Community Network guide
`http://http2.sils.umich.edu/~ckummer/commu-nity.html`
A WWW guide to community networking.

FREEnet INF-0001 General Information
`http://www.free.net/FREEnet/INF/INF-0001.en.html`
A network for research, education, and engineering.

Some Canadian Free-Nets on the Web
`http://www.synapse.net/~radio/freenet.htm`
Like the title says: some Canadian Free-Nets on the Web

Cleveland Free-Net
Telnet: freenet-in-a.cwru.edu, freenet-in-b.cwru.edu
or freenet-in-c.cwru.edu

City.Net

Hey. While we're on the topic of community computing, there many cities and towns with great WWW sites which organize everything going on in a city from jobs to entertainment. City.Net is "the most comprehensive international guide to communities around the world. City.Net is updated every day to provide easy and timely access to information on travel, entertainment, and local business, plus government and community services for all regions of the world." Check it out—see if a bunch of geeks have organized everything about where you live onto a WWW site. The URL for City.Net is:

`http://www.city.net`

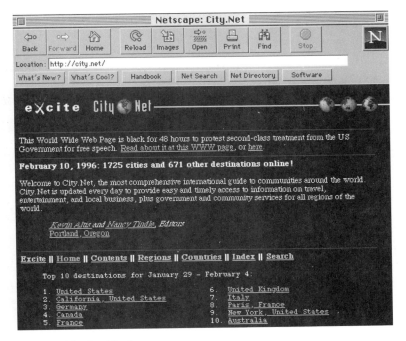

Figure 4.12: City.Net home page.

So, are we giving you some great places to go or what? Guess what. We made life easy for you. They're all included in Appendix C and as a bookmark file on the CD-ROM that comes with the book, remember? Look for a file named Cheesy.html.

There are a bunch of other great WWW sites we'd like to turn you on to. We're sure to miss some by the way. Some of those may even turn out to be your favorite. But we want to avoid page after page of boring black-and-white screen shots and instead just get you started. You'll do fine on your own out there.

On the Net there are so many wonderful sites covering every topic you could dream of. Jeff is a weather nut and goes to four to six great weather-related sites regularly. His favorites are the Storm Chaser page and WeatherNet at:

`http://taiga.geog.niu.edu/chaser/chaser.html`

and

`http://cirrus.sprl.umich.edu/wxnet/`

But the USA Today and CNN WWW sites also do good weather. Hey, it's fun to find and try different ones if weather is all you're into. In fact you could do nothing *but* weather sites on the Net if that's your trip. You'd be busy for a long, long time.

Here are a few more of our favorite sites. Some are very useful. Others are just fun. We're surfin' here, so don't look for a list that is organized by category. You can get that on the Net itself; we, on the other hand, are rambling, wandering kinds of guys.

Bob & Jeff Go Surfing

Epicurious

`http://www.epicurious.com/`

We get hungry just looking at this site. When are they going to have those Star Trek replicators on the Net?

Figure 4.13: Epicurious home page.

MTV, Music Television

http://www.mtv.com/

Is it just us or is their some retro thing going on? It's like the 1960s with no social or political activism all over again.

Figure 4.14: MTV home page.

Cool Site of the Day

http://www.infi.net/cool.html

Glenn Davis' opinion of what's cool. It's a popular stopping off spot.

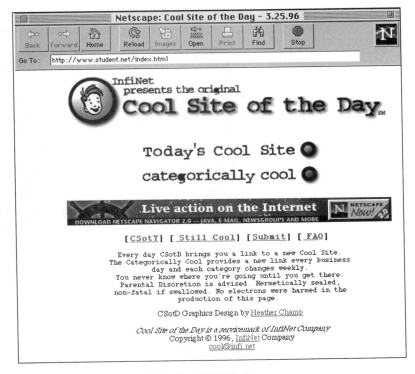

Figure 4.15: Cool Site of the Day WWW site.

The Virtual Tourist

http://www.vtourist.com/webmap/

So you've got two kids and a job and can't get off your duff
and see the world for a few years. Try this.

Figure 4.16: Virtual Tourist WWW site.

CBS Eye on the Net

http://www.cbs.com/

You can get to Letterman stuff from here if you don't get enough on the tube.

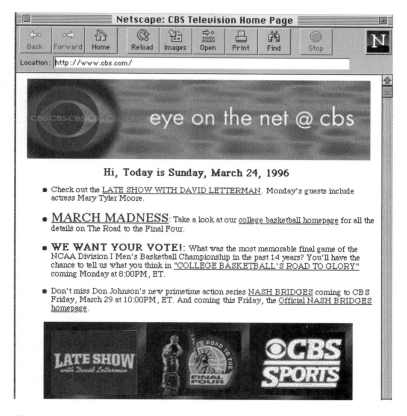

Figure 4.17: CBS WWW site home page.

Firehorse

http://www.peg.apc.org/~firehorse/welcome.html

A popular Aussie e-zine.

Figure 4.18: Firehorse WWW site.

Internet Underground Music Archive

http://www.iuma.com/

The Net's great hi-fi music archive.

Figure 4.19: Internet Underground Music WWW site.

Todd Rundgren's Freedom Fighters Home Base

http://www.iglou.com/scm/cgi-bin/todd.pl

Most of the stuff the Rundgren does pushes the envelope, gets you to step back and think a little for a change. Check it out.

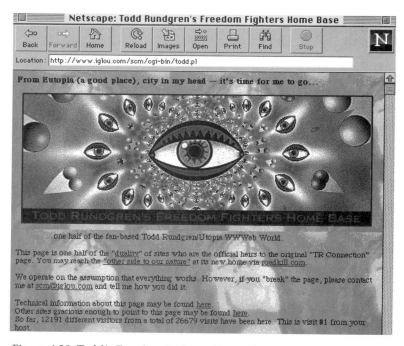

Figure 4.20: Todd's Freedom Fighters Home Base.

Suck

http://suck.com

"a fish, a barrel, and a smoking gun." Need we say more? Biting social and political satire mixed with unbelievable tales of mirth. Watch it get sucked into the dot on the home page. You'll get what we mean when you go there. Trust us.

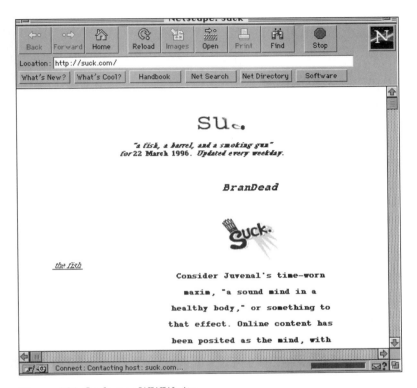

Figure 4.21: Suck.com WWW site.

We were also going to pick out some sites for great jokes and comic strips, but that gets to be a real personal thing for some people. Jeff gets tons of e-mail from friends who send him jokes. Most are dumb. He knows who compiles the good ones and uses that Eudora filter we told you about to blow through 'em. So you are on your own for a joke page. (Besides, it's a joke a minute reading this book, isn't it?)

We didn't think so. If you insist, go to Yahoo and follow the Entertainment link on the Yahoo home page to Comics and you'll be shocked by how much is there. You'll wonder, like we did, "where do all these people find the time to do all this?" In fact there's even a whole collection of over 100 "nothing but useless" pages listed at Yahoo. There are even whole WWW sites that specialize in combining their technological expertise with boredom to give us truly masterful pieces of nothingness.

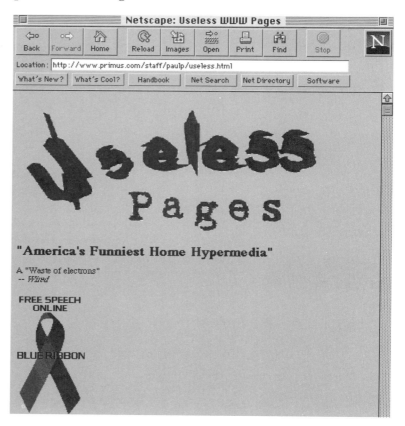

Figure 4.22: The Useless WWW site.

Bob & Jeff Go Shopping

Has all that got you itching to buy something? Even though lots of people are all flipped out about security and whether or not their credit card is going to get ripped off, electronic commerce is already starting to be a big reality on the Net. Getting ripped off probably happens more often in real life than in cyberspace. Besides, last time we checked the fine print on our credit cards we weren't liable for fraud if we didn't do it.

You can be sure that Visa and MasterCard and Bill Gates and Netscape will figure this all out and give the paranoid on Earth some peace of mind—about the issue of Net security at least. It's going to be a multi-billion-dollar-a-year industry.

We can hardly wait. Besides we can't stand all the junk mail catalogs our wives get. If only we could get them shopping on the Net. It might even get them to chill out on the consumer front for the time it takes them to learn their way around online ordering.

After that we're done for.

Hey—first stop on this shopping trip. Go to the Power Computing WWW site. Even if you're a DOS-head, Bill Gates groupie. They have a killer WWW site that lets you price a computer configuration online. You just click here and there, hit a "Submit" button, and blammo, instant price quote. You still have to call in and place the order last time we checked.

Great idea. Jeff's bought three or four Power Computing machines that way. Our friend, and writer-wannabeedoesn't-have-a-clue-how-much-work-it-is, Brian Combs did a great job putting the site together. (Disclaimer: Bob is Director of Evangelism for Power Computing, the first company granted a license for the Mac OS.)

Every day there are new places to shop popping up on the Net. Flowers, software, chocolate, collectibles, lawyers, mandolins—you get the idea. If it's not there yet it will be. Try these WWW sites or go to Yahoo and search for online shopping like we did. Keep in mind that sites come and go and that some sites are here today and gone by the time you buy the book.

Shop-The-Net

`http://www.shop-the-net.com/`

Shop 'til you drop.

Figure 4.23: Shop-the-Net WWW site.

1 World Plaza

http://www2.clever.net/1world/plaza/shop.htm

Even more great shopping.

Figure 4.24: 1 World Plaza WWW site.

1 Mall

http://www.1mall.com/

Secure online ordering and a great shopping basket way of buying.

Figure 4.25: 1 Mall WWW site.

1st Shopping Planet

http://www.shoppingplanet.com/

Computers, electronics, software, music, gifts, and then some.

Figure 4.26: 1st Shopping Planet WWW site.

American Internet Mall

http://www.ammall.com/

A higher class kind of shopping?

Figure 4.27: The American Internet Mall WWW site.

Dallas Market Center

http://www.the-center.com/

Wholesale merchandise—from home furnishings, lighting, and gifts to cowboy boots and kid's stuff.

Figure 4.28: The Dallas Market WWW site.

DreamShop

http://www.dreamshop.com

Eddie Bauer, The Horchow Collections, The Sharper Image, The Bombay Company, Time Warner's Viewer's Edge, Book of the Month Club, Spiegel, and then some.

Figure 4.29: Time Warner's Dream Shop WWW site.

The Front Page

http://www.thefrontpage.com/

Health products, marine products and services, professional services, video, arts, and much, much more stuff unrelated to each other.

Figure 4.30: The Front Page WWW home page.

InterArt

http://www.interart.net/

Nice gifts and arty artifacts—at least we thought so.

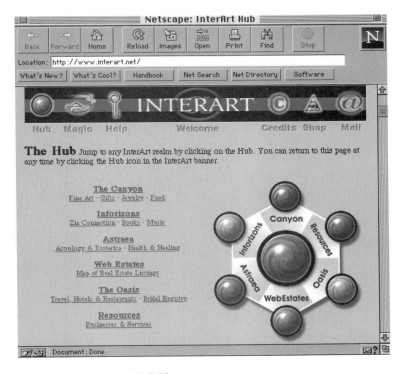

Figure 4.31: Interart's WWW home page.

MakeMusic.com

http://www.makemusic.com

Instruments, dealers, builders, musicians—the online site for the vintage string instruments. A killer site.

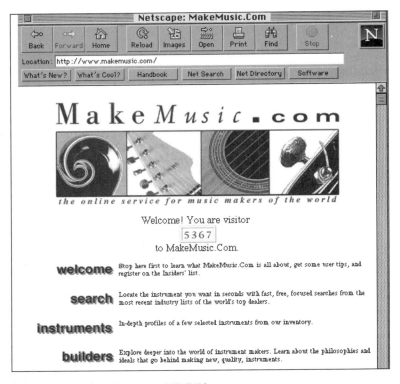

Figure 4.32: MakeMusic.com WWW home page.

Bob & Jeff Get Real

OK. Settle down. We're not going to keep on giving you list after list of places to go and tons of screen shots to tempt you to visit some of the sites we recommend you check out. We have only a few more of those to do before we're done with you. We don't want to turn this book into some out-of-date book of lists. Let's get back to some useful stuff. There's a ton more of it.

Hey. You're getting the idea, right? Anything you can think of is probably there on the Net. In spades. Just go to the big search engines and search. That's how we all do it.

Did we tell you about the All-In-One search site? Holy smokes. You gotta check this one out:

`http://www.albany.net/allinone/`

There are a couple of other types of Internet resources you should know about before we really get out there and show you where the newest things technologically that are happening on the Net can be found. We're saving that for last.

It's useful to know where you can find computer-related resources on the Net. If nothing else, the Net is the quickest way to get a software update for a version of a program you're running that keeps crashing your computer. It's also the best place to get the latest virus killer to deal with the attention deficit disorder creations of the teenage mutants.

Net Bugs, Viruses, and Stupid Toad-Heads

Face it. Viruses are a fact of life if you use a computer. They happen. For the most part they're a stupid nuisance and can be killed easily if they happen to find their way onto your hard drive. They're something you should check for regularly.

There are many good utilities on the Net and commercially that nail viruses. Symantec's Anti-Virus Research Center WWW site is at:

`http://www.symantec.com/avcenter/avcenter.html`

That is probably the best place to start looking for the latest info, alerts, and software dealing with viruses. They've got a solid list of associated links to other related sites off that address too.

There are many other computer-related resources on the Net. Just about every hardware and software manufacturer has a site now pitching their products. The sites listed below (yes, another list—but a good one!) are great resources. They're some of the biggies with a major Internet presence and are listed alphabetically. Microsoft has an excellent link to Internet resources off its home page by the way. They should, of course. And they do.

Apple Computer Inc.
`http://www.apple.com/`

Compaq Computer Corp.
`http://www.compaq.com/`

David Singer's OS/2 Page of Pointers
`http://index.almaden.ibm.com/`

Digital Equipment Corp.
`http://www.digital.com/`

Dell Computer Corp.
`http://www.us.dell.com`

Hewlett-Packard Co.
`http://www.hp.com`

IBM Corp.
`http://www.ibm.com`

IBM Personal Software Co.
`http://www.austin.ibm.com/pspinfo/`

Intel Corp.
`http://www.intel.com`

Lotus Development Corp.
`http://www.lotus.com`

Microsoft Corp.
`http://www.microsoft.com`

NEC Corp.
`http://www.nec.com`

Netcom Online Communication Services
`http://www.netcom.com`

Netscape Communications Corp.
`http://home.netscape.com`

Novell Inc.
`http://www.novell.com`

Performance Systems International Inc.
`http://www.psi.net`

Power Computing Corp.
`http://www.powercc.com`

Silicon Graphics Inc.
`http://www.sgi.com`

Spry Inc.
`http://www.spry.com`

Sun Microsystems Inc.
`http://www.sun.com`

UUNET Technologies
`http://www.uu.net`

Or you can save time and go to the C I Net Vendor Rolodex at:

```
http://www.cnet.com/Resources/Info/Vendor/
index.html
```

and do all your hunting around from there.

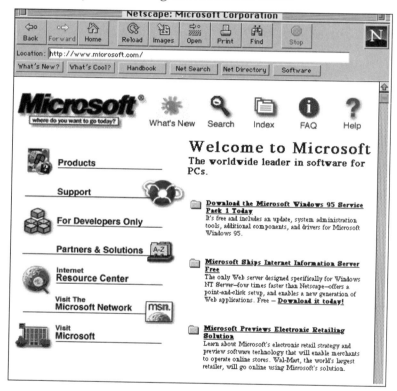

Figure 4.33: Microsoft WWW site home page.

You need to know a little about four more ways information on the Net is organized—FTP sites, newsgroups, mailing lists (often referred to as listservs), and Internet BBSs.

More important, you need to know where the good ones are, what they have, and how to use them.

FTP Sites

Let's start with FTP sites. You remember that FTP stand for File Transfer Protocol, right?

In addition to all the nonsense that's out there, it's time we turned you on to the spots to go get software, cheap and easily. Most of the software available on the Internet is freeware or "shareware." Freeware is free. Duh. Shareware is cheap and usually has a nominal fee of 10–20 bucks, sometimes a little more. The trick to nabbing software off the Net is to find a site that isn't swamped with a million other people doing the same thing. Sometimes you have to wait to get into an FTP site—like on the day Netscape Communications Corp. announces a new version of its Netscape Navigator software. Forget it. Wait a day or two or do it at 3 AM, when most sane people are sleeping.

Ask your friends. There are lots of hidden FTP sites that aren't publicized that have tons of software. But keep a good thing quiet when you find it. That's what we're going to do.

Keep away from private FTP sites and the pirate Internet bulletin board systems that have Photoshop and Marathon available to download. Don't tell us about them anyway. Keep it legal. And pay the shareware fees when you're supposed too. Don't be like the majority of online surfers who download shareware, use it regularly, and never send in the $10 it cost them. Don't be lame. It's bogus.

We recommend you just use your favorite Web browser software to search and download stuff. FTP is built into all the good Web browsers. You can use an FTP specific piece of software like WS-FTP (see Chapter 3 if you forgot about it) and usually increase the speed with which you can download a file—a little. Not enough, though, to notice for a beginner. And it's definitely more complicated than just using one application like Netscape or WinWeb to do everything. Instead of typing **http://** you type **ftp://** at the beginning of the URL address you are after. Here's an example that shows you AOL's FTP site. There are usually mirror sites for really big FTP sites like AOL's. Try both if you get a message that says the site is swamped with traffic. It help spreads the load.

AOL's master FTP site is at ftp://ftp.aol.com. Their mirror site's URL is ftp://mirror.aol.com. Sometimes the mirror is busier than the master.

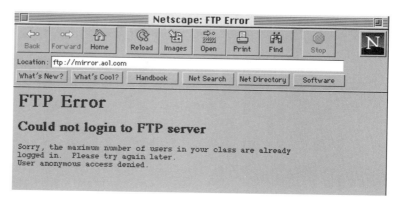

Figure 4.34: AOL FTP Server Unavailable Message.

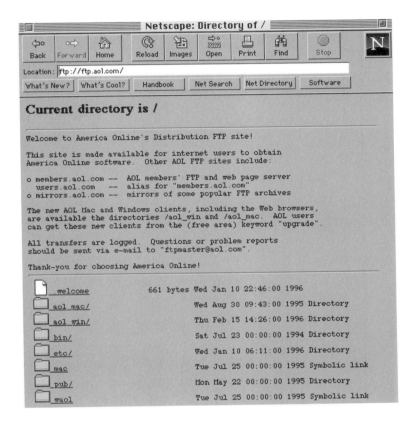

Figure 4.35: AOL FTP site at ftp://ftp.aol.com.

Most public FTP sites just let you log in as an anonymous user with a user id of "anonymous" and a password of "youremailaddress." It's rare that you have to even deal with entering that info when you're using a WWW browser to do FTP. Here's a quick list of great FTP sites for PC users on the Net:

AOL Mirror FTP Site
`ftp://mirror.aol.com/`

Washington U. PC Archives
`ftp://ftp.wustl.edu/systems/ibmpc`

UMass-Lowell PC Game Archives
`ftp://ftp.ulowell.edu/msdos/Games`

Michigan PC Archives
`http://www.umich.edu/~archive/msdos/`

OAK Software Depository
`http://www.acs.oakland.edu/oak.html`

C I Net's shareware.com
`http://www.shareware.com/`

There are lots more. One way to find them, of course, is to do that old search engine thing we've been harping on what must seem like every page. Try a different one this time. Have you been to the Infoseek WWW site yet? Go there. And don't use Yahoo this time. Sometimes it's painfully slow. Come on. Right now, while the iron's hot, get off your duff and go to Infoseek. Here's the URL so you don't have to dig around for it:

`http://www.infoseek.com`

Figure 4.36: Infoseek search results for PC Archives.

Usenet Newsgroups

Usenet is a worldwide hierarchical message system. It was started back in 1980 by four students on the Duke University campus and has grown to become the largest decentralized information repository in existence. A concise definition of what Usenet is and does is difficult to come by, so instead allow the following list of Usenet features help conjure up a working definition.

1. Usenet is not controlled or policed by anyone as a whole. No one has authority over Usenet; its users define what does and does not occur. No government owns or controls Usenet, other than standard national security restrictions. The owners of a local server have control over their server; it is up to them (commonly called "news administrators") to determine was is or isn't transmitted over their site. Individual users and moderators often try to regulate or control the content of specific newsgroups in order to maintain quality for all participants in a group with relative success.

2. Usenet is not an organization, company, or business. Other than the standards required to maintain universal compatibility between news servers, there is no widespread control over how Usenet functions or is used. Usenet is organized, or at least the foundations are organized—the resultant constructs on that basis are not always sound. There are specific organizational measures taken to insure that Usenet remains an easy-to-use information tool. But as with any activity which involves millions of people, some sloppiness and chaos is fated.

3. Usenet is not fair. Since there are no governing or controlling bodies restricting activities, anyone can post anything anywhere they want. Just another proof of the saying, "Life is not fair." You may be able to get away with a lot, but you may also get blamed for something you didn't do.

4. Usenet access is not part of the freedom of speech. The owners of the computers which house and transmit Usenet can and do restrict what is transmitted to or from their servers. If you want to have complete control over what you can say and read, buy your own server.

5. Usenet is not a publicly funded entity. It is funded by whatever means necessary to keep existing servers running and to add servers as needed. There is no large-scale organized effort to purchase and support equipment for the transmission of Usenet. Each individual or group maintains its servers at its own expense. Even without the direct funding of Usenet, it is carried over many publicly paid for types of equipment, such as university mainframes, government computers, and public telephone networks.

6. Usenet is not commercial. Even though most hosts are now owned by businesses, blatant widespread commercial advertising is often shunned. Usenet encompasses government agencies, educational facilities, businesses of all sizes, and individual home computers. Sections of Usenet are designated for specific uses based on the needs and desires of the owners and operators of the equipment. However, with proper planning and understanding of the newsgroups involved, personal or corporate gain via advertising can be accomplished successfully without offending the entire Usenet community.

7. Usenet is not the Internet. The Internet is a loose conglomeration of many information exchange, repository, and retrieval systems, only one of which is Usenet. Usenet can and does exist on servers which are not on the Internet. However, the Internet is an indispensable medium which Usenet travels over; if the Internet did not exist, neither would Usenet.

8. Usenet is not only in the United States. Like the Internet, Usenet is worldwide and is limited only by transmission lines and servers. Most of the Usenet's newsgroups can be accessed from all of the seven continents, including Antarctica!

9. Usenet is the collection of people who post articles to newsgroups. Usenet is not just the bits, the millions and millions of bits transmitted daily, it is the collection of people who care enough to send the very best (or the very worst, or at least what is mediocre and bland). Anyone from anywhere with anything to say about any subject with a connection to any communication network with Usenet access can post and retrieve articles. Usenet is the ultimate equal opportunity employer.

10. Usenet is not just one messaging system, but is many systems tied together which interact with and without human involvement. Most of Usenet exists on the Internet, but other electronic communication entities send and receive articles as well. Usenet can be accessed by e-mail, FTP, gopher, Web, and even Telnet, and that doesn't even cover all the methods possible.

That should just about clear it up. If you still don't have a good grasp of what Usenet is, there is plenty of material online available for you to chew on. First, grab yourself a newsreader (see the previous chapter), then visit one or more of the following newsgroups:

- news.announce.newusers

- news.announce.newgroups

- news.newusers.questions

- news.answers

- news.groups

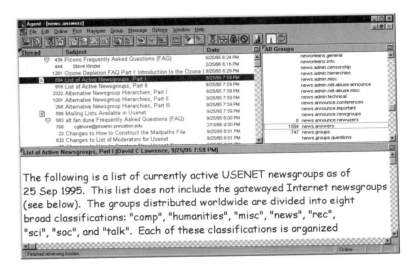

Figure 4.37: FreeAgent newsreader with news.answers newsgroup.

These newsgroups contain important Usenet-related FAQs and other information postings. If you take the time to read through the materials posted, you will learn more about what Usenet is and the wide range of activities and information which is available to you through Usenet. Some important topics you need to have a good grasp of are: netiquette, posting rules, tone, voice, smileys, group moderation, threads, test groups, signature files, cross-posting, subject lines, and distribution. The simple act of getting online and reading this information from Usenet will not only familiarize you with your newsreader but also give you first-hand experience using Usenet. For a humorous outage on the serious side of Usenet, take a peek at the "101 Ways to Be Obnoxious on Usenet" Web site at http://www.indirect.com/user/steiners/usenet.html.

Usenet has over 15,000 newsgroups and more are constantly being added. It would be a daunting task to list every significant group in the confines of this book.

Instead, in the next few paragraphs, we explain how to locate this information in Usenet itself.

Usenet is loosely organized into nine major categories:

- alt   limited distribution groups, often with a wider range of content

- biz   business

- comp   computers, software

- misc   anything that doesn't fit into another category

- news   news and topical subjects

- rec   recreation and entertainment

- sci   science

- soc   social issues and socializing

- talk   debate and discussion

Other categories exist but they are usually limited distribution groups for a specific group of people, such as the TX category, which focuses on Texas-related or -directed subjects. The subsequent portions of a newsgroup's name define its content and focus. Usually broad topics are used for the second name part and more specific and focused topics are included in further parts. Information about main and subcategory groups is often posted to an *.answers group. For information about the comp newsgroups, look in comp.answers.

Almost every newsgroup has a FAQ (frequently asked questions), which is a document containing the focus, purpose, posting limitations, and rules for the specific newsgroup. We strongly suggest (even insist) that you locate and read the FAQ for a newsgroup before you even think about posting. This will save you headaches, frustration, and long lectures or even flaming. Take our word for it—when in doubt about the rules of a newsgroup, DON'T. A newsgroup's FAQ is regularly posted to that group and to alt.answers, news.answers, or the *.answers group of its main category.

A few alternate locations for Usenet FAQs are:

- Usenet Graphics FAQs Web page. This site contains many graphical newsgroup and other related FAQs. `http://www.cis.ohio-state.edu/hyper-text/faq/usenet/graphics/top.html`

- Oxford's Usenet newsgroup hierarchy with searchable FAQ archive—a large collection of FAQs with search capabilities `http://www.lib.ox.ac.uk/internet/news/`

- Usenet newsgroups: Resources `http://scwww.ucs.indiana.edu/NetRsc/usenet.html`

- MIT FAQ FTP archive `ftp://rtfm.mit.edu/pub/usenet/news.answers/`

Oxford University Libraries Automation Service
World Wide Web Server

Newsgroups available in Oxford

Note: In order to use the **news:** * URLs on this and subsequent pages you must configure your browser to point at a suitable NNTP news server. Please refer to your browser documentation for details of how to do this.

[**FAQs by Category** | **FAQs by Newsgroup** | **Search FAQ archive** | **Help**]

- aa.read.this.newsgroup.first (FAQ) *Information for new Oxford users*
- **alt.*** ...
- **aus.*** ...
- **bionet.*** ...
- **bit.*** ...

Figure 4.38: Oxford's Usenet newsgroup hierarchy with searchable FAQ archive.

If you still feel inadequate to look for meaningful news-groups on your own, here is a list of Internet topical news-groups.

- alt.best.of.internet

- alt.internet.services

- comp.infosystems.*

- comp.internet

Welcome to the wild and woolly world of Usenet. BTW, be sure to tie a rope around your ankle in case someone has to drag you away from your computer. There is so much information in Usenet that is it impossible to read it all, so don't even try.

Mailing Lists

Mailing lists are e-mail–based discussion groups. There are countless thousands of mailing lists, from open discussion to highly moderated. Each mailing list is usually concentrated on a single topic or subject, but a narrow subject definition does not necessarily mean the content will stay focused. Mailing lists can be a regular synopsis of all submitted information or an avalanche of messages. If you are not careful when subscribing to mailing lists, you may find yourself flooded with useless messages. Before you sign up for a list, look for a FAQ or request the help or information file.

Most mailing lists are handled by standardized mailing list protocols. Each protocol has a set of controls or command words which are used to operate within the list. For current detailed information about mailing lists, how to subscribe, and even how to start your own, refer to the following Web URLs:

- Internet Mailing Lists Guides and Resources
  `http://www.nlc-bnc.ca/ifla/I/training /listserv/lists.htm`

- Liszt
  `http://www.liszt.com/`

- Search the List of Lists
  `http://catalog.com/vivian/interest- group-search.html`

- Publicly Accessible Mailing Lists
  `http://www.neosoft.com/internet/paml/ index.html`

Figure 4.39: Liszt WWW site.

There are a few extremely important pieces of mailing list etiquette you should be aware of. First, most mailing lists have two e-mail addresses associated with them. One is the administrative address and the other is the list address. The administrative address is the e-mail address you should use when subscribing, unsubscribing, getting help, requesting information, or altering the status or settings of your subscription. The list address is the e-mail address used to send messages to everyone subscribed to the list. Do not send administrative messages to the list address. The moderator of the list will ban you from his list faster than you can blink if you make that mistake. The second bit of mailing list information you should be aware of is that when you do send a message to the list address, be sure to send valuable content. Valuable content is more than quoting a previous message with one or two short comments added; it is giving quality information in a concise and direct manner. Leave message quoting to Usenet; you wouldn't want a mailbox full of useless replies, so don't send them out.

Most mailing lists use a set of four common commands: subscribe, unsubscribe, help, and info. Sending one of these commands as the body of an e-mail message to the administrative address of a mailing list will cause the action to be performed and usually a response message. Always ask for help and info before attempting to subscribe to a list. Usually the help or info message you receive will give detailed instructions and information about the list. The syntax of the subscribe commands varies depending on the type of list protocol used, so be sure to read the help/info messages to determine exactly how to join a list.

The four Web addresses mentioned earlier contain information which is vital to your Internet mailing list survival. If you are reading this paragraph and failed to visit the sites we listed, stop and go online and read the information provided for you. The only way for you to know what to do, what not to do, what you can do, and what you cannot do is to read and find out. Everything you will ever need to know about mailing lists is contained on or through these four Web sites. If you do not go online now and learn about mailing lists, we are going to call your mother.

If you are new to the Internet scene and want to get on a few mailing lists which will boost your Internet knowledge, let us make a few suggestions.

- The C I Net Online weekly newsletter—admin e-mail: subscribe@cnet.com; Subject: SUBSCRIBE DISPATCH; Body: SUBSCRIBE DISPATCH

- newbienewz-digest—admin e-mail: Majordomo@io.com; Body: info newbienewz-digest

- net-guide—admin e-mail: listserv@eff.org; Body: subscribe net-guide

Bob & Jeff Go Surreal and Show You the Really Cool Stuff

You've gotten Internet access, you downloaded a Web browser and have surfed the net—big deal, a bunch of people posting stupid pictures and blathering on about nothing, so what. Ha! If that's all you have seen of the Web, you have seen nothing yet baby! Yeah, sure the Web is based in a simple and easy-to-use protocol so anyone with a computer can post whatever they want (notice that having a brain is not a prerequisite). But the Web is also so versatile that interactive live multimedia can and is being transmitted over the Web. Have we piqued your interest? Gaining access to the really cool stuff on the Web is as simple as adding a few extras to your browser, then surfing to the right pages.

The extras you'll need to get the most out of the Web are usually called plug-ins (sometimes plugins), helper applications or add-ons. No matter what you call them, they all perform one unique function—they add features to your Web browser. There are a few rubs when using Web browser plug-ins. First, most plug-ins are designed for the Windows platforms and then later ported over to Macintosh, if at all. We could complain about this, but since this is a Windows book and a very large proportion of Internet surfers are Windows users, screw em. Second, most plug-ins are designed to work with only a limited number of browsers and often only one browser. Usually the one browser a plug-in is compatible with is the Netscape Navigator. And to be even more snobbish, often the only version of Netscape Navigator supported is the Windows 95 32-bit 2.0 version, so there. We have already explained at great length in earlier chapters about the wonders of Internet access using Windows 95 and Netscape Navigator, so that's our story and we are stick'n to it. All of the plug-ins listed here are fully compatible with Windows 95 and Netscape Navigator 2.0 for Windows 95. Some of these plug-ins are available for other browsers and other operating systems; please visit the listed Web sites to find out more information about other browser/OS combinations.

WARNING!!! The Web is a constantly expanding and changing environment. You may encounter some difficulty with plug-ins which are still in beta testing or are not properly configured for your system. The beta version of a software may be fully functional, but it also may be still full of bugs and errors. When you download and install a beta version of a plug-in, you are taking some risk that the software may not work properly or may damage or corrupt your system. Generally, when a beta fails to operate it simply doesn't work. Rarely will a plug-in harm your hard drive or operating system, but there is always that one in a million chance. You should be in the habit of backing up your system regularly, or at least before adding new software. So lets recap, BACKUP, BACKUP, BACKUP, then install.

One more item needs to be discussed before you dive head first into the ocean of the Web with these plug-ins—bandwidth. Bandwidth is the measurement of data that can be transmitted across a communications connection within a given amount of time. You are probably connecting to the Internet using a modem which means your maximum bandwith is 14.4Kbps or 28.8Kbps. While these are reasonable speeds for most Internet activities, you may find yourself growing impatient as you wait for a cool site to load. Many of the data files for the enhancement of Web pages which these plug-ins support are large, usually 500K to 5M each. If you want all the bells and whistles available on the Web, you'll need to wait for the transfer or lay out the cash for a faster Internet connection—such as ISDN. You've been warned, you will be waiting a lot to see some of the cool effects these plug-ins provide; those that support streaming—a continuous flow of data that is processed as it is received—are much more pleasant to use. The longer a data file takes to transfer to your system, the more opportunities there are for the data to be corrupted or interrupted during transfer. So when something doesn't work, try reloading it before giving up.

Oh yeah. Did we mention you need more RAM too?

You do.

About 16 Megs is the minimum. Barely. You really need at least 24 Megs to breathe easy.

The deal is, when you start banging around with plug-ins you're heading into the leading-edge stuff. The leading-edge geeks all have plenty of RAM and a big fat pipe of bandwidth.

You need both if you're going to surf with the big boys and girls.

Without further ado then, check out the brief descriptions that follow for a few of the major plug-ins. Then zip over to the Netscape plug-in page at:

`http://home.netscape.com/comprod/products/navigator/version_2.0/plug-ins/index.html`
(<—— how's that for an easy to remember URL. Not.)

Microsoft should have a plug-in page up by the time you read this too. Their Internet Explorer browser had just been released when we wrote this.

Hey, it was Netscape who did the deal with us for including their browser on the CD-ROM that comes with "Cheap & Easy."

And we didn't want to go back and redo the whole book from another browser's point of view.

Amber

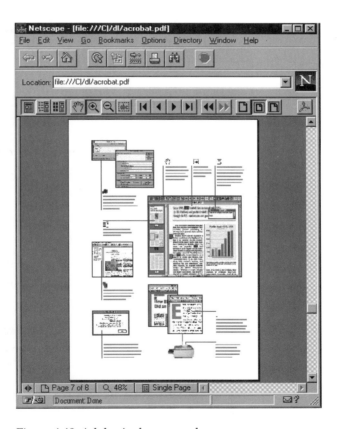

Figure 4.40: Adobe Amber example.

Amber is the Adobe Acrobat Reader plug-in which allows you to view Portable Document Format (PDF) files directly in your Netscape Navigator window. Amber is an browser plug-in adaptation of the free Adobe Acrobat Reader, which can also be configured as an external helper application. A PDF file is a unique cross-platform PostScript-based file format developed by Adobe which contains complete layout, graphic, and font information—on any platform, the document looks exactly like the original. This method of information exchange is quickly becoming a popular way to distribute layout-dependent information, such as manuals and legal forms. To obtain the Amber plug-in, please visit the Adobe Amber Web site at http://w1000.mv.us.adobe.com/Amber/Index.html.

Here's an example that will thrill you. Not.

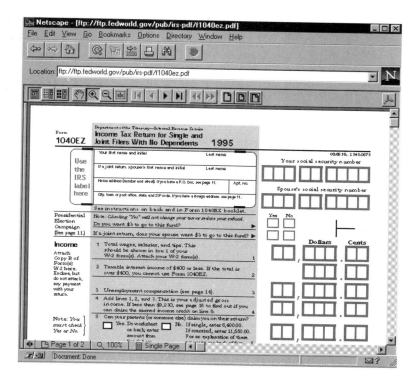

Figure 4.41: Bummer—the IRS does Amber too.

If you are interested in creating PDF files to distribute over the Web, there are a few options you can choose from. If you have a PostScript printer or a least a PostScript printer driver you can print to PDF. For more information about this process, visit http://w1000.mv.us.adobe.com/Amber/makepdf.html. Your second option is to purchase Adobe Exchange and Distiller, the PDF writer and creation tool. Detailed information about this product is available at http://w1000.mv.us.adobe.com/Acrobat/Exch.html.

Many Web sites have adopted the PDF file format as the dominant method of information exchange. Here are some sites which use PDF:

- Adobe. This one should be obvious; many of the manuals and product brochures are available online in PDF format: http://www.adobe.com

- Internal Revenue Service. The guys you love to hate have published most of the tax forms and documentation you'll need in PDF format. http://www.irs.ustreas.gov/

- New York Times Fax. A free daily service of highlights from the top news articles from the *New York Times* in PDF format. Once you fill out a simple registration form, you have access to the daily updated 8-page document. http://nytimesfax.com/

- Dial-A-Book. An online bookstore where PDF is the print medium. Pay a small fee to get an entire book over the Web. http://dab.psi.net/DialABook/

- Center for Disease Control: Morbidity and Mortality Weekly Report. A lively and informative publication from the people who take notice when you bite the big one. http://www.cdc.gov/epo/mmwr/mmwr_wk.html

Shockwave

Shockwave is the technology developed by Macromedia to allow Director multimedia presentations to be transmitted over the Web. Macromedia Director is the industry standard multimedia authoring tool for the creation of CD-ROM–based interactive software. The Shockwave plug-in lets you interact with Director presentations from your Web browser. Now, boring pages come to life with animation, movies, audio, interaction, and much, much more. To obtain the Shockwave plug-in, please visit the Macromedia Shockwave site at `http://www.macromedia.com/Tools/Shockwave/sdc/Plugin/index.htm`

Figure 4.42: ShockWave: Our pals do the multimedia thing.

If you are interested in creating your own Macromedia Director presentations for Web distribution, you will need to shell out the $1,000 or so for the full commercial package. To find out more detailed information about the Director authoring tool and other products from Macromedia, please visit http://www.macromedia.com.

Once you have the Shockwave plug-in installed, you will notice Shocked sites everywhere. A Shockwave movie will display the Macromedia background symbol in a box where a movie is being loaded (see Figure 4.43). When you see this type of image, wait for the movie to load and begin playing before you move on.

Figure 4.43: The Macromedia Shockwave background symbol displayed before a movie is played.

There are so many Shockwave-enhanced web sites that to mention one would be to fail to mention a thousand. So, instead visit the main Shockwave Gallery, where all the top Shocked sites are listed: `http://www.macromedia.com/Tools/Shockwave/Gallery/index.html`

Wait a sec, we did find one other Shockwave site collection page that is worth a little print space: ShockeR. ShockeR has a weekly top site and covers many amateur Shockwave sites which the Macromedia gallery overlooks. Take a short tour of the site and the collection of links at http://www.shocker.com/shocker/.

RealAudio

If you have been waiting for live audio on the Internet, then your sojourn is over. RealAudio has brought live FM-mono quality audio to your Web browser. Based on a proprietary compression technology and a streaming data protocol, RealAudio delivers great sound to your ears from across the globe. You need to have a 28.8 modem or faster in order to listen to uninterrupted audio. To obtain the RealAudio plug-in, visit the RealAudio Web site at http://www. realaudio.com. Here's a screen shot of RealAudio player. Hear it? If so, you're twisted.

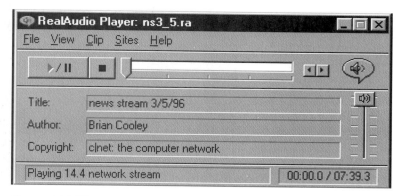

Figure 4.44: The RealAudio Player in action.

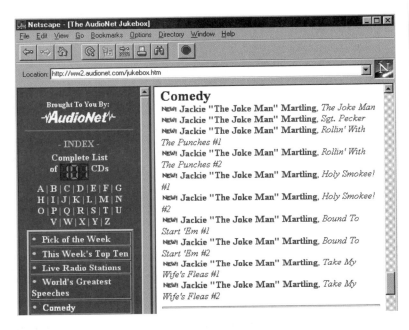

Figure 4.45: The AudioNet Jukebox WWW site.

If you are interested in producing your own RealAudio files for broadcasting over the Web, you will need to read about the RealAudio server and encoder. The encoder can be used free for creating audio-on-demand files. To set up a live audio broadcasting server, you will need to purchase the RealAudio server. All the information about these products is available from the RealAudio home page http://www.realaudio.com.

Some must-see RealAudio sites are:

• C | Net Radio—a daily Internet- and computer-related news and information broadcast.
  http://www.cnet.com/Content/Radio/index.html

- Net.Radio—live 24-hour-a-day Internet radio with rock and classical channels. http://www.netradio.net

- 1-800-MUSIC-NOW Online—"You Click, You Listen, You Like, You Buy." http://www.1800musicnow.mci.com

- Latest and Greatest RealAudio 2.0 sites—a collection of sites maintained by RealAudio. http://www.realaudio.com/products/ra2.0/sites/

Java

Java is a revolutionary programming language developed by Sun Microsystems which allows client-side execution of applications. Java applets can be quickly transmitted over the Internet and viewed in a Java-compatible browser. Video, sound, interaction, and other special effects are only some of the features this unique programming tool can provide. Java is no longer a plug-in but is now embedded into browsers which license Java from Sun. Currently, Netscape Navigator 2.0 is the only browser with built-in Java support outside the HotJava Sun browser. As you may have read in the previous chapter, Netscape far outbrews HotJava, so if you don't already use Netscape, go get it (http://www.netscape.com). For more information about Java, please visit Sun's Java Web site at http://java.sun.com.

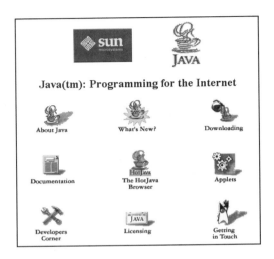

Figure 4.46: Sun's Java Web page.

If you are interested in creating your own Java applets for Web distribution, there are mountains of materials available online. However, you will need to be a fairly good programmer and have familiarity with C-based languages in order to write Java code. To get started, visit the Java Web site at http://java.sun.com and follow the About Java and Documentation links.

Java is being incorporated into many Web sites; to take a look at some of the best, visit http://www.gamelan.com/. Gamelan is a highly respected Java directory of Java-enhanced Web sites; however, it lists only sites with high-impact Java applications. There are a lot of sites on the Web which have Java applets subtly embedded into them, which you may not even notice. Properly designed Java applets become part of the page and do not seem like a separate entity. We are not complaining, seamless integration of multimedia and other Web enhancements is a very good thing. However, the best sites are often unnoticed because their authors did such a wonderful job of designing their presentation.

StreamWorks

Xing Technologies has developed a audio and video streaming delivery method called StreamWorks. Live video and audio are waiting for you on the Web; never watch cable TV again (yeah, right). This technology is extremely dependent on a fast and uninterrupted connection between your browser and the StreamWorks server out on the Internet. Once you get this bad boy configured and establish a good connection, entertainment beyond belief will be transmitted for your senses to bask in. To obtain the StreamWorks plug-in, please visit the Xing Technologies Web site at http://www.xingtech.com/.

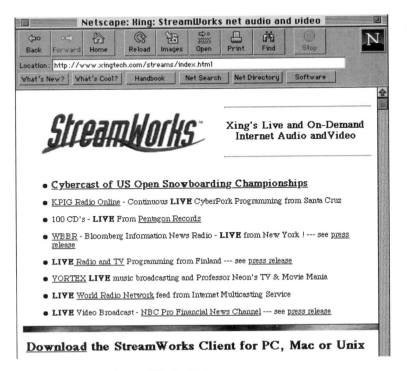

Figure 4.47: Xing's StreamWorks Web page.

If you are interested in producing StreamWork readable content for Web distribution, please read the information available from the Xing Technologies Web site. You should be warned, the server package is extremely expensive, not to mention the hardware and digital camera requirements.

If you download and install the StreamWorks plug-in, you'll have access to many predefined servers with numerous audio and video data streams. To explore other sites, go back to the StreamWorks Web site and visit the servers listed under the "StreamWorks on the Internet—publicly accessible servers" link.

VRML

Virtual Reality Modeling Language or VRML is a programming language that allows Web authors to build three-dimensional worlds which you can walk or fly through and explore inside, upside, and out. From simple box rooms to complete worlds with multimedia (audio, video, text, animation, and more), VRML is a step into the future of virtual reality interaction. It is difficult to describe or define the awe you will experience as you explore VRML worlds, they are simply mind boggling. Before you get too excited, you need to know that VRML is still under development and is unfortunately a bandwidth hog, but waiting for the data files to transfer is usually rewarded. For information about the VRML language itself and the ongoing development of the technology, visit the VRML Web site at http://www.vrml.org/.

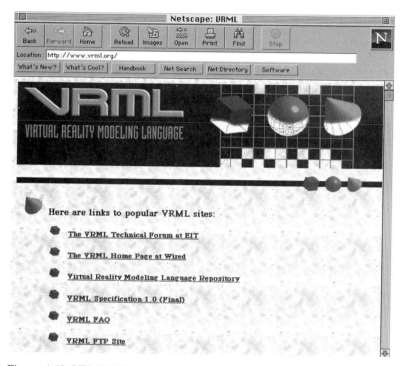

Figure 4.48: VRML Web site.

There are four good VRML plug-ins which are worth looking at. Each performs a little differently and has its own set
of movement controls. All of the plug-in creators claim that
their product is the best, but you will have to be the judge
of that. Be sure to read each plug-in's instructions before
trying to explore a VRML world, otherwise you may find
yourself up a creek without a paddle (or more likely outside the defined area with no reference point to find your
way back). Hey. Let us apologize in advance for some of
the screen shots you're about to see. They're kind of lame,
but there's not much more we can do on a two-dimensional
piece of paper to convey a 3-D object that floats around
when you move your mouse.

Once you get a VRML plug-in installed and configured, here are some great places (or should we say worlds) to get lost in:

- VRML Site of the Week—A weekly showing of the best VRML world on the Net.
  http://www.virtus.com/modmonth.html

- Aereal Serch—Search for VRML worlds or look at the daily VRML site.
  http://www.virtpark.com/theme/cgi-bin/serch.html

- VRML Review—A large collection of links to worlds and other information.
  http://www.imaginative.com/Chuck/vrml/

- Proteinman's Top Ten VRML Worlds— A rotating list of the 10 best worlds.
  http://www.virtpark.com/theme/proteinman/

Live3D

Live3D is a VRML extension developed by Netscape and Paper, Inc. for the Navigator 2.0 Web browser. Live3D is the updated, expanded, and enhanced plug-in which was previously known as WebFX. This plug-in supports the new Moving Worlds VRML 2.0 specification developed by Netscape and Silicon Graphics (which is still pending approval from the VRML Architecture Group at this time). It also supports Java and streaming audio and video. If you are a Netscape user, this is the VRML plug-in for you. To obtain the Live3D plug-in, please visit the Live3D Web page at http://home.netscape.com/comprod/products/navigator/live3d/index.html. You can also find information about Live3D and other Paper, Inc. projects from the Paper, Inc. Web site at http://www.paperinc.com/.

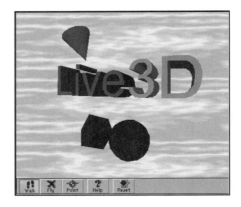

Figure 4.49: Live3D in a VRML floating world.

From both the Netscape and Paper, Inc. pages, you will find links to information about developing your own Live3D VRML worlds and example sites using Live3D.

VR Scout

VR Scout by Chaco has been rated as one of the fastest VRML engines currently in use. VR Scout fully supports the VRML 1.0 specifications, uses multithreading to download scenes, and has a headlight for illuminating poorly lit scenes. To obtain the VR Scout plug-in, please visit the VR Scout Web site at http://www.chaco.com/vrscout/.

Chaco encourages first-time users of the VR Scout plug-in to visit the Jack O' Lantern page at http://www.chaco.com /~glenn/jack/.

Figure 4.50: A scene from the Jack O' Lantern VRML site.

VRealm

VRealm by Integrated Data Systems is another popular VRML plug-in. This VRML tool has excellent high color performance, is fully VRML 1.0 compliant, and has a great navigation tool bar. VRealm seamlessly integrates into Netscape Navigator 2.0, unlike other VRML tools. To obtain the VRealm plug-in, please visit the IDS VRealm Web site at http://www.ids-net.com/.

Figure 4.51: Integrated Data Systems' Web site.

IDS has collected a good list of quality VRML worlds which you can explore with the VRealm plug-in. Go to the IDS Web site and follow the Worlds to Explore link.

WIRL

WIRL by VREAM is a step above the rest (or so it claims). With the standard VRML 1.0 compliancy, VREAM has added object interactivity, VREAMScripting, true color support, and much more. To get the feel for this VRML tool, you'll need to experience it first hand. To obtain the WIRL plug-in, please visit the VREAM WIRL page at http://www.vream.com/3dl1.html.

Figure 4.52: VREAM's Web site.

VREAM has collected a good list of VRML sites for you to explore. To get there, visit the main Web page at http://www.vream.com and follow the Cool 3D Sites link.

OK. So those screen shots were more than just a little lame. They bring lame to new heights. Beats us how to do it. Think of those shots as nice text-breaker-uppers for your eyes.

QuickTime VR

The QuickTime VR "helper app" allows your Web browser to display the virtual reality worlds created using QuickTime movies. This technology is different from VRML. In VRML, the images you see must be painstakingly drawn or a multimedia image is pasted onto a surface. Thus the world can be a little edgy. With QuickTime VR, movies are made using a video camera of real-world places or using 3-D modeling software to create animation. These movies, once they have been properly processed, give the illusion of reality much better than current VRML standards. Quicktime VR not only displays great three-dimensional spaces, it also has interactive objects which you can manipulate. To use the plug-in you will need to have Apple QuickTime installed on your system. The plug-in is still in beta testing; but it works great. You can find complete information and installation instructions at the QuickTime VR Web site at http://qtvr.quicktime.apple. com/. If you are running Windows 95, get the newest release of the 32-bit QuickTime Player from http://quicktime.apple.com/.

Figure 4.53: Apple QuickTime VR Web site.

Internet Telephone

You may have heard the rumor that you can bypass long-distance charges by using your Internet connection as a telephone link to anywhere in the world. Well, the rumor is true, but you can't just dial any phone anywhere, you can only contact other people who have Internet access and the same communications protocol as you. This isn't that difficult of a hurdle to jump over, just send your best pal across the big blue pool a message to buy or download the software with the same protocol that you have and arrange a time to make contact.

Before you rush to get an Internet phone connection going, you'll need to check your system for certain hardware. You must have a sound card with speakers (or headphones) and a microphone; a 16-bit Sound Blaster is the preferred standard. You will also need a direct PPP connection to the Internet, which implies a 14.4 modem (28.8 preferable) and 16550 UART serials or better. Your system will need to be a 486DX33 (a Pentium 75 or better is preferable) and at least 8M of RAM (we always use 16 or more). If you want to get into videoconferencing, you'll need a video capture board and a digital camera (an easy $800 to $4,000) or the $100 Connectix QuickCam (our choice as well!)(visit http://www.connectix.com/ for Connectix product information).

For more information about using the Internet for worldwide "free" communications, check out:

• The Internet Telephony Page—
  http://rpcp.mit.edu/~asears/main.html

• FAQ: "How can I use the Internet as a telephone?"—
  http://www.northcoast.com/savetz/voice-faq.html.

There are many good commercial Internet phone communications packages available, from $35 to $500. Often these products will allow you to share or spawn a second copy of the software to the site you wish to connect to. However, if you want a broader range of connection sites and want to be able to join in on impromptu Internet talk sessions, try using one of the shareware packages such as Speak Freely or CUSeeMe.

Speak Freely

Speak Freely for Windows by John Walker is one of the best Internet phone utilities available for free. It offers many features more advanced than commercial software, such as voice mail, multicasting, encryption, and excellent sound quality. This software is available through the Speak Freely Web site at http://www.fourmilab.ch/netfone/windows/speak_freely.html.

CUSeeMe

CUSeeMe is a project of Cornell University and supports both audio only and videoconferencing over the Internet with up to eight simultaneous connections. To video conference you will need a digital video camera (such as the Connectix QuickCam). CUSeeMe is currently the only free software which supports real-time two-way video conferencing over the Internet. This software is available through the CUSeeMe Web site at http://cu-seeme.cornell.edu/

Figure 4.54: CUSeeMe Web site.

Better Late Than Never

If these plug-ins have not satisfied your need for more, more, more on the Web, there are still other places to locate other browser plug-ins. Take a gander at these sites.

`http://home.netscape.com/comprod/products/navigator/version_2.0/plug-ins/index.html`

`http://www2.netscape.com/assist/helper_apps/windowhelper.html`

```
http://charlotte.acns.nwu.edu/internet/
helper/

http://wwwhost.cc.utexas.edu/learn/use/
helper.html

http://www.ncsa.uiuc.edu/SDG/Software/
WinMosaic/viewers.htm
```

Summary

Hopefully you have figured out by now that no single book or information repository can contain all of the current information about the Internet. You'll need to take the time to explore and search for new materials, enhanced software, and improved information. In this chapter, we tried to give you insight into the amazing world of entertainment, education, and productivity that exists on the Internet. But don't take our word for it, go surfing for yourself.

Appendix A—Glossary

Our friends who do Internet training at LearningCurve, Inc. here in Austin have helped us put together a useful little glossary of Internet terms you come across all the time. Thanks Rachal!

Hey, if you ever make it to Austin and still haven't figured this Internet thing out, be sure to pay them a visit. They'll hold your hand, give you a glass of water, pat you on the back, and help you out. You can check out their WWW site at http://www.learningcurve.com.

ARPANET
Advanced Research Projects Agency Network. TCP/IP-based international network. The precursor to the Internet. Developed in the late 1960s and early 1970s by the U.S. Department of Defense as an experiment in wide-area networking that would survive a nuclear war.

ASCII
American Standard Code for Information Interchange—the de facto worldwide standard for the code numbers used by computers to represent all the uppercase and lowercase Latin letters, numbers, punctuation, etc. There are 128 standard ASCII codes, each of which can be represented by a 7-digit binary number: 0000000 through 1111111.

BACKBONE

High-speed connection within a network which connects shorter (usually slower) branch circuits. A high-speed line or series of connections that forms a major pathway within a network. The term is relative, as a backbone in a small network may be much smaller than many nonbackbone lines in a large network.

BANDWIDTH

The difference, in hertz (Hz), between the highest and lowest frequencies of a transmission channel; the greater the bandwidth, the "faster" the line. Also refers to how much information you can send through a connection. Usually measured in bits per second. A full page of English text is about 16,000 bits. A fast modem can move about 15,000 bits in 1 second. Full-motion, full-screen video would require roughly 10,000,000 bits per second, depending on compression. Also creeping into common usage to indicate time and availability, as in: "I wanted to meet with them, but I didn't have the bandwidth."

BASEBAND

Characteristic of any network like Ethernet that uses a single carrier frequency and requires all stations attached to the network to participate in every transmission.

BAUD

Unit of measure of data transmission speed; usually bits/second. In common usage the "baud rate" of a modem is how many bits it can send or receive per second. Technically, "baud" is the number of times per second that the carrier signal shifts value—so a 2400-bit-per-second modem actually runs at 300 baud, but it moves 4 bits per baud (4 x 300 = 2400 bits per second).

BITNET

Because It's Time Network. TCP/IP-based international network.

BPS

Bits per second. A measure of the rate of data transmission. A 28.8 modem can move 28,800 bits per second.

BROADCAST

A packet delivery system that delivers a copy of a given packet to all hosts that attach to it is said to "broadcast" the packet.

BROWSER

A client program (software) that is used to look at various kinds of Internet resources.

CLIENT

The user of a network service, or a software program that is used to contact and obtain data from a server software program on another computer, often across a great distance. Each client program is designed to work with one or more specific kinds of server programs, and each server requires a specific kind of client.

COAX

Coaxial cable, comprised of a central wire surrounded by dielectric insulator, all encased in a protective sheathing.

COM

One of the top-level domains. Stands for commercial and includes commercial enterprises. For example: info@learningcurve.com

COM PORT

Communications port. Also known as a serial port. On a PC, there are up to four serial ports designated COM1, COM2, COM3, and COM4. Special hardware can allow for more ports. A serial port on a PC has 9 or 25 pins and is generally where an external modem would be connected, using a serial cable. Internal modems also require that a COM port be designated for them, usually selectable on the modem card itself or through software.

CYBERSPACE

The term was originated by author William Gibson in his novel "Neuromancer". The word cyberspace is currently used to describe the whole range of information resources available through computer networks.

DEFAULT GATEWAY

The first destination for data you wish to send over the Internet, usually the IP address of a router of some kind. Your service provider can tell you what your default gateway will be. Also see "gateway."

DIAL-UP CONNECTION

A connection between machines through a phone line. Modem, ISDN, and other high-speed connections can be loosely defined as dial-up connections if they are not 24-hour-a-day dedicated connections.

DOMAIN

In the Internet, a part of the naming hierarchy. Syntactically, a domain name consists of a sequence of names separated by dots.

DOMAIN NAME

The unique name that identifies an Internet site. Domain names always have two or more parts, separated by dots. The part on the left is the most specific, and the part on the right is the most general. It is possible for a domain name to exist but not be connected to an actual machine. This is often done so that a group or business can have an Internet e-mail address without having to establish a real Internet site. In these cases, one's ISP must handle the mail on behalf of the listed domain name.

EDU

One of the top-level domains. Stands for educational and includes educational institutions. For example: bob@utexas.edu.

E-MAIL

Electronic mail. Messages, usually text, sent from one person to another via computer. E-mail can also be sent automatically to a large number of addresses.

ETHERNET

A very common method of networking computers in a LAN. Ethernet will handle about 10,000,000 bits per second and can be used with almost any kind of computer.

FAQ

Frequently asked questions. FAQs are documents that list and answer the most common questions on a particular subject.

FTP

File Transfer Protocol. A user-level protocol and program that you can use to transfer files over the network. A very common method of moving files between two Internet sites. FTP is a special way to log in to another Internet site for the purpose of retrieving and/or sending files. There are many Internet sites that have established publicly accessible libraries of material that can be obtained using FTP, by logging in using the account name "anonymous"; thus these sites are called "anonymous ftp servers."

GATEWAY

A device that acts as a connector between two logically separate networks. It has interfaces to more than one network and can translate the packets of one network to another, possibly dissimilar, network. For example, Prodigy has a gateway that translates between its internal, proprietary e-mail format and Internet e-mail format. Another, sloppier meaning of gateway is to describe any mechanism for providing access to another system; e.g., AOL might be called a gateway to the Internet.

GOPHER

An older and widely successful method of making menus of material available over the Internet. Gopher is a client and server style program, which requires that the user have a Gopher client program. Although Gopher spread rapidly across the globe in only a couple of years, it is being largely supplanted by Hypertext, also known as WWW (World Wide Web). There are still thousands of Gopher servers on the Internet and we can expect they will remain for a while.

GOV

One of the top-level domains. Stands for government and includes governmental organizations. For example: smith@nssdca.gsfc.nasa.gov.

"HAYES" COMMAND SET

Also known as the "AT" command set. A standard set of modem commands first developed by the Hayes modem company. Most modems have adopted this standard. All commands sent to the modem begin with the characters "AT" for "Attention."

HOST

Any computer on a network that is a repository for services available to other computers on the network. It is quite common to have one host machine provide several services, such as WWW and Usenet.

HTML

HyperText Markup Language. The coding language used create hypertext documents for use on the World Wide Web. HTML looks a lot like old-fashioned typesetting code, where you surround a block of text with instructions that indicate how it should appear. In addition, in HTML you can specify that a block of text, or a word, is "linked" to another file on the Internet. HTML files are meant to be viewed using a World Wide Web client program (browser), such as Mosaic or Netscape.

HTTP

HyperText Transport Protocol. The protocol for moving hypertext files across the Internet. Requires an HTTP client program on one end and an HTTP server program on the other end. HTTP is the primary protocol used in the World Wide Web (WWW).

HYPERTEXT

Generally, any text that contains "links" to other documents—words or phrases in the document that can be chosen by a reader using a browser and which cause another document to be retrieved and displayed.

INTERNET

Physically, a collection of packet-switching networks interconnected by gateways along with protocols that allow them to function logically as a single, large, virtual network. When written in uppercase, Internet refers specifically to the DARPA Internet and the TCP/IP protocols it uses.

INTERNET

The collection of networks and gateways, including the ARPANET, MILNET, and NSFnet, that use the TCP/IP protocol suite and function as a single, cooperative virtual network. The Internet reaches many universities, government research labs, and military installations.

INTERNET ACCESS PROVIDER

See ISP.

INTERNET ADDRESS

The address assigned to hosts that want to participate in the Internet using TCP/IP. This unique number consists of four parts separated by dots, e.g., 165.113.245.2. Every machine that is on the Internet has a unique IP number—if a machine does not have an IP number, it is not really on the Internet.

INTEROPERABILITY

The ability of software and hardware on multiple machines from multiple vendors to communicate meaningfully.

IP

Internet protocol. The Internet standard protocol that defines the Internet datagram as the unit of information passes across the Internet and provides the basis for the Internet connectionless, best-effort packet delivery service.

IP ADDRESS

See "Internet address." Your IP address will either be given to you by your service provider for permanent use or assigned to you dynamically when you connect.

IRQ

Interrupt request. Hardware on a PC uses an interrupt request "channel" to tell the CPU that its normal processing needs to be interrupted to handle a request by the hardware. Serial ports, printer ports, network cards, and sound cards all use interrupts. The range of IRQs on 386 PCs or better is from 2 to 15. Generally, each piece of hardware will need a unique IRQ associated with it. Many PC problems involving modems and network cards are due to IRQ conflicts.

ISDN

Integrated Services Digital Network. Basically a way to move more data over existing regular phone lines. ISDN is only slowly becoming available in the USA, but where it is available it can provide speeds of 64,000 bits per second over a regular phone line at almost the same cost as a normal phone call.

ISP

Internet service provider (or Internet access provider). A company which provides Internet access and other Internet-related services to businesses or individuals. For example: Netcom and OuterNet.

KERNAL

The level of an operating system or networking system that contains the system-level commands or all of the functions hidden from the user. In a UNIX system, the kernal is a program that contains the device drivers, the memory management routines, the scheduler, and system calls. This program is always running while the system is operating.

LAN

Local area network. A high-speed network connecting machines at one physical site.

LEASED LINE

Refers to a phone line that is rented for exclusive 24-hour, 7-days-a-week use from your location to another location. The highest speed data connections require a leased line.

LISTSERV

The most common kind of mail list. Listservs originated on BITNET, but they are now common on the Internet.

MAIL GATEWAY

A machine that connects to two or more electronic mail systems (especially dissimilar mail systems on two different networks) and transfers mail messages among them.

MAILLIST

A (usually automated) system that allows people to send e-mail to one address, whereupon their message is copied and sent to all of the other subscribers to the maillist. In this way, people who have many different kinds of e-mail access can participate in discussions together.

MIL

One of the top-level domains. Stands for military and includes military organizations. For example: clyde@hqafsc.af.mil.

MODEM

MOdulator, DEModulator. A device that you connect to your computer and to a phone line that allows the computer to talk to other computers through the phone system. Basically, modems do for computers what a telephone does for humans.

MTU

Maximum transmission unit. The size of the packet which can be sent. If you are using TCP/IP on an Ethernet, this will be 1500. If you are using SLIP or PPP, obtain this value from your service provider.

NAME SERVER

A machine which translates Internet host and domain names into IP addresses (e.g., draconis.outer.net   204.96.12.9). Where your connection or network software requests this, enter the IP address of your name server. You can get these numbers from your service provider.

NET

One of the top-level domains. Stands for network and includes network service centers, network information centers, and other organizations that have a hand in network management. For instance: sue@austinfree.net.

NETMASK

A network mask which prevents your system from broadcasting packets to too many other systems. What your netmask is will depend on the size of the network you're on. For example, the netmask for a Class C network (204.96.12.0–204.96.12.255) is 255.255.255.0. Your service provider can tell you what your netmask will be.

NETWORK

A group of machines connected together so they can transmit information to one another. Any time you connect two or more computers together so that they can share resources you have a computer network. Connect two or more networks together and you have an internet.

NETWORK PATH

A series of machine names used to direct electronic mail from one user to another.

NEWSGROUPS
The name for discussion groups on Usenet.

NSFNET
National Science Foundation network. TCP/IP-based network.

ONLINE SERVICE PROVIDER
A company which offers a variety of services on their own private computer network, which customers can dial in to. Most of these companies have connected their private networks to the Internet and now offer some Internet services. For example: America Online and CompuServe.

ORG
One of the top-level domains. Encompasses nonprofit organizations.

PACKET
A unit of data sent across a packet-switching network.

PACKET DRIVER
A network software driver which allows data to be sent to and from a networked DOS or Windows machine in the form of packets. Most network cards for PCs will include packet driver software. When used in conjunction with TCP/IP stack software, such as Trumpet Winsock, a packet driver allows a PC to communicate using TCP/IP over a network.

PACKET SWITCHING
Data transmission technique in which data is segmented and routed in packets. The method used to move data around on the Internet. In packet switching, all the data coming out of a machine is broken up into chunks; each chunk has the address of where it came from and where it is going. This enables chunks of data from many different sources to move on the same lines and be sorted and directed to different routes by special machines along the way. This way many people can use the same lines at the same time.

PPP
Point to Point Protocol. Most well known as a protocol that allows a computer to use a regular telephone line and a modem to make a TCP/IP connection and thus be really and truly on the Internet. PPP is gradually replacing SLIP for this purpose.

PROTOCOL

A formal set of rules governing the format, timing, and error control of transmissions on a network or the protocol that networks use to communicate with each other.

ROUTE

The path that network traffic takes from its source to its destination.

ROUTER

A hardware and software device that connects hosts on different networks. A special-purpose computer (or software package) that handles the connection between two or more networks. Routers spend all their time looking at the destination addresses of the packets passing through them and deciding which route to send them on.

ROUTING

The process of selecting the correct path (circuit) for a transmission over a network.

SERVER

A computer, or a software package, that provides a specific kind of service to client software running on other computers. The term can refer to a particular piece of software, such as a WWW server, or to the machine on which the software is running, e.g., "Our mail server is down today, that's why e-mail isn't getting out." A single server machine could have several different server software packages running on it, thus providing many different services to clients on the network.

SLIP

Serial Line Internet Protocol. A standard for using a regular telephone line (a "serial line") and a modem to connect a computer as a real Internet site. SLIP is gradually being replaced by PPP.

SMTP

Simple Mail Transfer Protocol. The Internet standard protocol for transferring electronic mail messages from one machine to another.

T1

AT&T term for digital circuit carrying transmissions at a rate of 1,544,000 bits/second. At maximum theoretical capacity, a T1 line could move a megabyte in less than 10 seconds.

T3

Transmission rate on this type of circuit is 45,000,000 bits per second. This is more than enough to do full-screen, full-motion video.

TCP

Transmission Control Protocol. The Internet standard transport level protocol that provides the reliable, full duplex, stream service on which many application protocols depend.

TRUMPET WINSOCK

A shareware program developed by Peter Tattam of Trumpet Software International. It provides a winsock library, an internal SLIP and PPP driver, a Windows packet driver, and a convenient dialer. It's available from ftp.trumpet.com.au.

UNIX

A computer operating system (the basic software running on a computer, underneath things like word processors and spreadsheets). UNIX is designed to be used by many people at the same time (it is "multiuser") and has TCP/IP built in. It is the most common operating system for servers on the Internet.

URL

Uniform (or Universal) Resource Locator. The standard way to define the address of any resource on the Internet that is part of the World Wide Web (WWW).

USENET

A worldwide system of discussion groups, with comments passed among hundreds of thousands of machines. Not all Usenet machines are on the Internet. Usenet is completely decentralized, with over 15,000 discussion areas, called newsgroups.

USER-LEVEL PROTOCOLS

Protocols, such as Telnet, SMTP, and FTP, which allow you to perform operations via client-side applications on the network.

UUCP

UNIX to UNIX Copy Program.

VIRTUAL CIRCUIT

A network service that allows two processes to communicate as if they were directly connected to each other. A virtual circuit is similar to a UNIX pipe.

VJ COMPRESSION

Van Jacobson Compression. A technique used to compress data going through a SLIP or PPP connection. Ask your service provider if they support VJ compression.

WAN
Wide-area network.

WINSOCK
Winsock is the general name for a software specification which provides a standard TCP/IP networking layer for Windows systems. The official name for this specification is Windows Sockets, and the software routines for TCP/IP networking are generally found in a Windows library file called WINSOCK.DLL. Winsocks are available from Microsoft, IBM, Internet in a Box, Chameleon, Trumpet, and other Internet packages.

WWW
World Wide Web. Two meanings. First, loosely used, the whole constellation of resources that can be accessed using a variety of tools and protocols. Second, the universe of hypertext servers, which are the servers that allow text, graphics, and sound files to be mixed together and linked using hypertext markup language to define addresses.

Appendix B—Internet Service Providers

Here's the latest list of Internet Service Providers courtesy of Paul Celestin. The most current version is available by sending an email to info@celestin.com with the words SEND POCIA.TXT in the subject line of the message. There's another good source for Internet Service Providers available on the WWW at http://thelist.com —it's searchable by all sorts of categories and is very well organized. Check it out too if you're ISP shopping.

All of the information in this directory was supplied to Celestin Company directly by the service providers and is subject to change without notice. Celestin Company does not endorse any of the providers in this directory. If you do not see a provider listed for your area, please do not ask them or us about it, as we both only know about providers in this directory. This directory is brought to you as a public service. Celestin Company does not receive any compensation from the providers listed here, and neither do we. Since Internet service providers come and go and frequently change their offers, we strongly urge you to contact them for additional information and/or restrictions.

The latest version of this document is available at the following location:

```
ftp://ftp.celestin.com/biz/celestin/pocia/p
ocia.txt
```

If you have Web access, try http://www.celestin.com /pocia/ for the hypertext version of this list, which includes addresses, telephone numbers, fax numbers, e-mail addresses, and pricing.

DOMESTIC

A listing of Internet service providers in the U.S. and Canada, sorted by area code. Fields are area code, service provider name, voice phone number, and e-mail address for more information.

Free Service Providers

For the cost of a long-distance phone call, you can dial any of these Internet providers and give the Internet a try.

Free.org (shell,slip,ppp) modem ->   715 743 1600 info@free.org
Free.I.Net (must dial via AT&T) modem ->   801 471 2266 info@free.i.net
SLIPNET (shell,slip,ppp)   modem -> 217 792 2777 info@slip.net

Nationwide Service Providers

The following access providers provide service to more than just one part of the United States/Canada. Many of them provide service regardless of your geographic location, but may charge a higher price than local service providers.

AGIS (Apex Global Information Services)	313 730 1130 info@agis.net
ANS	703 758 7700 info@ans.net
BBN Planet	617 873 2905 net-info@bbnplanet.com
Concentric Research Corp.	800 745 2747 info@cris.com
CRL Network Services	415 837 5300 sales@crl.com
DataXchange Network, Inc.	800 863 1550 info@dx.net
Delphi Internet Services Corp.	800 695 4005 info@delphi.com
EarthLink Network, Inc.	213 644 9500 sales@earthlink.net
Exodus Communications, Inc.	408 522 8450 info@exodus.net
4GL Corp.	713 589 8077 info@4gl.com
Global Connect, Inc.	804 229 4484 info@gc.net
Information Access Technologies (Holonet)	510 704 0160 info@holonet.net
Institute for Global Communications	415 442 0220 igc-info@igc.apc.org
Liberty Information Network	800 218 5157 info@liberty.com
MIDnet	800 682 5550 info@mid.net
Moran Communications	716 639 1254 info@moran.com
NETCOM On-Line Communications Services	408 554 8649 info@netcom.com
Netrex, Inc.	800 3 NETREX info@netrex.com
Network 99, Inc.	800 NET 99IP net99@cluster.mcs.net
Performance Systems International	800 827 7482 all-info@psi.com
Portal Information Network	408 973 9111 info@portal.com
SprintLink - Nationwide 56K - 45M access	800 817 7755 info@sprint.net
The ThoughtPort Authority, Inc.	800 ISP 6870 info@thoughtport.com
WareNet	714 348 3295 info@ware.net
Zocalo Engineering	510 540 8000 info@zocalo.net

Toll-Free Service Providers

These access providers allow you to dial a toll-free 800 number to connect to the Internet. Most of them charge for this privilege, but it may save you money over long-distance charges if you do not have local Internet access.

Allied Access Inc.	618 684 2255 sales@intrnet.net
ARInternet Corp.	301 459 7171 info@ari.net
American Information Systems, Inc.	708 413 8400 info@ais.net
Association for Computing Machinery	817 776 6876 account-info@acm.org
CICNet, Inc.	313 998 6103 info@cic.net
Cogent Software, Inc.	818 585 2788 info@cogsoft.com
Cyberius Online, Inc.	613 233 1215 info@cyberus.ca
Colorado SuperNet, Inc.	303 296 8202 info@csn.org
EarthLink Network, Inc.	213 644 9500 sales@earthlink.net
Global Connect, Inc.	804 229 4484 info@gc.net
Internet Express	719 592 1240 info@usa.net
Iowa Network Services	800 546 6587 service@netins.net
Mnematics, Inc.	914 359 4546 service@mne.com
Msen, Inc.	313 998 4562 info@msen.com
NeoSoft, Inc.	713 684 5969 info@neosoft.com
NETCOM On-Line Communications Services	408 554 8649 info@netcom.com
New Mexico Technet, Inc.	505 345 6555 granoff@technet.nm.org
Pacific Rim Network, Inc.	360 650 0442 info@pacificrim.net
Rocky Mountain Internet	800 900 7644 info@rmii.com
Synergy Communications, Inc.	800 345 9669 info@synergy.net
VivaNET, Inc.	800 836 UNIX info@vivanet.com
VoiceNet	800 835 5710 info@voicenet.com
WLN	800 342 5956 info@wln.com

Regional Service Providers

These access providers specialize in particular regions, some as small as a town of a thousand people, others as large as the San Francisco Bay Area.

201 Carroll-Net, Inc.	201 488 1332 info@carroll.com
201 Crystal Palace Networking, Inc.	201 300 0881 info@crystal.palace.net
201 Digital Express Group	301 847 5000 info@digex.net
201 Eclipse Internet Access	800 483 1223 info@eclipse.net
201 Galaxy Networks	201 825 2310 info@galaxy.net
201 GBN InternetAccess	201 343 6427 gbninfo@gbn.net
201 I-2000, Inc.	800 464 3820 info@i-2000.com
201 INTAC Access Corp.	800 504 6822 info@intac.com
201 Interactive Networks, Inc.	201 881 1878 info@interactive.net
201 Intercall, Inc.	800 758 7329 sales@intercall.com
201 InterCom Online	212 714 7183 info@intercom.com
201 The Internet Connection Corp.	201 435 4414 info@cnct.com
201 Internet Online Services	x226 -> 201 928 1000 help@ios.com
201 Lightning Internet Services, LLC	516 248 8400 sales@lightning.net
201 Mordor International BBS	201 433 4222 ritz@mordor.com
201 New York Net	718 776 6811 sales@new-york.net
201 NIC - Neighborhood Internet Connection	201 934 1445 info@nic.com
201 Openix - Open Internet Exchange	201 443 0400 info@openix.com
201 Planet Access Networks	201 691 4704 info@planet.net
201 ZONE One Network Exchange	212 824 4000 info@zone.net
202 American Information Network	410 855 2353 info@ai.net
202 ARInternet Corp.	301 459 7171 info@ari.net
202 CAPCON Library Network	202 331 5771 info@capcon.net
202 Charm.Net	410 558 3900 info@charm.net
202 Cyber Services, Inc.	703 749 9590 info@cs.com
202 Digital Express Group	301 847 5000 info@digex.net
202 Genuine Computing Resources	703 878 4680 info@gcr.com
202 I-Link, Ltd.	800 ILINK 99 info@i-link.net
202 Internet Online, Inc.	301 652 4468 info@intr.net
202 Interpath	800 849 6305 info@interpath.net
202 LaserNet	703 591 4232 info@laser.net
202 Quantum Networking Solutions, Inc.	805 538 2028 info@qnet.com
202 RadixNet Internet Services	301 567 9831 info@radix.net
202 Smartnet Internet Services, LLC	301 470 3400 info@smart.net
202 SONNETS, Inc.	703 502 8589 office@sonnets.net
202 UltraPlex Information Providers	301 598 6UPX info@upx.net
202 Universal Telecomm Corp.	703 758 0550 root@utc.net

202 US Net, Inc.   301 572 5926 info@us.net
202 World Web Limited   703 838 2000 info@worldweb.net
202 Xpress Internet Services   301 601 5050 info@xis.com

203 Computerized Horizons   203 335 7431 sysop@fcc.com
203 Connix: Connecticut Internet Exchange   860 349 7059 office@connix.com
203 Continuum Communications, Inc.   203 885 3576 gph@q.continuum.net
203 Futuris Networks, Inc.   203 359 8868 info@futuris.net
203 I-2000, Inc.   800 464 3820 info@i-2000.com
203 imagine.com   860 527 9245 Postmaster@imagine.com
203 Lightning Internet Services, LLC   516 248 8400 sales@lightning.net
203 MCIX, Inc.   860 572 8720 info@mcix.com
203 Mindport Internet Services, Inc.   860 892 2081 staff@mindport.net
203 NETPLEX   203 233 1111 info@ntplx.net
203 North American Internet Company   800 952 INET info@nai.net
203 Paradigm Communications, Inc.   203 250 7397 info@pcnet.com
203 ZONE One Network Exchange   212 824 4000 info@zone.net

204 Cycor Communications, Inc.   902 892 7354 signup@cycor.ca
204 Gate West Communications   204 663 2931 info@gatewest.net

205 AIRnet Internet Services, Inc.   800 247 6388 efelton@AIRnet.net
205 Community Internet Connect, Inc.   205 722 0199 info@cici.com
205 HiWAAY Information Services   205 533 3131 info@HiWAAY.net
205 Hub City Area Access   601 268 6156 info@hub1.hubcity.com
205 interQuest, Inc.   205 464 8280 info@iquest.com
205 MindSpring Enterprises, Inc.   800 719 4332 info@mindspring.com
205 Renaissance Internet Services   205 535 2113 info@ro.com
205 Scott Network Services, Inc.   205 987 5889 info@scott.net

206 Blarg! Online Services   206 782 6578 info@blarg.net
206 Cyberspace   206 281 5397 info@cyberspace.com
206 Digital Forest   206 487 6414 info@forest.net
206 Eskimo North   206 367 7457 nanook@eskimo.com
206 I-Link, Ltd.   800 ILINK 99 info@i-link.net
206 InEx Net   206 670 1131 info@inex.com
206 Interconnected Associates, Inc. (IXA)   206 622 7337 mike@ixa.com
206 Internet Express   719 592 1240 info@usa.net

206 ISOMEDIA.COM	206 881 8769 info@isomedia.com
206 Northwest Nexus, Inc.	206 455 3505 info@nwnexus.wa.com
206 NorthWestNet	206 562 3000 info@nwnet.net
206 Olympic Computing Solutions	206 989 6698 ocs@oz.net
206 Oregon Information Technology Centeres	503 469 6699 hmaster@harborside.com
206 Pacific Rim Network, Inc.	x11 -> 360 650 0442 info@pacificrim.net
206 Seanet Online Services	206 343 7828 info@seanet.com
206 SenseMedia	408 335 9400 sm@picosof.com
206 Structured Network Systems, Inc.	503 656 3530 info@structured.net
206 Teleport, Inc.	503 223 4245 info@teleport.com
206 Transport Logic	503 243 1940 sales@transport.com
206 WLN	800 342 5956 info@wln.com
207 Agate Internet Services	207 947 8248 ais@agate.net
207 Internet Maine	207 780 0416 info@mainelink.net
207 MaineStreet Communications	207 657 5078 rainmaker@maine.com
207 Midcoast Internet Solutions	207 594 8277 accounts@midcoast.com
207 MV Communications, Inc.	603 429 2223 info@mv.mv.com
207 Northern Lights Internet Services	207 773 4941 jkilday@nlbbs.com
208 Micron Internet Services	208 368 5400 sales@micron.net
208 Minnesota Regional Network	612 342 2570 info@mr.net
208 NICOH Net	208 233 5802 info@nicoh.com
208 NorthWestNet	206 562 3000 info@nwnet.net
208 Primenet	602 870 1010 info@primenet.com
208 SRVnet	208 524 6237 nlp@srv.net
208 Structured Network Systems, Inc.	503 656 3530 info@structured.net
208 Transport Logic	503 243 1940 sales@transport.com
209 The Computer Depot	209 223 5043 admin@cdepot.net
209 Cybergate Information Services	209 486 4283 cis@cybergate.com
209 Infonet Communications, Inc.	209 446 2360 mikeb@icinet.net
209 InReach Internet Communications	800 446 7324 info@inreach.com
209 InterNex Tiara	408 496 5466 info@internex.net
209 Primenet	602 870 1010 info@primenet.com
209 ValleyNet Communications	209 486 8638 info@valleynet.com
209 West Coast Online	707 586 3060 info@calon.com

210 Connect International, Inc.	210 341 2599 info@connecti.com
210 Delta Design and Development, Inc.	800 763 8265 sales@deltaweb.com
210 The Eden Matrix	512 478 9900 info@eden.com
210 I-Link, Ltd.	800 ILINK 99 info@i-link.net
210 Phoenix DataNet, Inc.	713 486 8337 info@phoenix.net
212 Advanced Standards, Inc advn.com	212 302 3366 kolian@advn.com
212 Alternet (UUNET Technologies, Inc.)	703 204 8000 info@alter.net
212 Blythe Systems	212 226 7171 infodesk@blythe.org
212 BrainLINK	718 805 6559 info@beast.brainlink.com
212 bway.net / Outernet, Inc.	212 982 9800 info@bway.net
212 Calyx Internet Access	212 475 5051 info@calyx.net
212 Creative Data Consultants (SILLY.COM)	718 229 0489 info@silly.com
212 Digital Express Group	301 847 5000 info@digex.net
212 Echo Communications Group	212 255 3839 info@echonyc.com
212 escape.com - Kazan Corp	212 888 8780 info@escape.com
212 I-2000, Inc.	800 464 3820 info@i-2000.com
212 I-Link, Ltd.	800 ILINK 99 info@i-link.net
212 Ingress Communications, Inc.	212 679 2838 info@ingress.com
212 INTAC Access Corp.	800 504 6822 info@intac.com
212 Intellitech Walrus	212 406 5000 info@walrus.com
212 Interactive Networks, Inc.	201 881 1878 info@interactive.net
212 Intercall, Inc.	800 758 7329 sales@intercall.com
212 InterCom Online	212 714 7183 info@intercom.com
212 The Internet Connection Corp.	201 435 4414 info@cnct.com
212 Internet Online Services	x226 -> 201 928 1000 help@ios.com
212 Internet QuickLink Corp.	212 307 1669 info@quicklink.com
212 Interport Communications Corp.	212 989 1128 info@interport.net
212 Lightning Internet Services, LLC	516 248 8400 sales@lightning.net
212 Long Island Internet HeadQuarters	516 439 7800 support@pb.net
212 Mordor International BBS	201 433 4222 ritz@mordor.com
212 Mnematics, Inc.	914 359 4546 service@mne.com
212 New World Data	718 962 1725 dmk@nwdc.com
212 New York Net	718 776 6811 sales@new-york.net
212 NY WEBB, Inc.	800 458 4660 wayne@webb.com
212 NYSERNet	800 493 4367 sales@nysernet.org
212 Panix (Public Access uNIX)	212 741 4400 info@panix.com
212 Phantom Access Technologies, Inc.	212 989 2418 bruce@phantom.com

212 Pipeline New York	212 267 3636 info@pipeline.com
212 Real Life Pictures RealNet	212 366 4434 reallife@walrus.com
212 Spacelab.Net	212 966 8844 mike@mxol.com
212 The ThoughtPort Authority, Inc.	800 ISP 6870 info@thoughtport.com
212 ThoughtPort of New York City	212 645 7970 info@precipice.com
212 tunanet/InfoHouse	212 229 8224 info@tunanet.com
212 ZONE One Network Exchange	212 824 4000 info@zone.net
213 ArtNetwork	800 395 0692 info@artnet.net
213 BeachNet Internet Access	310 823 3308 info@beachnet.com
213 Cogent Software, Inc.	818 585 2788 info@cogsoft.com
213 Cyberverse Online	310 643 3783 info@cyberverse.com
213 Delta Internet Services	714 778 0370 info@deltanet.com
213 DigiLink Network Services	310 542 7421 info@digilink.net
213 DirectNet	213 383 3144 info@directnet.com
213 Electriciti	619 338 9000 info@powergrid.electriciti.com
213 Exodus Communications, Inc.	408 522 8450 info@exodus.net
213 Flamingo Communications, Inc.	310 532 3533 sales@fcom.com
213 I-Link, Ltd.	800 ILINK 99 info@i-link.net
213 Instant Internet Corp. (InstaNet)	818 772 0097 charlyg@instanet.com
213 InterWorld Communications, Inc.	310 726 0500 sales@interworld.net
213 The Loop Internet Switch Co.	213 465 1311 info@loop.com
213 KAIWAN Internet	714 638 2139 info@kaiwan.com
213 KTB Internet Online	818 240 6600 info@ktb.net
213 Leonardo Internet	310 395 5500 jimp@leonardo.net
213 Liberty Information Network	800 218 5157 info@liberty.com
213 Network Intensive	714 450 8400 info@ni.net
213 Online-LA	310 967 8000 sales@online-la.com
213 OutWest Network Services	818 545 1996 info@outwest.net
213 Primenet	602 870 1010 info@primenet.com
213 QuickCom Internet Communcations	213 634 7735 info@quickcom.net
213 Saigon Enterprises	818 246 0689 info@saigon.net
213 ViaNet Communications	415 903 2242 info@via.net
214 Alternet (UUNET Technologies, Inc.)	703 204 8000 info@alter.net
214 CompuTek	214 994 0190 info@computek.net
214 Connection Technologies - ConnectNet	214 490 7100 sales@connect.net
214 Delta Design and Development, Inc.	800 763 8265 sales@deltaweb.com

214	DFW Internet Services, Inc.	817 332 5116 info@dfw.net
214	I-Link, Ltd.	800 ILINK 99 info@i-link.net
214	OnRamp Technologies, Inc.	214 746 4710 info@onramp.net
214	Texas Metronet, Inc.	214 705 2900 info@metronet.com
215	Cheap Net	302 993 8420 sammy@ravenet.com
215	Digital Express Group	301 847 5000 info@digex.net
215	epix	800 374 9669 karndt@epix.net
215	FishNet	610 337 9994 info@pond.com
215	GlobalQUEST, Inc.	610 696 8111 info@globalquest.net
215	I-2000, Inc.	800 464 3820 info@i-2000.com
215	Internet Tidal Wave	610 770 6187 steve@itw.com
215	InterNetworking Technologies	302 398 4369 itnt.com@itnt.com
215	The Magnetic Page	302 651 9753 info@magpage.com
215	Microserve Information Systems	717 779 4430 info@microserve.com
215	Net Access	215 576 8669 support@netaxs.com
215	NetReach, Inc.	215 283 2300 info@netreach.net
215	Network Analysis Group	800 624 9240 nag@good.freedom.net
215	OpNet	610 520 2880 info@op.net
215	RaveNet Systems, Inc.	302 993 8420 waltemus@ravenet.com
215	VivaNET, Inc.	800 836 UNIX info@vivanet.com
215	VoiceNet	800 835 5710 info@voicenet.com
215	You Tools Corp. / FASTNET	610 954 5910 info@fast.net
216	APK Public Access UNI Site	216 481 9436 info@wariat.org
216	Branch Information Services	313 741 4442 branch-info@branch.com
216	CanNet Internet Services	216 484 2260 info@cannet.com
216	CommercePark Interactive, Ltd.	216 523 2240 info@commercepark.com
216	ExchangeNet	216 261 4593 info@en.com
216	Gateway to Internet Services	216 656 5511 ytc@gwis.com
216	Multiverse, Inc.	216 344 3080 multiverse.com
216	New Age Consulting Service	216 524 3162 damin@nacs.net
216	OARnet (corporate clients only)	614 728 8100 info@oar.net
217	Allied Access, Inc.	618 684 2255 sales@intrnet.net
217	Net66	217 328 0066 sales@net66.com
217	Shouting Ground Technologies, Inc.	217 351 7921 admin@shout.net
217	Sol Tec, Inc.	317 920 1SOL info@soltec.com

218 Minnesota OnLine   612 225 1110 info@mn.state.net
218 Red River Net   701 232 2227 info@rrnet.com
218 Protocol Communications, Inc.   612 541 9900 info@protocom.com

219 Custom Logic Systems   219 255 5201 info@cl-sys.com
219 Wink Communications Group, Inc.   708 310 9465 sales@winkcomm.com

301 ABSnet Internet Services   410 361 8160 info@abs.net
301 American Information Network   410 855 2353 info@ai.net
301 ARInternet Corp.   301 459 7171 info@ari.net
301 Charm.Net   410 558 3900 info@charm.net
301 Clark Internet Services, Inc. ClarkNet   410 995 0691 info@clark.net
301 Cyber Services, Inc.   703 749 9590 info@cs.com
301 Digital Express Group   301 847 5000 info@digex.net
301 FredNet   301 631 5300 info@fred.net
301 Genuine Computing Resources   703 878 4680 info@gcr.com
301 Internet Online, Inc.   301 652 4468 info@intr.net
301 Kompleat Internet Services LLC   301 293 4333 netadmin@kis.net
301 LaserNet   703 591 4232 info@laser.net
301 Quantum Networking Solutions, Inc.   805 538 2028 info@qnet.com
301 RadixNet Internet Services   301 567 9831 info@radix.net
301 Smartnet Internet Services, LLC   301 470 3400 info@smart.net
301 SONNETS, Inc.   703 502 8589 office@sonnets.net
301 SURAnet   301 982 4600 marketing@sura.net
301 UltraPlex Information Providers   301 598 6UPX info@upx.net
301 Universal Telecomm Corp.   703 758 0550 root@utc.net
301 US Net, Inc.   301 572 5926 info@us.net
301 World Web Limited   703 838 2000 info@worldweb.net
301 Xpress Internet Services   301 601 5050 info@xis.com

302 Cheap Net   302 993 8420 sammy@ravenet.com
302 Delaware Common Access Network   302 654 1019 info@dca.net
302 First State Web, Inc.   302 234 0721 info@wittnet.com
302 InterNetworking Technologies   302 398 4369 itnt.com@itnt.com
302 The Magnetic Page   302 651 9753 info@magpage.com
302 RaveNet Systems, Inc.   302 993 8420 waltemus@ravenet.com
302 SSNet, Inc.   302 378 1386 info@ssnet.com
302 VoiceNet   800 835 5710 info@voicenet.com

303 ABWAM, Inc. 303 730 6050 info@entertain.com
303 Colorado SuperNet, Inc. 303 296 8202 info@csn.org
303 CSDC, Inc. 303 665 8053 support@ares.csd.net
303 The Denver Exchange, Inc. 303 455 4252 info@tde.com
303 ENVISIONET, Inc. 303 770 2408 info@envisionet.net
303 EZLink Internet Access 970 482 0807 ezadmin@ezlink.com
303 I-Link, Ltd. 800 ILINK 99 info@i-link.net
303 Indra's Net, Inc. 303 546 9151 info@indra.com
303 Internet Express 719 592 1240 info@usa.net
303 NETConnect 800 689 8001 office@tcd.net
303 NetWay 2001, Inc. 303 794 1000 info@netway.net
303 New Mexico Technet, Inc. 505 345 6555 granoff@technet.nm.org
303 Online Network Enterprises, Inc. 303 444 2522 info@netONE.com
303 Rocky Mountain Internet 800 900 7644 info@rmii.com
303 Shaman Exchange, Inc. 303 674 9784 info@dash.com
303 Stonehenge Internet Communications 800 RUN INET info@henge.com

304 RAM Technologies, Inc. 800 950 1726 info@ramlink.net

305 Acquired Knowledge Systems, Inc. 305 525 2574 info@aksi.net
305 CyberGate, Inc. 305 428 4283 sales@gate.net
305 Electronic Link 305 378 1128 info@elink.net
305 The EmiNet Domain 407 731 0222 info@emi.net
305 ICANECT 305 621 9200 sales@icanect.net
305 InteleCom Data Systems, Inc. 401 885 6855 info@ids.net
305 Internet Providers of Florida, Inc. 305 273 7978 office@ipof.fla.net
305 Internet World Information Network 305 535 3090 webmaster@winnet.net
305 Magg Information Services, Inc. 407 642 9841 help@magg.net
305 NetMiami Internet Corp. 305 554 4463 picard@netmiami.com
305 Netpoint Communications, Inc. 305 891 1955 info@netpoint.net
305 Paradise Communications, Inc. 404 980 0078 info@paradise.net
305 PSS InterNet Services 800 463 8499 support@america.com
305 SatelNET Communications, Inc. 305 434 8738 admin@satelnet.org
305 Shadow Information Services, Inc. 305 594 2450 admin@shadow.net
305 WebIMAGE, an internet presence provider 407 723 0001 info@webimage.com
305 Zimmerman Communications 954 584 0199 bob@zim.com

306 Cycor Communications, Inc. 902 892 7354 signup@cycor.ca

307 CoffeyNet	307 234 5443 web@coffey.com
307 NETConnect	800 689 8001 office@tcd.net
307 wyoming.com	307 332 3030 info@wyoming.com
308 Synergy Communications, Inc.	800 345 9669 info@synergy.net
309 CICNet, Inc.	313 998 6103 info@cic.net
309 Driscoll Communications	309 367 2006 info@dris.com
309 Interactive Communications & Explorations	309 454 4638 icenet@ice.net
310 ArtNetwork	800 395 0692 info@artnet.net
310 BeachNet Internet Access	310 823 3308 info@beachnet.com
310 Business Access Technologies	714 577 8978 Techs@batech.com
310 Cloverleaf Communications	714 895 3075 sales@cloverleaf.com
310 Cogent Software, Inc.	818 585 2788 info@cogsoft.com
310 CruzNet	714 680 6600 info@cruznet.net
310 Cyberverse Online	310 643 3783 info@cyberverse.com
310 Delta Internet Services	714 778 0370 info@deltanet.com
310 DigiLink Network Services	310 542 7421 info@digilink.net
310 Exodus Communications, Inc.	408 522 8450 info@exodus.net
310 Flamingo Communications, Inc.	310 532 3533 sales@fcom.com
310 Instant Internet Corp. (InstaNet)	818 772 0097 charlyg@instanet.com
310 InterWorld Communications, Inc.	310 726 0500 sales@interworld.net
310 KAIWAN Internet	714 638 2139 info@kaiwan.com
310 KTB Internet Online	818 240 6600 info@ktb.net
310 Leonardo Internet	310 395 5500 jimp@leonardo.net
310 Liberty Information Network	800 218 5157 info@liberty.com
310 Lightside, Inc.	818 858 9261 Lightside@Lightside.Com
310 The Loop Internet Switch Co.	213 465 1311 info@loop.com
310 Network Intensive	714 450 8400 info@ni.net
310 Online-LA	310 967 8000 sales@online-la.com
310 OutWest Network Services	818 545 1996 info@outwest.net
310 QuickCom Internet Communcations	213 634 7735 info@quickcom.net
310 QuickNet, Inc.	714 969 1091 sales@quick.net
310 Saigon Enterprises	818 246 0689 info@saigon.net
310 SoftAware	310 305 0275 info@softaware.com
310 ViaNet Communications	415 903 2242 info@via.net

312 American Information Systems, Inc.   708 413 8400 info@ais.net
312 CICNet, Inc.   313 998 6103 info@cic.net
312 CIN.net Computerese Information Network 708 310 1188 info@cin.net
312 Compunet Technology Consultants   708 355 XNET webmaster@ms.com-punet.com
312 InterAccess Co.   708 498 2542 info@interaccess.com
312 Interactive Network Systems, Inc.   312 881 3039 info@insnet.com
312 MCSNet   312 803 6271 info@mcs.net
312 Ripco Communications, Inc.   312 477 6210 info@ripco.com
312 Tezcatlipoca, Inc.   312 850 0181 info@tezcat.com
312 The ThoughtPort Authority, Inc.   800 ISP 6870 info@thoughtport.com
312 Wink Communications Group, Inc.   708 310 9465 sales@winkcomm.com
312 WorldWide Access   708 367 1870 info@wwa.com
312 XNet Information Systems   708 983 6064 info@xnet.com

313 Branch Information Services   313 741 4442 branch-info@branch.com
313 CICNet, Inc.   313 998 6103 info@cic.net
313 Great Lakes Information Systems   810 786 0454 info@glis.net
313 ICNET / Innovative Concepts   313 998 0090 info@ic.net
313 Isthmus Corp.   313 973 2100 info@izzy.net
313 Michigan Internet Cooperative Assn   810 355 1438 info@coop.mica.net
313 Mich.com, Inc.   810 478 4300 info@mich.com
313 Msen, Inc.   313 998 4562 info@msen.com
313 RustNet, Inc.   810 650 6812 info@rust.net
313 Voyager Information Networks, Inc.   517 485 9068 help@voyager.net

314 accessU.S., Inc.   800 638 6373 info@accessus.net
314 Allied Access, Inc.   618 684 2255 sales@intrnet.net
314 Inlink   314 432 0935 support@inlink.com
314 NeoSoft, Inc.   713 684 5969 info@neosoft.com
314 Online Information Access Network   618 692 9813 info@oia.net
314 MVP-Net, Inc.   314 731 2252 info@MO.NET
314 SOCKET Internet Services Corp.   314 499 9131 office@socketis.net
314 Tetranet Communications, Inc.   314 256 4495 info@tetranet.net
314 The ThoughtPort Authority, Inc.   800 ISP 6870 info@thoughtport.com

315 NYSERNet   800 493 4367 sales@nysernet.org
315 ServiceTech, Inc.   716 263 3360 info@servtech.com
315 Spectra.net   607 798 7300 info@spectra.net

315 Syracuse Internet	315 233 1948 info@vcomm.net
315 VivaNET, Inc.	800 836 UNIX info@vivanet.com
316 Elysian Fields, Inc.	316 267 2636 info@elysian.net
316 Future Net, Inc.	316 652 0070 rgmann@fn.net
316 SouthWind Internet Access, Inc.	316 263 7963 info@southwind.net
317 HolliCom Internet Services	317 883 4500 cale@holli.com
317 IQuest Internet, Inc.	317 259 5050 info@iquest.net
317 Metropolitan Data Networks Limited	317 449 0539 info@mdn.com
317 Net Direct	317 251 5252 kat@inetdirect.net
317 Sol Tec, Inc.	317 920 1SOL info@soltec.com
318 Linknet Internet Services	318 442 5465 rdalton@linknet.net
318 Net-Connect, Ltd.	318 234 4396 services@net-connect.net
319 Freese-Notis Weather.Net	515 282 9310 hfreese@weather.net
319 ia.net	319 393 1095 info@ia.net
319 INTERLINK L.C.	319 524 2895 postmaster@interl.net
319 Iowa Network Services	800 546 6587 service@netins.net
334 Datasync Internet Services	601 872 0001 info@datasync.com
334 Gulf Coast Internet Company	904 438 5700 info@gulf.net
334 OnLine Montgomery	334 271 9576 rverble@bbs.olm.com
334 MindSpring Enterprises, Inc.	800 719 4332 info@mindspring.com
334 Scott Network Services, Inc.	205 987 5889 info@scott.net
334 WSNetwork Communications Services, Inc.	334 263 5505 custserv@wsnet.com
360 The Bellingham Internet Cafe	360 650 0442 tonys@inet-cafe.com
360 Interconnected Associates, Inc. (IXA)	206 622 7337 mike@ixa.com
360 NorthWest CommLink	360 336 0103 info@nwcl.net
360 NorthWestNet	206 562 3000 info@nwnet.net
360 Olympia Networking Services	360 753 3636 info@olywa.net
360 Olympic Net	360 692 0651 info@olympic.net
360 Olympus	360 385 0464 info@olympus.net
360 Pacifier Computers	360 693 2116 info@pacifier.com
360 Pacific Rim Network, Inc.	x11 -> 360 650 0442 info@pacificrim.net
360 Premier1 Internet Services	360 793 3658 info@premier1.net

360 Skagit On-Line Services	360 755 0190 info@sos.net
360 Structured Network Systems, Inc.	503 656 3530 info@structured.net
360 Teleport, Inc.	503 223 4245 info@teleport.com
360 Transport Logic	503 243 1940 sales@transport.com
360 TSCNet, Inc.	360 613 0708 info@tscnet.com
360 Whidbey Connections, Inc.	360 678 1070 info@whidbey.net
360 WLN	800 342 5956 info@wln.com
401 brainiac services, Inc.	401 539 9050 info@brainiac.com
401 CompUtopia	401 732 5588 allan@computopia.com
401 InteleCom Data Systems, Inc.	401 885 6855 info@ids.net
401 The Internet Connection, Inc.	508 261 0383 info@ici.net
401 MCIX, Inc.	860 572 8720 info@mcix.com
401 Plymouth Commercial Internet Exchange	617 741 5900 info@pcix.com
401 Saturn Internet Corp.	617 451 9121 info@saturn.net
402 Greater Omaha Public Access Unix Corp.	402 558 5030 info@gonix.com
402 Internet Nebraska	402 434 8680 info@inetnebr.com
402 Iowa Network Services	800 546 6587 service@netins.net
402 The Online Pitstop	402 291 1542 bob@top.net
402 Pioneer Internet	712 271 0101 info@pionet.net
402 ProLinx Communications, Inc.	402 551 3036 techsupport@nfinity.nfinity.com
402 Synergy Communications, Inc.	800 345 9669 info@synergy.net
402 Zelcom International, Inc.	402 333 2441 administration-dept@zelcom.com
403 AGT Limited	800 608 1155 info@agt.net
403 Alberta SuperNet, Inc.	403 441 3663 info@supernet.ab.ca
403 CCI Networks	403 450 6787 info@ccinet.ab.ca
403 Cycor Communications, Inc.	902 892 7354 signup@cycor.ca
403 Debug Computer Services	403 248 5798 root@debug.cuc.ab.ca
403 TST Consulting	403 529 1560 sales@TST-MedHat.com
403 UUNET Canada, Inc.	416 368 6621 info@uunet.ca
404 CyberNet Communications Corp.	404 518 5711 sfeingold@atlwin.com
404 Digital Service Consultants, Inc.	770 455 9022 info@dscga.com
404 First Internet Resources	800 577 5969 jcarter@1stresource.com
404 I-Link, Ltd.	800 ILINK 99 info@i-link.net
404 Internet Atlanta	404 410 9000 info@atlanta.com

404 MindSpring Enterprises, Inc.	800 719 4332 info@mindspring.com
404 NetDepot, Inc.	770 434 5595 info@netdepot.com
404 Paradise Communications, Inc.	404 980 0078 info@paradise.net
404 Random Access, Inc.	404 804 1190 sales@randomc.com
404 vividnet	770 933 0999 webadmin@vivid.net
405 Internet Oklahoma	405 721 1580 info@ionet.net
405 Questar Network Services	405 848 3228 info@qns.net
406 CyberPort Montana	406 863 3221 skippy@cyberport.net
406 Internet Montana	406 255 9699 support@comp-unltd.com
406 Montana Internet Cooperative	406 443 3347 admin@mt.net
406 Montana Online	406 721 4952 info@montana.com
406 NorthWestNet	206 562 3000 info@nwnet.net
407 Acquired Knowledge Systems, Inc.	305 525 2574 info@aksi.net
407 CyberGate, Inc.	305 428 4283 sales@gate.net
407 The EmiNet Domain	407 731 0222 info@emi.net
407 Florida Online	407 635 8888 info@digital.net
407 GS-Link Systems, Inc.	407 671 8682 info@gslink.net
407 I-Link, Ltd.	800 ILINK 99 info@i-link.net
407 ICANECT	305 621 9200 sales@icanect.net
407 InteleCom Data Systems, Inc.	401 885 6855 info@ids.net
407 Internet Providers of Florida, Inc.	305 273 7978 office@ipof.fla.net
407 InternetU	407 952 8487 info@iu.net
407 Magg Information Services, Inc.	407 642 9841 help@magg.net
407 MagicNet, Inc.	407 657 2202 info@magicnet.net
407 MetroLink Internet Services	407 726 6707 jtaylor@metrolink.net
407 PSS InterNet Services	800 463 8499 support@america.com
407 Shadow Information Services, Inc.	305 594 2450 admin@shadow.net
407 WAM / NetRunner	407 392 9422 wam@wamsyst.com
407 WebIMAGE, an internet presence provider	407 723 0001 info@webimage.com
408 A-Link Network Services, Inc.	408 720 6161 info@alink.net
408 Aimnet Information Services	408 257 0900 info@aimnet.com
408 Alternet (UUNET Technologies, Inc.)	703 204 8000 info@alter.net
408 Bay Area Internet Solutions	408 447 8690 tjw00@bayarea.net
408 Brainstorm's Internet Power Connection	415 473-6411 info@brainstorm.net

408 BTR Communications Company	415 966 1429 support@btr.com
408 Click.Net	415 579 2535 info@click.net
408 Cruzio	408 423 1162 office@cruzio.com
408 Direct Network Access	510 649 6110 support@dnai.com
408 The Duck Pond Public Unix	modem -> 408 249 9630 postmaster@kfu.com
408 Electriciti	619 338 9000 info@powergrid.electriciti.com
408 Exodus Communications, Inc.	408 522 8450 info@exodus.net
408 GST Net	510 792 0768 info@gst.net
408 ICOnetworks	408 461 4638 info@ico.net
408 Infoserv Connections	408 335 5600 root@infoserv.com
408 Internet Avenue	408 727 0777 sales@ave.net
408 InterNex Tiara	408 496 5466 info@internex.net
408 ISP Networks	408 653 0100 info@isp.net
408 Liberty Information Network	800 218 5157 info@liberty.com
408 meernet	415 428 7111 info@meer.net
408 Monterey Bay Internet	408 642 6100 info@mbay.net
408 NetGate Communications	408 565 9601 sales@netgate.net
408 Network Solutions	408 946 6895 info@inow.com
408 San Jose Co-op	408 978 3958 sales@sj-coop.net
408 Scruz-Net	408 457 5050 info@scruz.net
408 SenseMedia	408 335 9400 sm@picosof.com
408 South Valley Internet	408 683 4533 info@garlic.com
408 Silicon Valley Public Access Link	408 448 3071 abem@svpal.org
408 West Coast Online	707 586 3060 info@calon.com
408 zNET	619 755 7772 info@znet.com
408 Zocalo Engineering	510 540 8000 info@zocalo.net
409 Brazos Information Highway Services	409 693 9336 info@bihs.net
409 CVTV - Internet	800 247 8885 cyndyz@cvtv.net
409 Cybercom Corp.	409 268 0771 www@cy-net.net
409 Delta Design and Development Inc.	800 763 8265 sales@deltaweb.com
409 Fayette Area Internet Services	409 968 3999 mcooper@fais.net
409 Internet Connect Services, Inc.	512 572 9987 info@icsi.net
409 PERnet Communications, Inc.	409 729 4638 info@mail.pernet.net
409 Phoenix DataNet, Inc.	713 486 8337 info@phoenix.net
410 ABSnet Internet Services	410 361 8160 info@abs.net
410 American Information Network	410 855 2353 info@ai.net

410 ARInternet Corp.	301 459 7171 info@ari.net
410 BayServe Technologies, Inc.	410 360 2216 sales@bayserve.net
410 CAPCON Library Network	202 331 5771 info@capcon.net
410 Charm.Net	410 558 3900 info@charm.net
410 Clark Internet Services, Inc. ClarkNet	410 995 0691 info@clark.net
410 Cyber Services, Inc.	703 749 9590 info@cs.com
410 Digital Express Group	301 847 5000 info@digex.net
410 jaguNET Access Services	410 931 3157 info@jagunet.com
410 Smartnet Internet Services, LLC	410 792 4555 info@smart.net
410 Softaid Internet Services Inc.	410 290 7763 sales@softaid.net
410 UltraPlex Information Providers	410 880 4604 info@upx.net
410 US Net, Inc.	301 572 5926 info@us.net
412 CityNet, Inc.	412 481 5406 info@city-net.com
412 epix	800 374 9669 karndt@epix.net
412 FYI Networks	412 898 2323 info@fyi.net
412 Pittsburgh OnLine, Inc.	412 681 6130 sales@pgh.net
412 Stargate Industries, Inc.	412 942 4218 info@sgi.net
412 Telerama Public Access Internet	412 481 3505 info@telerama.lm.com
412 The ThoughtPort Authority, Inc.	800 ISP 6870 info@thoughtport.com
412 USA OnRamp	412 391 4382 info@usaor.com
412 Westmoreland Online Inc.	412 830 4900 sales@westol.com
413 Mallard Electronics, Inc.	413 732 0214 gheacock@map.com
413 ShaysNet.COM	413 772 3774 staff@shaysnet.com
413 SoVerNet, Inc.	802 463 2111 info@sover.net
413 the spa!, inc.	413 539 9818 info@the-spa.com
414 Excel.Net, Inc.	414 452 0455 manager@excel.net
414 Exec-PC, Inc.	414 789 4200 info@execpc.com
414 FullFeed Communications	608 246 4239 info@fullfeed.com
414 Internet Access LLC	414 648 3837 info@intaccess.com
414 MIX Communications	414 351 1868 info@mixcom.com
414 NetNet, Inc.	414 499 1339 info@netnet.net
414 The Peoples Telephone Company	414 326 3151 info@peoples.net
414 TRC Access	414 827 9111 info@trcaccess.net
414 Wink Communications Group, Inc.	708 310 9465 sales@winkcomm.com

415 A-Link Network Services, Inc.	408 720 6161 info@alink.net
415 Aimnet Information Services	408 257 0900 info@aimnet.com
415 Alternet (UUNET Technologies, Inc.)	703 204 8000 info@alter.net
415 APlatform	415 941 2647 support@aplatform.com
415 Bay Area Internet Solutions	408 447 8690 tjw00@bayarea.net
415 Beckemeyer Development	510 530 9637 info@bdt.com
415 Brainstorm's Internet Power Connection	415 473-6411 info@brainstorm.net
415 BTR Communications Company	415 966 1429 support@btr.com
415 Click.Net	415 579 2535 info@click.net
415 Community ConneXion - NEXUS-Berkeley	510 549 1383 info@c2.org
415 Datatamers	415 367 7919 info@datatamers.com
415 Direct Network Access	510 649 6110 support@dnai.com
415 emf.net	510 704 2929 sales@emf.net
415 Exodus Communications, Inc.	408 522 8450 info@exodus.net
415 GST Net	510 792 0768 info@gst.net
415 I-Link, Ltd.	800 ILINK 99 info@i-link.net
415 Idiom Consulting	510 644 0441 info@idiom.com
415 InReach Internet Communications	800 446 7324 info@inreach.com
415 InterNex Tiara	408 496 5466 info@internex.net
415 ISP Networks	408 653 0100 info@isp.net
415 LanMinds, Inc.	510 843 6389 info@lanminds.com
415 Liberty Information Network	800 218 5157 info@liberty.com
415 LineX Communications	415 455 1650 info@linex.com
415 meernet	415 428 7111 info@meer.net
415 MobiusNet	415 821 0600 info@mobius.net
415 NetGate Communications	408 565 9601 sales@netgate.net
415 Network Solutions	408 946 6895 info@inow.com
415 QuakeNet	415 655 6607 info@quake.net
415 San Francisco Online (Televolve, Inc.)	415 861 7712 info@sfo.com
415 Sirius	415 284 4700 info@sirius.com
415 SLIPNET	415 281 3132 info@slip.net
415 Silicon Valley Public Access Link	408 448 3071 abem@svpal.org
415 Ultima Tool	415 775 8960 info@ultima.org
415 Value Net Internetwork Services	510 943 5769 info@value.net
415 ViaNet Communications	415 903 2242 info@via.net
415 The WELL	415 332 4335 info@well.com
415 22 Solutions	415 431 9903 info@catch22.com
415 West Coast Online	707 586 3060 info@calon.com

415 zNET	619 755 7772 info@znet.com
415 Zocalo Engineering	510 540 8000 info@zocalo.net
416 ComputerLink/Internet Direct	416 233 7150 info@idirect.com
416 Cycor Communications, Inc.	902 892 7354 signup@cycor.ca
416 HookUp Communications	905 847 8000 info@hookup.net
416 Internex Online, Inc.	416 363 8676 support@io.org
416 InterLog Internet Services	416 975 2655 internet@interlog.com
416 Internet Light and Power	416 502 1512 staff@ilap.com
416 Magic Online Services International, Inc.	416 591 6490 info@magic.ca
416 Neptune Internet Services	905 895 0898 info@neptune.on.ca
416 UUNET Canada, Inc.	416 368 6621 info@uunet.ca
417 DialNet (Digital Internet Access Link)	417 873 3425 sales@dialnet.net
417 Panther Creek Information Services	417 767 2126 info@pcis.net
417 Woodtech Information Systems, Inc.	417 886 0234 info@woodtech.com
418 autoroute.net	514 333 3145 info@autoroute.net
418 UUNET Canada, Inc.	416 368 6621 info@uunet.ca
419 Branch Information Services	313 741 4442 branch-info@branch.com
419 GlassNet Communications, LTD.	419 382 6800 info@glasscity.net
419 OARnet (corporate clients only)	614 728 8100 info@oar.net
419 Primenet	602 870 1010 info@primenet.com
423 accessU.S., Inc.	800 638 6373 info@accessus.net
423 MindSpring Enterprises, Inc.	800 719 4332 info@mindspring.com
423 Preferred Internet, Inc.	615 323 1142 info@preferred.com
423 Virtual Interactive Center	423 544 7902 info@vic.com
501 A2ZNET	901 854 1871 webmaster@a2znet.com
501 Aristotle Internet Access	501 374 4638 info@aristotle.net
501 Cloverleaf Technologies	903 832 1367 helpdesk@clover.cleaf.com
501 IntelliNet ISP	501 376 7676 info@intellinet.com
502 accessU.S., Inc.	800 638 6373 info@accessus.net
502 IgLou Internet Services	800 436 4456 info@iglou.com
502 Mikrotec Internet Services, Inc.	606 225 1488 info@mis.net

503 Alternet (UUNET Technologies, Inc.)   703 204 8000 info@alter.net
503 aracnet.com   503 626 8696 info@aracnet.com
503 aVastNet   503 263 0912 info@vastnet.com
503 Cascade Connection   503 282 8303 info@casconn.com
503 Cenornet   503 557 9047 info@cenornet.com
503 Colossus, Inc.   x19 -> 312 528 1000 colossus@romney.mtjeff.com
503 Data Research Group, Inc.   503 465 3282 info@ordata.com
503 Gorge Networks   503 386 8300 postmaster@gorge.net
503 Europa   503 222 9508 info@europa.com
503 Hevanet Communications   503 228 3520 info@hevanet.com
503 I-Link, Ltd.   800 ILINK 99 info@i-link.net
503 Interconnected Associates, Inc. (IXA)   206 622 7337 mike@ixa.com
503 Internet Communications   503 848 8139 info@iccom.com
503 NorthWestNet   206 562 3000 info@nwnet.net
503 Open Door Networks, Inc.   503 488 4127 info@opendoor.com
503 Oregon Information Technology Centeres   503 469 6699 hmaster@harborside.com
503 Pacifier Computers   360 693 2116 info@pacifier.com
503 RainDrop Laboraties/Agora   503 293 1772 info@agora.rdrop.com
503 Structured Network Systems, Inc.   503 656 3530 info@structured.net
503 Teleport, Inc.   503 223 4245 info@teleport.com
503 Transport Logic   503 243 1940 sales@transport.com
503 WLN   800 342 5956 info@wln.com

504 AccessCom Internet Services   504 887 0022 info@accesscom.net
504 Communique, Inc.   504 527 6200 info@communique.net
504 Cyberlink   504 277 4186 cladmin@eayor.cyberlink-no.com
504 Hollingsworth Information Services, Inc.   504 769 2156 webmaster@rouge.net
504 Hub City Area Access   601 268 6156 info@hub1.hubcity.com
504 I-Link, Ltd.   800 ILINK 99 info@i-link.net
504 InterSurf Online, Inc.   504 755 0500 info@intersurf.net
504 JAMNet Internet Services, Inc.   504 361 3492 info@jis.net
504 NeoSoft, Inc.   713 684 5969 info@neosoft.com

505 Computer Systems Consulting   505 984 0085 info@spy.org
505 Internet Direct, Inc.   800 879 3624 info@direct.net
505 Internet Express   719 592 1240 info@usa.net
505 Network Intensive   714 450 8400 info@ni.net
505 New Mexico Internet Access   505 877 0617 info@nmia.com

505 New Mexico Technet, Inc.	505 345 6555 granoff@technet.nm.org
505 Southwest Cyberport	505 271 0009 info@swcp.com
505 WhiteHorse Communications, Inc.	915 584 6630 whc.net.html
505 ZyNet SouthWest	505 343 8846 zycor@zynet.com
506 Agate Internet Services	207 947 8248 ais@agate.net
506 Cycor Communications, Inc.	902 892 7354 signup@cycor.ca
507 Desktop Media	507 373 2155 isp@dm.deskmedia.com
507 Internet Connections, Inc.	507 625 7320 info@ic.mankato.mn.us
507 Millennium Communications, Inc.	612 338 5509 info@millcomm.com
507 Minnesota OnLine	612 225 1110 info@mn.state.net
507 Minnesota Regional Network	612 342 2570 info@mr.net
507 Protocol Communications, Inc.	612 541 9900 info@protocom.com
508 Argo Communications	508 261 6121 info@argo.net
508 Channel 1	617 864 0100 support@channel1.com
508 CompUtopia	401 732 5588 allan@computopia.com
508 The Destek Group, Inc.	603 635 3857 inquire@destek.net
508 Empire.Net, Inc.	603 889 1220 info@empire.net
508 FOURnet Information Network	508 291 2900 info@four.net
508 The Internet Access Company (TIAC)	617 276 7200 info@tiac.net
508 The Internet Connection, Inc.	508 261 0383 info@ici.net
508 Intuitive Information, Inc.	508 342 1100 info@iii.net
508 Kersur Technologies, Inc.	508 384 1404 info@kerser.net
508 MV Communications, Inc.	603 429 2223 info@mv.mv.com
508 PICTAC	508 999 1565 sales@pictac.com
508 Pioneer Global Telecommunications, Inc.	617 375 0200 info@pn.com
508 Plymouth Commercial Internet Exchange	617 741 5900 info@pcix.com
508 Saturn Internet Corp.	617 451 9121 info@saturn.net
508 Shore.Net	617 593 3110 info@shore.net
508 StarNet	508 922 8238 info@venus.star.net
508 TerraNet, Inc.	617 450 9000 info@terra.net
508 UltraNet Communications, Inc.	508 229 8400 info@ultranet.com
508 USAinternet, Inc.	800 236 9737 info@usa1.com
508 The World	617 739 0202 info@world.std.com
508 Wilder Systems, Inc.	617 933 8810 info@id.wing.net

509 Cascade Connections, Inc.   509 663 4259 carrie@cascade.net
509 Interconnected Associates, Inc. (IXA)   206 622 7337 mike@ixa.com
509 Internet On-Ramp, Inc.   509 624 RAMP info@on-ramp.ior.com
509 NorthWestNet   206 562 3000 info@nwnet.net
509 Structured Network Systems, Inc.   503 656 3530 info@structured.net
509 Transport Logic   503 243 1940 sales@transport.com
509 WLN   800 342 5956 info@wln.com

510 A-Link Network Services, Inc.   408 720 6161 info@alink.net
510 Aimnet Information Services   408 257 0900 info@aimnet.com
510 Alternet (UUNET Technologies, Inc.)   703 204 8000 info@alter.net
510 Beckemeyer Development   510 530 9637 info@bdt.com
510 BTR Communications Company   415 966 1429 support@btr.com
510 Community ConneXion - NEXUS-Berkeley   510 549 1383 info@c2.org
510 Direct Network Access   510 649 6110 support@dnai.com
510 emf.net   510 704 2929 sales@emf.net
510 Exodus Communications, Inc.   408 522 8450 info@exodus.net
510 GST Net   510 792 0768 info@gst.net
510 Idiom Consulting   510 644 0441 info@idiom.com
510 InterNex Tiara   408 496 5466 info@internex.net
510 LanMinds, Inc.   510 843 6389 info@lanminds.com
510 Liberty Information Network   800 218 5157 info@liberty.com
510 LineX Communications   415 455 1650 info@linex.com
510 MobiusNet   415 821 0600 info@mobius.net
510 Network Solutions   408 946 6895 info@inow.com
510 San Francisco Online (Televolve, Inc.)   415 861 7712 info@sfo.com
510 Sirius   415 284 4700 info@sirius.com
510 SLIPNET   415 281 3132 info@slip.net
510 22 Solutions   415 431 9903 info@catch22.com
510 Ultima Tool   415 775 8960 info@ultima.org
510 Value Net Internetwork Services   510 943 5769 info@value.net
510 West Coast Online   707 586 3060 info@calon.com
510 Zocalo Engineering   510 540 8000 info@zocalo.net

512 @sig.net   512 306 0700 sales@aus.sig.net
512 CVTV - Internet   800 247 8885 cyndyz@cvtv.net
512 Delta Design and Development Inc.   800 763 8265 sales@deltaweb.com
512 The Eden Matrix   512 478 9900 info@eden.com

512 I-Link, Ltd.   800 ILINK 99 info@i-link.net
512 Illuminati Online   512 462 0999 info@io.com
512 Internet Connect Services, Inc.   512 572 9987 info@icsi.net
512 Onramp Access, Inc.   512 322 9200 info@onr.com
512 OuterNet Connection Strategies   512 345 3573 question@outer.net
512 Phoenix DataNet, Inc.   713 486 8337 info@phoenix.net
512 Real/Time Communications   512 451 0046 info@realtime.net
512 Turning Point Information Services, Inc.   512 499 8400 info@tpoint.net
512 Zilker Internet Park, Inc.   512 206 3850 info@zilker.net

513 The Dayton Network Access Company   513 237 6868 info@dnaco.net
513 IgLou Internet Services   800 436 4456 info@iglou.com
513 Internet Access Cincinnati   513 887 8877 info@iac.net
513 Local Internet Gateway Co.   510 503 9227 sdw@lig.net
513 OARnet (corporate clients only)   614 728 8100 info@oar.net
513 Premier Internet Cincinnati, Inc.   513 561 6245 pic@cinti.net

514 Accent Internet   514 737 6077 admin@accent.net
514 autoroute.net   514 333 3145 info@autoroute.net
514 CiteNet Telecom, Inc.   514 721 1351 info@citenet.net
514 Communication Accessibles Montreal   514 288 2581 info@cam.org
514 Communications Inter-Acces   514 367 0002 info@interax.net
514 Cycor Communications, Inc.   902 892 7354 signup@cycor.ca
514 Odyssee Internet   514 861 3432 info@odyssee.net
514 UUNET Canada, Inc.   416 368 6621 info@uunet.ca

515 Freese-Notis Weather.Net   515 282 9310 hfreese@weather.net
515 ia.net   319 393 1095 info@ia.net
515 Iowa Network Services   800 546 6587 service@netins.net
515 JTM MultiMedia, Inc.   515 277 1990 jtm@ecity.net
515 Minnesota OnLine   612 225 1110 info@mn.state.net
515 Synergy Communications, Inc.   800 345 9669 info@synergy.net

516 ASB Internet Services   516 981 1953 info@asb.com
516 bway.net / Outernet, Inc.   212 982 9800 info@bway.net
516 Creative Data Consultants (SILLY.COM)   718 229 0489 info@silly.com
516 Echo Communications Group   212 255 3839 info@echonyc.com
516 I-2000, Inc.   800 464 3820 info@i-2000.com

516 INTAC Access Corp.   800 504 6822 info@intac.com
516 LI Net, Inc.   516 476 1168 info@li.net
516 Lightning Internet Services, LLC   516 248 8400 sales@lightning.net
516 Long Island Information, Inc.   516 294 0124 info@liii.com
516 Long Island Internet HeadQuarters   516 439 7800 support@pb.net
516 Network Internet Services   516 543 0234 info@netusa.net
516 New World Data   718 962 1725 dmk@nwdc.com
516 NYSERNet   800 493 4367 sales@nysernet.org
516 Panix (Public Access uNIX)   212 741 4400 info@panix.com
516 Pipeline New York   212 267 3636 info@pipeline.com
516 Real Life Pictures RealNet   212 366 4434 reallife@walrus.com
516 ZONE One Network Exchange   212 824 4000 info@zone.net

517 Branch Information Services   313 741 4442 branch-info@branch.com
517 Freeway, Inc. (tm)   616 347 2400 info@freeway.net
517 The Internet Ramp   800 502 0620 newaccts@tir.com
517 Mich.com, Inc.   810 478 4300 info@mich.com
517 Msen, Inc.   313 998 4562 info@msen.com
517 Voyager Information Networks, Inc.   517 485 9068 help@voyager.net

518 AlbanyNet   518 462 6262 info@albany.net
518 epix   800 374 9669 karndt@epix.net
518 Global One, Inc.   518 452 1465 lorin@global1.net
518 Klink Net Communications   518 725 3000 admin@klink.net
518 NetHeaven   800 910 6671 info@netheaven.com
518 NYSERNet   800 493 4367 sales@nysernet.org
518 SoVerNet, Inc.   802 463 2111 info@sover.net
518 Wizvax Communications   518 273 4325 info@wizvax.com

519 Electro-Byte Technologies   519 332 8235 info@ebtech.net
519 Execulink Internet Services Corp.   519 451 4288 info@execulink.com
519 FastLane.Net Ltd.   519 679 0908 info@fastlane.ca
519 headwaters network   519 940 9252 sales@headwaters.com
519 HookUp Communications   905 847 8000 info@hookup.net
519 HyperNet   519 652 3790 Admin@L2.lonet.ca
519 Information Gateway Services   519 884 7200 info@kw.igs.net
519 Inter•Com Information Services   519 679 1620 info@icis.on.ca
519 Magic Online Services International, Inc.   416 591 6490 info@magic.ca

519 MGL Systems Computer Technologies, Inc.   519 836 1295 info@mgl.ca
519 Network Enterprise Technology, Inc.   905 525 4555 info@netinc.ca
519 UUNET Canada, Inc.   416 368 6621 info@uunet.ca
519 Windsor Infromation Network Company   519 945 9462 kim@wincom.net

520 InfoMagic, Inc.   520 526 9565 info@infomagic.com
520 Internet Direct, Inc.   800 879 3624 info@direct.net
520 Opus One   602 324 0494 sales@opus1.com
520 Primenet   602 870 1010 info@primenet.com
520 RTD Systems & Networking, Inc.   602 318 0696 info@rtd.com
520 Sedona Internet Services, Inc.   520 204 2247 info@sedona.net

540 Cyber Services, Inc.   703 749 9590 info@cs.com

541 aVastNet   503 263 0912 info@vastnet.com

601 A2ZNET   901 854 1871 webmaster@a2znet.com
601 Datasync Internet Services   601 872 0001 info@datasync.com
601 Gulfcoast On-Line Development, Inc.   601 864 2423 info@goldinc.com
601 Hub City Area Access   601 268 6156 info@hub1.hubcity.com

602 Crossroads Communications   602 813 9040 crossroads@xroads.com
602 I-Link, Ltd.   800 ILINK 99 info@i-link.net
602 InfoMagic, Inc.   520 526 9565 info@infomagic.com
602 Internet Direct, Inc.   800 879 3624 info@direct.net
602 Internet Express   719 592 1240 info@usa.net
602 New Mexico Technet, Inc.   505 345 6555 granoff@technet.nm.org
602 Opus One   602 324 0494 sales@opus1.com
602 Phoenix Computer Specialists   602 265 9188 info@pcslink.com
602 Primenet   602 870 1010 info@primenet.com
602 RTD Systems & Networking, Inc.   602 318 0696 info@rtd.com
602 StarLink Internet Services   602 878 7001 sysop@starlink.com
602 Systems Solutions, Inc.   602 955 5566 support@syspac.com

603 Agate Internet Services   207 947 8248 ais@agate.net
603 Empire.Net, Inc.   603 889 1220 info@empire.net
603 The Destek Group, Inc.   603 635 3857 inquire@destek.net
603 MV Communications, Inc.   603 429 2223 info@mv.mv.com

603 NETIS Public Access Internet   603 437 1811 epoole@leotech.mv.com
603 Rocket Science Computer Services, Inc. 603 334 6444 info@rscs.com
603 SoVerNet, Inc.   802 463 2111 info@sover.net
603 StarNet   508 922 8238 info@venus.star.net
603 UltraNet Communications, Inc.   508 229 8400 info@ultranet.com

604 AMT Solutions Group, Inc. Island Net   604 727 6030 info@islandnet.com
604 auroraNET, Inc.   604 294 4357 sales@aurora.net
604 Cycor Communications, Inc.   902 892 7354 signup@cycor.ca
604 Fairview Technology Centre, Ltd.   604 498 4316 bwklatt@ftcnet.com
604 The InterNet Shop, Inc.   604 376 3719 info@netshop.net
604 Mind Link!   604 534 5663 info@mindlink.bc.ca
604 Okanagan Internet Junction   604 549 1036 info@junction.net
604 Sunshine Net, Inc.   604 886 4120 admin@sunshine.net
604 UUNET Canada, Inc.   416 368 6621 info@uunet.ca

605 Internet Services of the Black Hills   605 642 2244 postmaster@blackhills.com
605 Pioneer Internet   712 271 0101 info@pionet.net

606 IgLou Internet Services   800 436 4456 info@iglou.com
606 Internet Access Cincinnati   513 887 8877 info@iac.net
606 Mikrotec Internet Services, Inc.   606 225 1488 info@mis.net
606 RAM Technologies, Inc.   800 950 1726 info@ramlink.net

607 Art Matrix - Lightlink   607 277 0959 info@lightlink.com
607 Clarity Connect, Inc.   607 257 2070 chuck@baka.com
607 epix   800 374 9669 karndt@epix.net
607 NYSERNet   800 493 4367 sales@nysernet.org
607 ServiceTech, Inc.   716 263 3360 info@servtech.com
607 Spectra.net   607 798 7300 info@spectra.net

608 BOSSNet Internet Services   608 362 1340 mbusam@bossnt.com
608 Exec-PC, Inc.   414 789 4200 info@execpc.com
608 FullFeed Communications   608 246 4239 info@fullfeed.com

609 CyberComm Online Services   908 506 6651 info@cybercomm.net
609 Cyberenet (Kaps, Inc.)   609 753 9840 access-sales@cyberenet.net

609 Digital Express Group   301 847 5000 info@digex.net
609 Eclipse Internet Access   800 483 1223 info@eclipse.net
609 InterActive Network Services   609 227 6380 info@jersey.net
609 K2NE Software   609 893 0673 vince-q@k2nesoft.com
609 Net Access   215 576 8669 support@netaxs.com
609 NetReach, Inc.   215 283 2300 info@netreach.net
609 New Jersey Computer Connection   609 896 2799 info@pluto.njcc.com
609 Texel International   908 297 0290 info@texel.com
609 VoiceNet   800 835 5710 info@voicenet.com

610 Cheap Net   302 993 8420 sammy@ravenet.com
610 Digital Express Group   301 847 5000 info@digex.net
610 ENTER.Net   610 366 1300 info@enter.net
610 epix   800 374 9669 karndt@epix.net
610 FishNet   610 337 9994 info@pond.com
610 GlobalQUEST, Inc.   610 696 8111 info@globalquest.net
610 Internet Tidal Wave   610 770 6187 steve@itw.com
610 InterNetworking Technologies   302 398 4369 itnt.com@itnt.com
610 The Magnetic Page   302 651 9753 info@magpage.com
610 Microserve Information Systems   717 779 4430 info@microserve.com
610 Net Access   215 576 8669 support@netaxs.com
610 NetReach, Inc.   215 283 2300 info@netreach.net
610 Network Analysis Group   800 624 9240 nag@good.freedom.net
610 Night Vision   610 366 9767 info@n-vision.com
610 SSNet, Inc.   302 378 1386 info@ssnet.com
610 Oasis Telecommunications, Inc.   610 439 8560 staff@oasis.ot.com
610 OpNet   610 520 2880 info@op.net
610 RaveNet Systems Inc.   302 993 8420 waltemus@ravenet.com
610 VivaNET, Inc.   800 836 UNIX info@vivanet.com
610 VoiceNet   800 835 5710 info@voicenet.com
610 You Tools Corp. / FASTNET   610 954 5910 info@fast.net

612 Cloudnet   612 240 8243 info@cloudnet.com
612 DCC, Inc.   612 378 4000 kgastony@dcc.com
612 Freese-Notis Weather.Net   515 282 9310 hfreese@weather.net
612 GlobalCom   612 920 9920 info@globalc.com
612 James River Group, Inc.   612 339 2521 jriver@jriver.jriver.COM
612 Millennium Communications, Inc.   612 338 5509 info@millcomm.com

612 Minnesota OnLine   612 225 1110 info@mn.state.net
612 Minnesota Regional Network   612 342 2570 info@mr.net
612 Orbis Internet Services, Inc.   612 645 9663 info@orbis.net
612 pclink.com   612 541 5656 infomatic@pclink.com
612 Primenet   602 870 1010 info@primenet.com
612 Protocol Communications, Inc.   612 541 9900 info@protocom.com
612 Sihope Communications   612 829 9667 info@sihope.com
612 Sound Communications Internet   612 722 8470 root@scc.net
612 StarNet Communications, Inc.   612 941 9177 info@winternet.com
612 Synergy Communications, Inc.   800 345 9669 info@synergy.net
612 Vector Internet Services, Inc.   612 288 0880 info@visi.com

613 autoroute.net   514 333 3145 info@autoroute.net
613 Cyberius Online, Inc.   613 233 1215 info@cyberus.ca
613 Cycor Communications, Inc.   902 892 7354 signup@cycor.ca
613 Information Gateway Services (Ottawa)   613 592 5619 info@igs.net
613 Interactive Telecom, Inc.   613 727 5258 info@intertel.net
613 HookUp Communications   905 847 8000 info@hookup.net
613 Magma Communications, Ltd.   613 228 3565 info@magmacom.com
613 o://info.web   613 225 3354 kevin@magi.com
613 UUNET Canada, Inc.   416 368 6621 info@uunet.ca

614 ASCInet (Columbus)   614 798 5321 info@ascinet.com
614 Branch Information Services   313 741 4442 branch-info@branch.com
614 Internet Access Cincinnati   513 887 8877 info@iac.net
614 OARnet (corporate clients only)   614 728 8100 info@oar.net
614 RAM Technologies, Inc.   800 950 1726 info@ramlink.net

615 accessU.S., Inc.   800 638 6373 info@accessus.net
615 ERC, Inc. / The Edge   615 455 9915 staff@edge.ercnet.com
615 First Internet Resources   800 577 5969 jcarter@1stresource.com
615 GoldSword Systems   615 691 6498 info@goldsword.com
615 ISDN-Net, Inc.   615 377 7672 jdunlap@rex.isdn.net
615 MindSpring Enterprises, Inc.   800 719 4332 info@mindspring.com
615 Preferred Internet, Inc.   615 323 1142 info@preferred.com
615 The Telalink Corp.   615 321 9100 sales@telalink.net
615 The Tri-Cities Connection   615 378 5355 info@tricon.net
615 U.S. Internet   615 522 6788 info@usit.net

615 Virtual Interactive Center   423 544 7902 info@vic.com

616 Branch Information Services   313 741 4442 branch-info@branch.com
616 Freeway, Inc. (tm)   616 347 2400 info@freeway.net
616 The iserv Co.   616 281 5254 info@iserv.net
616 Mich.com, Inc.   810 478 4300 info@mich.com
616 Msen, Inc.   313 998 4562 info@msen.com
616 NetLink Systems L.L.C.   616 345 LINK info@serv01.net-link.net
616 Novagate Communications Corp.   616 847 0910 info@novagate.com
616 RustNet, Inc.   810 650 6812 info@rust.net
616 Traverse Communication Company   616 935 1705 info@traverse.com
616 Voyager Information Networks, Inc.   517 485 9068 help@voyager.net

617 Alternet (UUNET Technologies, Inc.)   703 204 8000 info@alter.net
617 Argo Communications   508 261 6121 info@argo.net
617 Channel 1   617 864 0100 support@channel1.com
617 CompUtopia   401 732 5588 allan@computopia.com
617 COWZ Technologies   617 497 0058 system@cow.net
617 Cyber Access Internet Communications, Inc.   617 396 0491 info@cybercom.net
617 FOURnet Information Network   508 291 2900 info@four.net
617 The Internet Access Company (TIAC)   617 276 7200 info@tiac.net
617 The Internet Connection, Inc.   508 261 0383 info@ici.net
617 Intuitive Information, Inc.   508 342 1100 info@iii.net
617 Pioneer Global Telecommunications, Inc.   617 375 0200 info@pn.com
617 Plymouth Commercial Internet Exchange   617 741 5900 info@pcix.com
617 Saturn Internet Corp.   617 451 9121 info@saturn.net
617 Shore.Net   617 593 3110 info@shore.net
617 TerraNet, Inc.   617 450 9000 info@terra.net
617 UltraNet Communications, Inc.   508 229 8400 info@ultranet.com
617 USAinternet, Inc.   800 236 9737 info@usa1.com
617 The World   617 739 0202 info@world.std.com
617 Wilder Systems, Inc.   617 933 8810 info@id.wing.net
617 The Xensei Corp.   617 376 6342 info@xensei.com

618 accessU.S., Inc.   800 638 6373 info@accessus.net
618 Allied Access, Inc.   618 684 2255 sales@intrnet.net
618 Applied Personal Computing, Inc.   618 632 7282 spider@apci.net
618 Online Information Access Network   618 692 9813 info@oia.net

618 MVP-Net, Inc.   314 731 2252 info@MO.NET

619 CONNECTnet Internet Network Services   619 450 0254 info@connectnet.com
619 CTS Network Services   619 637 3637 info@cts.com
619 Cyberg8t Internet Services   909 398 4638 sales@cyberg8t.com
619 Delta Internet Services   714 778 0370 info@deltanet.com
619 The Cyberspace Station   619 634 2894 info@cyber.net
619 Electriciti   619 338 9000 info@powergrid.electriciti.com
619 I-Link, Ltd.   800 ILINK 99 info@i-link.net
619 Liberty Information Network   800 218 5157 info@liberty.com
619 Primenet   602 870 1010 info@primenet.com
619 RidgeNET   619 371 3501 saic@owens.ridgecrest.ca.us
619 Sierra-Net   702 831 3353 giles@sierra.net
619 WANet, Software Design Associates, Inc.   619 679 5900 info@WANet.net

701 NorthWestNet   206 562 3000 info@nwnet.net
701 Red River Net   701 232 2227 info@rrnet.com

702 @wizard.com   702 871 4461 info@wizard.com
702 Connectus, Inc.   702 323 2008 info@connectus.com
702 Great Basin Internet Services   702 829 2244 info@greatbasin.com
702 InterMind   702 878 6111 support@terminus.intermind.net
702 NETConnect   800 689 8001 office@tcd.net
702 Sierra-Net   702 831 3353 giles@sierra.net
702 Skylink Networks, Inc.   702 368 0700 sales@skylink.net

703 Alternet (UUNET Technologies, Inc.)   703 204 8000 info@alter.net
703 ARInternet Corp.   301 459 7171 info@ari.net
703 CAPCON Library Network   202 331 5771 info@capcon.net
703 Charm.Net   410 558 3900 info@charm.net
703 Clark Internet Services, Inc. ClarkNet   410 995 0691 info@clark.net
703 Cyber Services, Inc.   703 749 9590 info@cs.com
703 Digital Express Group   301 847 5000 info@digex.net
703 Genuine Computing Resources   703 878 4680 info@gcr.com
703 Internet Online, Inc.   301 652 4468 info@intr.net
703 Interpath   800 849 6305 info@interpath.net
703 LaserNet   703 591 4232 info@laser.net
703 Preferred Internet, Inc.   615 323 1142 info@preferred.com

703 Quantum Networking Solutions, Inc.	805 538 2028 info@qnet.com
703 RadixNet Internet Services	301 567 9831 info@radix.net
703 Smartnet Internet Services, LLC	410 792 4555 info@smart.net
703 SONNETS, Inc.	703 502 8589 office@sonnets.net
703 UltraPlex Information Providers	410 880 4604 info@upx.net
703 Universal Telecomm Corp.	703 758 0550 root@utc.net
703 US Net, Inc.	301 572 5926 info@us.net
703 World Web Limited	703 838 2000 info@worldweb.net
703 Xpress Internet Services	301 601 5050 info@xis.com
704 Interpath	800 849 6305 info@interpath.net
704 SunBelt.Net	803 328 1500 info@sunbelt.net
704 Vnet Internet Access	704 334 3282 info@vnet.net
705 Barrie Connex, Inc.	705 725 0819 info@bconnex.net
705 Magic Online Services International Inc.	416 591 6490 info@magic.ca
705 Mindemoya Computing	705 523 0243 info@mcd.on.ca
705 Neptune Internet Services	905 895 0898 info@neptune.on.ca
705 SooNet Corp.	705 253 4700 service@soonet.ca
706 Athens' ISP, Inc.	706 613 0611 info@athens.net
706 InteliNet	803 279 9775 administrator@intelinet.net
706 internet@Dalton	706 673 4715 support@dalton.net
706 Internet Atlanta	404 410 9000 info@atlanta.com
706 MindSpring Enterprises, Inc.	800 719 4332 info@mindspring.com
707 Beckemeyer Development	510 530 9637 info@bdt.com
707 CASTLES Information Network	707 422 7311 info@castles.com
707 Datatamers	415 367 7919 info@datatamers.com
707 InReach Internet Communications	800 446 7324 info@inreach.com
707 Liberty Information Network	800 218 5157 info@liberty.com
707 Value Net Internetwork Services	510 943 5769 info@value.net
707 West Coast Online	707 586 3060 info@calon.com
707 Zocalo Engineering	510 540 8000 info@zocalo.net
708 American Information Systems, Inc.	708 413 8400 info@ais.net
708 CICNet, Inc.	313 998 6103 info@cic.net
708 CIN.net Computerese Information Network	708 310 1188 info@cin.net

708 Compunet Technology Consultants   708 355 XNET webmaster@ms.com-punet.com
708 I Connection, Inc.   708 662 0877 info@iconnect.net
708 InterAccess Co.   708 498 2542 info@interaccess.com
708 Interactive Network Systems, Inc.   312 881 3039 info@insnet.com
708 MCSNet   312 803 6271 info@mcs.net
708 Ripco Communications, Inc.   312 477 6210 info@ripco.com
708 TensorNet Co.   708 665 3637 info@tensornet.com
708 Tezcatlipoca, Inc.   312 850 0181 info@tezcat.com
708 Wink Communications Group, Inc.   708 310 9465 sales@winkcomm.com
708 WorldWide Access   708 367 1870 info@wwa.com
708 XNet Information Systems   708 983 6064 info@xnet.com

709 InterActions Limited   709 745 4638 connect@nfld.com

712 Freese-Notis Weather.Net   515 282 9310 hfreese@weather.net
712 Greater Omaha Public Access Unix Corp   402 558 5030 info@gonix.com
712 ia.net   319 393 1095 info@ia.net
712 Iowa Network Services   800 546 6587 service@netins.net
712 The Online Pitstop   402 291 1542 bob@top.net
712 Pioneer Internet   712 271 0101 info@pionet.net
712 ProLinx Communications, Inc.   402 551 3036 techsupport@nfinity.nfinity.com
712 Synergy Communications, Inc.   800 345 9669 info@synergy.net
712 Zelcom International, Inc.   402 333 2441 administration-dept@zelcom.com

713 Alternet (UUNET Technologies, Inc.)   703 204 8000 info@alter.net
713 The Black Box   713 480 2684 info@blkbox.com
713 Delta Design and Development, Inc.   800 763 8265 sales@deltaweb.com
713 ELECTROTEX, Inc.   713 526 3456 info@electrotex.com
713 I-Link, Ltd.   800 ILINK 99 info@i-link.net
713 Internet Connect Services, Inc.   512 572 9987 info@icsi.net
713 NeoSoft, Inc.   713 684 5969 info@neosoft.com
713 OnRamp Technologies, Inc.   214 746 4710 info@onramp.net
713 Phoenix DataNet, Inc.   713 486 8337 info@phoenix.net
713 South Coast Computing Services, Inc.   713 917 5000 info@houston.net
713 USiS   713 682 1666 admin@usis.com

714 Argonet   714 261 7511 postmaster@argonet.net
714 ArtNetwork   800 395 0692 info@artnet.net

714 Business Access Technologies	714 577 8978 Techs@batech.com
714 Cloverleaf Communications	714 895 3075 sales@cloverleaf.com
714 Cogent Software, Inc.	818 585 2788 info@cogsoft.com
714 CruzNet	714 680 6600 info@cruznet.net
714 DPC Systems Beach.Net	714 443 4172 connect@beach.net
714 Delta Internet Services	714 778 0370 info@deltanet.com
714 DigiLink Network Services	310 542 7421 info@digilink.net
714 EDM NetWORK	714 476 0416 info@edm.net
714 Electriciti	619 338 9000 info@powergrid.electriciti.com
714 Exodus Communications, Inc.	408 522 8450 info@exodus.net
714 InterNex Tiara	408 496 5466 info@internex.net
714 InterWorld Communications, Inc.	310 726 0500 sales@interworld.net
714 KAIWAN Internet	714 638 2139 info@kaiwan.com
714 Liberty Information Network	800 218 5157 info@liberty.com
714 Lightside, Inc.	818 858 9261 Lightside@Lightside.Com
714 The Loop Internet Switch Co.	213 465 1311 info@loop.com
714 NetQuest	714 379 8228 info@net-quest.com
714 Network Intensive	714 450 8400 info@ni.net
714 OutWest Network Services	818 545 1996 info@outwest.net
714 Primenet	602 870 1010 info@primenet.com
714 QuickNet, Inc.	714 969 1091 sales@quick.net
715 FullFeed Communications	608 246 4239 info@fullfeed.com
715 Minnesota OnLine	612 225 1110 info@mn.state.net
716 Blue Moon Online System Internet Svcs	716 447 5629 sales@net.bluemoon.net
716 BuffNET	800 463 6499 info@buffnet.net
716 E-Znet, Inc.	716 262 2485
716 epix	800 374 9669 karndt@epix.net
716 NYSERNet	800 493 4367 sales@nysernet.org
716 ServiceTech, Inc.	716 263 3360 info@servtech.com
716 VivaNET, Inc.	800 836 UNIX info@vivanet.com
717 epix	800 374 9669 karndt@epix.net
717 The Internet Cafe	717 344 1969 info@lydian.scranton.com
717 Keystone Information Access Systems	717 741 2626 office@yrkpa.kias.com
717 Microserve Information Systems	717 779 4430 info@microserve.com
717 Oasis Telecommunications, Inc.	610 439 8560 staff@oasis.ot.com

717 PenNet   717 368 1577 safrye@pennet.net
717 Red Rose SuperNet   800 222 2517 info@redrose.net
717 Spectra.net   607 798 7300 info@spectra.net
717 VoiceNet   800 835 5710 info@voicenet.com
717 You Tools Corp. / FASTNET   610 954 5910 info@fast.net

718 Advanced Standards, Inc. advn.com   212 302 3366 kolian@advn.com
718 Blythe Systems   212 226 7171 infodesk@blythe.org
718 BrainLINK   718 805 6559 info@beast.brainlink.com
718 bway.net / Outernet, Inc.   212 982 9800 info@bway.net
718 Creative Data Consultants (SILLY.COM)   718 229 0489 info@silly.com
718 escape.com - Kazan Corp   212 888 8780 info@escape.com
718 Ingress Communications, Inc.   212 679 2838 info@ingress.com
718 INTAC Access Corp.   800 504 6822 info@intac.com
718 Intellitech Walrus   212 406 5000 info@walrus.com
718 Intercall, Inc.   800 758 7329 sales@intercall.com
718 InterCom Online   212 714 7183 info@intercom.com
718 Internet QuickLink Corp.   212 307 1669 info@quicklink.com
718 Interport Communications Corp.   212 989 1128 info@interport.net
718 Lightning Internet Services, LLC   516 248 8400 sales@lightning.net
718 Long Island Information, Inc.   516 294 0124 info@liii.com
718 Long Island Internet HeadQuarters   516 439 7800 support@pb.net
718 Mnematics, Inc.   914 359 4546 service@mne.com
718 Mordor International BBS   201 433 4222 ritz@mordor.com
718 New World Data   718 962 1725 dmk@nwdc.com
718 Panix (Public Access uNIX)   212 741 4400 info@panix.com
718 Phantom Access Technologies, Inc.   212 989 2418 bruce@phantom.com
718 Pipeline New York   212 267 3636 info@pipeline.com
718 Real Life Pictures RealNet   212 366 4434 reallife@walrus.com
718 Spacelab.Net   212 966 8844 mike@mxol.com
718 ThoughtPort of New York City   212 645 7970 info@precipice.com
718 tunanet/InfoHouse   212 229 8224 info@tunanet.com
718 ZONE One Network Exchange   212 824 4000 info@zone.net

719 Colorado SuperNet, Inc.   303 296 8202 info@csn.org
719 Internet Express   719 592 1240 info@usa.net
719 Old Colorado City Communications   719 528 5849 thefox@oldcolo.com
719 Rocky Mountain Internet   800 900 7644 info@rmii.com

770 Digital Service Consultants, Inc.   770 455 9022 info@dscga.com
770 MindSpring Enterprises, Inc.   800 719 4332 info@mindspring.com
770 Paradise Communications, Inc.   404 980 0078 info@paradise.net
770 Random Access, Inc.   404 804 1190 sales@randomc.com
770 vividnet   770 933 0999 webadmin@vivid.net

801 I-Link, Ltd.   800 ILINK 99 info@i-link.net
801 Internet Technology Systems (ITS)   801 375 0538 admin@itsnet.com
801 NETConnect   800 689 8001 office@tcd.net
801 The ThoughtPort Authority, Inc.   800 ISP 6870 info@thoughtport.com
801 Utah Wired/The Friendly Net   801 532 1117 sales@utw.com
801 Vyzynz International   801 568 0999 info@vii.com
801 XMission   801 539 0852 support@xmission.com

802 The Plainfield Bypass   802 426 3963 questions@plainfield.bypass.com
802 SoVerNet, Inc.   802 463 2111 info@sover.net

803 A World of Difference, Inc.   803 769 4488 info@awod.com
803 CetLink.Net   803 327 2754 info@cetlink.net
803 Global Vision, Inc.   803 241 0901 info@globalvision.net
803 Hargray Telephone Company   803 686 5000 info@hargray.com
803 InteliNet   803 279 9775 administrator@intelinet.net
803 Interpath   800 849 6305 info@interpath.net
803 SIMS, Inc.   803 762 4956 info@sims.net
803 South Carolina SuperNet, Inc.   803 212 4400 info@scsn.net
803 SunBelt.Net   803 328 1500 info@sunbelt.net
803 Teleplex Communications, Inc.   803 585 PLEX info@teleplex.net

804 Widomaker Communication Service   804 253 7621 bloyall@widowmaker.com

805 The Catalina BBS InterNet Services fax->   805 687 1185 help@catalina.org
805 The Central Connection   818 735 3000 info@centcon.com
805 Cogent Software, Inc.   818 585 2788 info@cogsoft.com
805 Delta Internet Services   714 778 0370 info@deltanet.com
805 Fishnet Internet Services, Inc.   805 650 1844 info@fishnet.net
805 Instant Internet Corp. (InstaNet)   818 772 0097 charlyg@instanet.com
805 Internet Access of Ventura County   805 383 3500 info@vcnet.com
805 KAIWAN Internet   714 638 2139 info@kaiwan.com

805 KTB Internet Online   818 240 6600 info@ktb.net
805 Lancaster Internet (California)   805 943 2112 dennis@gargamel.ptw.com
805 Liberty Information Network   800 218 5157 info@liberty.com
805 The Loop Internet Switch Co.   213 465 1311 info@loop.com
805 Netport Internet Access   805 538 2860 info@netport.com
805 Network Intensive   714 450 8400 info@ni.net
805 OutWest Network Services   818 545 1996 OWInfo@outwest.com
805 Quantum Networking Solutions, Inc.   805 538 2028 info@qnet.com
805 Regional Alliance for Info Networking   805 967 7246 info@rain.org
805 Saigon Enterprises   818 246 0689 info@saigon.net
805 Silicon Beach Communications   805 730 7740 help@silcom.com
805 Tehachapi Mountain Internet   805 822 7803 info@tminet.com
805 ValleyNet Communications   209 486 8638 info@valleynet.com
805 WestNet Communications, Inc.   805 892 2133 info@west.net

806 HubNet   806 792 4482 info@HUB.ofthe.NET
806 OnRamp Technologies, Inc.   214 746 4710 info@onramp.net

807 Pronet Internet Services   807 622 5915 info@mail.procom.net

808 FlexNet, Inc.   808 732 8849 info@aloha.com
808 Hawaii OnLine   808 533 6981 support@aloha.net
808 Inter-Pacific Network Services   808 935 5550 sales@interpac.net
808 LavaNet, Inc.   808 545 5282 info@lava.net
808 Pacific Information Exchange, Inc.   808 596 7494 info@pixi.com

810 Branch Information Services   313 741 4442 branch-info@branch.com
810 Freeway, Inc. (tm)   616 347 2400 info@freeway.net
810 Great Lakes Information Systems   810 786 0454 info@glis.net
810 ICNET / Innovative Concepts   313 998 0090 info@ic.net
810 The Internet Ramp   800 502 0620 newaccts@tir.com
810 Michigan Internet Cooperative Association   810 355 1438 info@coop.mica.net
810 Mich.com, Inc.   810 478 4300 info@mich.com
810 Msen, Inc.   313 998 4562 info@msen.com
810 RustNet, Inc.   810 650 6812 info@rust.net
810 Voyager Information Networks, Inc.   517 485 9068 help@voyager.net

812 accessU.S., Inc.   800 638 6373 info@accessus.net

812 HolliCom Internet Services	317 883 4500 cale@holli.com
812 IgLou Internet Services	800 436 4456 info@iglou.com
812 World Connection Services	812 479 1700 info@evansville.net
813 Bay-A-Net	813 988 7772 info@bayanet.com
813 Centurion Technology, Inc.	813 538 1919 info@tpa.cent.com
813 CFTnet	813 980 1317 sales@cftnet.com
813 CocoNet Corp.	813 945 0055 info@coconet.com
813 CyberGate, Inc.	305 428 4283 sales@gate.net
813 Florida Online	407 635 8888 info@digital.net
813 Intelligence Network Online, Inc. x22 ->	813 442 0114 info@intnet.net
813 PacketWorks, Inc.	813 446 8826 info@packet.net
813 Shadow Information Services, Inc.	305 594 2450 admin@shadow.net
813 The ThoughtPort Authority, Inc.	800 ISP 6870 info@thoughtport.com
813 WebIMAGE, an internet presence provider	407 723 0001 info@webimage.com
814 North Coast Internet	814 838 6386 info@ncinter.net
814 Penncom Internet Co.	814 723 4141 admin@penn.com
814 PenNet	717 368 1577 safrye@pennet.net
815 American Information Systems, Inc.	708 413 8400 info@ais.net
815 BOSSNet Internet Services	608 362 1340 mbusam@bossnt.com
815 CIN.net Computerese Information Network	708 310 1188 info@cin.net
815 InterAccess Co.	708 498 2542 info@interaccess.com
815 The Software Farm	815 246 7295 info@softfarm.com
815 T.B.C. Online Data-Net	815 758 5040 info@tbcnet.com
815 Wink Communications Group, Inc.	708 310 9465 sales@winkcomm.com
816 fyi@unicom.net	913 383 8466 fyi@unicom.net
816 Interstate Networking Corp.	816 472 4949 staff@interstate.net
816 Primenet	602 870 1010 info@primenet.com
817 Association for Computing Machinery	817 776 6876 account-info@acm.org
817 CompuTek	214 994 0190 info@computek.net
817 Connection Technologies - ConnectNet	214 490 7100 sales@connect.net
817 Delta Design and Development Inc.	800 763 8265 sales@deltaweb.com
817 DFW Internet Services, Inc.	817 332 5116 info@dfw.net
817 OnRamp Technologies, Inc.	214 746 4710 info@onramp.net

817	Texas Metronet, Inc.	214 705 2900 info@metronet.com
818	ArtNetwork	800 395 0692 info@artnet.net
818	BeachNet Internet Access	310 823 3308 info@beachnet.com
818	The Central Connection	818 735 3000 info@centcon.com
818	Cogent Software, Inc.	818 585 2788 info@cogsoft.com
818	CruzNet	714 680 6600 info@cruznet.net
818	Cyberg8t Internet Services	909 398 4638 sales@cyberg8t.com
818	Cyberverse Online	310 643 3783 info@cyberverse.com
818	Delta Internet Services	714 778 0370 info@deltanet.com
818	DigiLink Network Services	310 542 7421 info@digilink.net
818	Exodus Communications, Inc.	408 522 8450 info@exodus.net
818	Flamingo Communications, Inc.	310 532 3533 sales@fcom.com
818	Instant Internet Corp. (InstaNet)	818 772 0097 charlyg@instanet.com
818	InterNex Tiara	408 496 5466 info@internex.net
818	InterWorld Communications, Inc.	310 726 0500 sales@interworld.net
818	KAIWAN Internet	714 638 2139 info@kaiwan.com
818	KTB Internet Online	818 240 6600 info@ktb.net
818	Leonardo Internet	310 395 5500 jimp@leonardo.net
818	Liberty Information Network	800 218 5157 info@liberty.com
818	Lightside, Inc.	818 858 9261 Lightside@Lightside.Com
818	The Loop Internet Switch Co.	213 465 1311 info@loop.com
818	Network Intensive	714 450 8400 info@ni.net
818	Online-LA	310 967 8000 sales@online-la.com
818	OutWest Network Services	818 545 1996 info@outwest.net
818	Primenet	602 870 1010 info@primenet.com
818	QuickCom Internet Communcations	213 634 7735 info@quickcom.net
818	Regional Alliance for Info Networking	805 967 7246 info@rain.org
818	Saigon Enterprises	818 246 0689 info@saigon.net
818	ViaNet Communications	415 903 2242 info@via.net
819	Information Gateway Services (Ottawa)	613 592 5619 info@igs.net
819	Interactive Telecom, Inc.	613 727 5258 info@intertel.net
819	Magma Communications, Ltd.	613 228 3565 info@magmacom.com
819	o://info.web	613 225 3354 kevin@magi.com
860	Connix: Connecticut Internet Exchange	860 349 7059 office@connix.com
860	imagine.com	860 527 9245 Postmaster@imagine.com

860 MCIX, Inc.   860 572 8720 info@mcix.com
860 Mindport Internet Services, Inc.   860 892 2081 staff@mindport.net
860 Paradigm Communications, Inc.   203 250 7397 info@pcnet.com

864 Global Vision, Inc.   803 241 0901 info@globalvision.net

901 accessU.S., Inc.   800 638 6373 info@accessus.net
901 A2ZNET   901 854 1871 webmaster@a2znet.com
901 ISDN-Net, Inc.   615 377 7672 jdunlap@rex.isdn.net
901 Magibox, Inc.   901 757 7835 info@magibox.net
901 U.S. Internet   615 522 6788 info@usit.net

902 Cycor Communications, Inc.   902 892 7354 signup@cycor.ca

903 Cloverleaf Technologies   903 832 1367 helpdesk@clover.cleaf.com
903 Delta Design and Development, Inc.   800 763 8265 sales@deltaweb.com
903 Phoenix DataNet, Inc.   713 486 8337 info@phoenix.net
903 Rapid Ramp, Inc.   903 759 0705 help@rapidramp.com
903 StarNet Online Systems   903 785 5533 lrhea@stargate.1starnet.com

904 CyberGate, Inc.   305 428 4283 sales@gate.net
904 Florida Online   407 635 8888 info@digital.net
904 Gulf Coast Internet Company   904 438 5700 info@gulf.net
904 Internet Connect Company   904 375 2912 info@atlantic.net
904 Jax Gateway to the World   904 730 7692 sales@gttw.com
904 MagicNet, Inc.   407 657 2202 info@magicnet.net
904 Polaris Network, Inc.   904 878 9745 staff@polaris.net
904 PSS InterNet Services   800 463 8499 support@america.com
904 SymNet   904 385 1061 info@symnet.net
904 WebIMAGE, an internet presence provider   407 723 0001 info@webimage.com

905 ComputerLink/Internet Direct   416 233 7150 info@idirect.com
905 Cycor Communications Inc.   902 892 7354 signup@cycor.ca
905 eagle.ca - Northumbria Associates   905 373 9313 info@eagle.ca
905 HookUp Communications   905 847 8000 info@hookup.net
905 iCOM Internet Services   905 522 1220 sales@icom.ca
905 InterLog Internet Services   416 975 2655 internet@interlog.com
905 Internet Access Worldwide   905 714 1400 info@iaw.on.ca

905 Internet Connect Niagara, Inc.   905 988 9909 info@niagara.com
905 Internex Online, Inc.   416 363 8676 support@io.org
905 Magic Online Services International, Inc.   416 591 6490 info@magic.ca
905 Neptune Internet Services   905 895 0898 info@neptune.on.ca
905 Network Enterprise Technology, Inc.   905 525 4555 info@netinc.ca
905 Times.net   905 775 4471 rfonger@times.net
905 Vaxxine Computer Systems, Inc.   905 562 3500 admin@vaxxine.com

906 Branch Information Services   313 741 4442 branch-info@branch.com
906 Mich.com, Inc.   810 478 4300 info@mich.com
906 Msen, Inc.   313 998 4562 info@msen.com
906 The Portage at Micro + Computers   906 487 9832 admin@mail.portup.com

907 Alaska Information Technology   907 258 1881 info@anc.ak.net
907 Internet Alaska   907 562 4638 info@alaska.net
907 Micronet Communications   907 333 8663 info@micronet.net
907 NorthWestNet   206 562 3000 info@nwnet.net

908 BLASTNET Internet Service   908 534 5881 mcp@blast.net
908 Castle Network, Inc.   908 548 8881 request@castle.net
908 CyberComm Online Services   908 506 6651 info@cybercomm.net
908 Crystal Palace Networking, Inc.   201 300 0881 info@crystal.palace.net
908 Digital Express Group   301 847 5000 info@digex.net
908 Eclipse Internet Access   800 483 1223 info@eclipse.net
908 I-2000, Inc.   800 464 3820 info@i-2000.com
908 INTAC Access Corp.   800 504 6822 info@intac.com
908 Intercall, Inc.   800 758 7329 sales@intercall.com
908 Internet For 'U'   800 NET WAY1 info@ifu.net
908 Internet Online Services   x226 -> 201 928 1000 help@ios.com
908 Lightning Internet Services, LLC   516 248 8400 sales@lightning.net
908 Openix - Open Internet Exchange   201 443 0400 info@openix.com
908 Planet Access Networks   201 691 4704 info@planet.net
908 TechnoCore Communications, Inc.   908 928 7400 info@thecore.com
908 Texel International   908 297 0290 info@texel.com
908 You Tools Corp. / FASTNET   610 954 5910 info@fast.net

909 Cogent Software, Inc.   818 585 2788 info@cogsoft.com
909 CONNECTnet Internet Network Services   619 450 0254 info@connectnet.com

909	CruzNet	714 680 6600 info@cruznet.net
909	Cyberg8t Internet Services	909 398 4638 sales@cyberg8t.com
909	DiscoverNet	909 335 1209 info@discover.net
909	DPC Systems Beach.Net	714 443 4172 connect@beach.net
909	Delta Internet Services	714 778 0370 info@deltanet.com
909	EmpireNet	909 787 4969 support@empirenet.com
909	InterWorld Communications, Inc.	310 726 0500 sales@interworld.net
909	KAIWAN Internet	714 638 2139 info@kaiwan.com
909	Keyway Internet Access	909 933 3650 sales@keyway.net
909	Liberty Information Network	800 218 5157 info@liberty.com
909	Lightside, Inc.	818 858 9261 Lightside@Lightside.Com
909	Network Intensive	714 450 8400 info@ni.net
909	Primenet	602 870 1010 info@primenet.com
909	Saigon Enterprises	818 246 0689 info@saigon.net
910	Interpath	800 849 6305 info@interpath.net
910	NetDepot, Inc.	770 434 5595 info@netdepot.com
910	Netpath, Inc.	910 226 0425 info@netpath.net
910	Red Barn Data Center	910 750 9809 tom@rbdc.rbdc.com
910	SpyderByte Communications	910 643 6999 info@spyder.net
910	Vnet Internet Access	704 334 3282 info@vnet.net
912	Hargray Telephone Company	803 686 5000 info@hargray.com
912	Homenet Communications, Inc.	912 329 8638 info@hom.net
912	Internet Atlanta	404 410 9000 info@atlanta.com
912	MindSpring Enterprises, Inc.	800 719 4332 info@mindspring.com
913	Flint Hills Computers, Inc.	913 776 4333 gil@flinthills.com
913	fyi@unicom.net	913 383 8466 fyi@unicom.net
913	Interstate Networking Corp.	816 472 4949 staff@interstate.net
913	Tri-Rivers Internet	913 826 2595 staff@tri.net
914	bway.net / Outernet, Inc.	212 982 9800 info@bway.net
914	Cloud 9 Internet	914 682 0626 info@cloud9.net
914	Computer Net	914 773 1130 paul@computer.net
914	Creative Data Consultants (SILLY.COM)	718 229 0489 info@silly.com
914	epix	800 374 9669 karndt@epix.net
914	GBN InternetAccess	201 343 6427 gbninfo@gbn.net

914 ICU On-Line   914 627 3800 info@icu.com
914 INTAC Access Corp.   800 504 6822 info@intac.com
914 I-2000, Inc.   800 464 3820 info@i-2000.com
914 InteleCom Data Systems, Inc.   401 885 6855 info@ids.net
914 Lightning Internet Services, LLC   516 248 8400 sales@lightning.net
914 Long Island Internet HeadQuarters   516 439 7800 support@pb.net
914 MHVNet (Computer Solutions by Hawkinson)   914 473 0844 info@mhv.net
914 Mnematics, Inc.   914 359 4546 service@mne.com
914 New World Data   718 962 1725 dmk@nwdc.com
914 NYSERNet   800 493 4367 sales@nysernet.org
914 Panix (Public Access uNIX)   212 741 4400 info@panix.com
914 Pipeline New York   212 267 3636 info@pipeline.com
914 TZ-Link Internet   914 353 5443 info@j51.com
914 WestNet Internet Services   914 967 7816 info@westnet.com
914 ZONE One Network Exchange   212 824 4000 info@zone.net

915 Delta Design and Development, Inc.   800 763 8265 sales@deltaweb.com
915 New Mexico Technet, Inc.   505 345 6555 granoff@technet.nm.org
915 Primenet   602 870 1010 info@primenet.com
915 TexNet Internet Services   915 857 1800 jcoving@tnis.net
915 WhiteHorse Communications ,Inc.   915 584 6630 whc.net.html

916 CASTLES Information Network   707 422 7311 info@castles.com
916 Connectus, Inc.   702 323 2008 info@connectus.com
916 Great Basin Internet Services   702 829 2244 info@greatbasin.com
916 mother.com   916 757 8070 info@mail.mother.com
916 InterStar Network Services   916 224 6866 gfrank@shasta.com
916 ORONET   916 477 6650 info@oro.net
916 NetLink Data-Communications, Inc.   916 447 3025 info@netlink.net
916 Psyberware Internet Access   916 645 9451 info@psyber.com
916 R C Concepts Foothill-Net   916 367 3818 sales@foothill.net
916 Sacramento Network Access   916 565 4500 info@sna.com
916 Sierra-Net   702 831 3353 giles@sierra.net
916 SnowCrest Computer Specialties   916 926 2526 root@snowcrest.net
916 Sutter Yuba Internet Exchange   916 755 1751 dave@syix.com
916 TTCI.net   916 895 1609 info@ttci.net
916 VFR, Inc.   916 652 7237 vfr@vfr.net
916 West Coast Online   707 586 3060 info@calon.com

916 Zocalo Engineering	510 540 8000 info@zocalo.net
917 ZONE One Network Exchange	212 824 4000 info@zone.net
918 Galaxy Star Systems	918 835 3655 info@galstar.com
918 Internet Oklahoma	918 583 1161 info@ionet.net
918 South Coast Computing Services, Inc.	713 917 5000 info@houston.net
919 Interpath	800 849 6305 info@interpath.net
919 MCS Internet Services	919 751 5777 shultz@mail.gld.com
919 Vnet Internet Access	704 334 3282 info@vnet.net
941 Centurion Technology, Inc.	813 538 1919 info@tpa.cent.com
941 Net Sarasota	941 371 1966 info@netsrq.com
941 PacketWorks, Inc.	813 446 8826 info@packet.net
941 USA Computers	941 939 5630 info@usacomputers.net
954 Acquired Knowledge Systems, Inc.	305 525 2574 info@aksi.net
954 ICANECT	305 621 9200 sales@icanect.net
954 Shadow Information Services, Inc.	305 594 2450 admin@shadow.net
954 Zimmerman Communications	954 584 0199 bob@zim.com
970 EZLink Internet Access	970 482 0807 ezadmin@ezlink.com
970 Frontier Internet, Inc.	970 385 4177 info@frontier.net
970 Rocky Mountain Internet	800 900 7644 info@rmii.com
970 Verinet Communications, Inc.	970 416 9152 info@verinet.com

FOREIGN

A listing of Internet service providers in countries other than the U.S. and Canada, sorted by country. Fields are country, service provider name, voice phone number, and e-mail address for more information.

Antigua/Barbuda Cable & Wireless (WI) Ltd.   +1 809 462 0840 scholla@candw.ag

Australia AusNet Services Pty., Ltd. +61 2 241 5888 sales@world.net
Australia Byron Public Access +61 18 823 541 admin@byron.apana.org.au
Australia Corporate Internet Pty., Ltd . +61 2 391 3489 admin@corpnet.com.au
Australia DIALix Services +61 2 948 6995 justin@sydney.dialix.oz.au
Australia Global Data Access +61 9 421 1222 info@ednet.com.au
Australia Highway 1 +61 9 370 4584 info@highway1.com.au
Australia Hilink Communications Pty. +61 3 9528 2018 info@hilink.com.au
Australia Hunter Network Association +61 49 621783 mbrown@hna.com.au
Australia iiNet Technologies +61 9 3071183iinet@iinet.com.au
Australia Kralizec Dialup Unix System +61 2 837 1397 nick@kralizec.zeta.org.au
Australia Informed Technology +61 9 245 2279 info@it.com.au
Australia The Message eXchange Pty., Ltd. +61 2 550 5014 info@tmx.com.au
Australia Microplex Pty., Ltd. +61 2 888 3685 info@mpx.com.au
Australia Pegasus Networks Pty., Ltd. +61 7 257 1111 fwhitmee@peg.apc.org
Australia PPIT Pty., Ltd. (059 051 320) +61 3 747 9823 info@ppit.com.au
Australia Stour System Services +61 9 571 1949 stour@stour.net.au
AustraliaWinthrop Technology +61 9 380 3564 wthelp@yarrow.wt.uwa.edu.au
Australia Zip Australia Pty., Ltd. +61 2 482 7015 info@zip.com.au

Austria ARGE DATEN +43 1 4897893info@email.ad.or.at
Austria EUnet EDV +43 1 3174969info@austria.eu.net
Austria Hochschuelerschaft... +43 1 586 1868 sysop@link-atu.comlink.apc.org
Austria Net4You +43 4242 257367 office@net4you.co.at
Austria netwing +43 5337 65315 info@netwing.at
Austria PING EDV +43 1 3194336info@ping.at
Austria simon media +43 316 813 8240 info@sime.com
Austria Vianet Austria, Ltd. +43 1 5892920info@via.at

Bashkiria UD JV 'DiasPro' +7 3472 387454 iskander@diaspro.bashkiria.su

Belarus Open Contact, Ltd. +7 017 2206134 admin@brc.minsk.by

Belgium EUnet Belgium NV +32 16 236099info@belgium.eu.net
Belgium Infoboard Telematics +32 2 475 22 99 info@infoboard.be
Belgium INnet NV/SA +32 14 319937info@inbe.net
Belgium KnoopPunt VZW +32 9 2333 686 support@knooppunt.be
Belgium Netropolis Belgium +32 2 6493693info@netropolis.be

Bulgaria EUnet Bulgaria   +359 52 259135 info@bulgaria.eu.net

Denmark DKnet / EUnet Denmark   +45 3917 9900info@dknet.dk

Finland Clinet, Ltd.   +358 0 437 5209 clinet@clinet.fi
Finland EUnet Finland, Ltd.   +358 0 400 2060 helpdesk@eunet.fi

France CalvaCom   +33 1 3463 1919 fb101@calvacom.fr
France French Data Network   +33 1 4797 5873 info@fdn.org
France Internet Way   +33 1 4143 2110 info@iway.fr
France OLEANE   +33 1 4328 3232 info-internet@oleane.net
France REMCOMP SARL   +33 1 4479 0642 info@liber.net

Georgia Mimosi Hard   +7 8832 232857 kisho@sanet.ge

Germany bbTT Electronic Networks   +49 30 817 42 06 willem@b-2.de.contrib.net
Germany ccn computer consultant net   +49 89 29164023 info@ccn.de
Germany EUnet Germany GmbH   +49 231 972 2222 info@germany.eu.net
Germany ILK INternet GmbH   +49 721 9100 0 info@ilk.de
Germany Individual Network e.V.   +49 441 980 8556 in-info@individual.net
Germany INS Inter Networking Systems   +49 2305 356505 info@ins.net
Germany Internet PoP Frankfurt   +49 69 94439192 joerg@pop-frankfurt.com
Germany ISC Dr.-Ing. Nepustil   +49 7123 93102 1 Info@Nepustil.NET
Germany Knipp Medien & Kommunikation   +49 231 9703 0 info@knipp.de
Germany Lemke & Fuerst GbR   +49 711 7189847 info@lf.net
Germany LyNet Kommunikation   +49 451 6101056 info@lynet.de
Germany MUC.DE e.V.   +49 89 324 683 0 postmaster@muc.de
Germany Onlineservice Nuernberg   +49 911 9933882 info@osn.de
Germany PFM News & Mail Xlink POP   +49 171 331 0862 info@pfm.pfm-mainz.de
Germany Point of Presence GmbH   +49 40 2519 2025 info@pop.de
Germany POP Contrib.Net Netzdienste   +49 521 9683011 info@teuto.de
Germany SpaceNet GmbH   +49 89 324 683 0 info@space.net
Germany TouchNET GmbH   +49 89 5447 1111 info@touch.net
Germany Westend GbR   +49 241 911879 info@westend.com

Ghana Chonia Informatica   +233 21 66 94 20 info@ghana.net

Greece Ariadne   +30 1 651 3392 dialup@leon.nrcps.ariadne-t.gr

Greece Foundation of Research	+30 81 221171 forthnet-pr@forthnet.gr
Greece Hellenic Informatics	+30 1 620 3040 info@hol.gr
Hong Kong Asia On-Line Limited	+852 2866 6018 info@asiaonline.net
Hong Kong Asia Pacific CompuNet, Ltd.	+852 2976 9995 info@ap.net.hk
Hong Kong Hong Kong SuperNet	+852 358 7924 trouble@hk.super.net
Hungary iSYS Hungary	+36 1 266 6090 info@isys.hu
Iceland SURIS / ISnet	+354 1 694747 isnet-info@isnet.is
Ireland Cork Internet Services	+353 21 277124 info@cis.ie
Ireland Ieunet Limited	+353 1 679 0832 info@ieunet.ie
Ireland Ireland On-Line	+353 91 592727 info@iol.ie
Israel ACTCOM	+972 4 676115 office@actcom.co.il
Israel Elronet	+972 313534 info@elron.net
Israel NetMedia, Ltd.	+972 2 795 861 info@netmedia.co.il
Israel NetVision, Ltd.	+972 550330 info@netvision.net.il
Italy Abacom s.a.s.	+39 434 660911 info@system.abacom.it
Italy I.NET S.p.A.	+39 2 26162258 info@inet.it
Italy ITnet S.p.A.	+39 10 6563324 info@it.net
Italy Spin	+39 40 8992 286 info@spin.it
Italy Tex.NET TELECOMUNICAZIONI	+39 574 35038 texnet@texnet.it
Italy Video On Line	+39 70 659 625 info@vol.it
Jamaica Jamaica Online Information	+1 809 960 8209 info@jol.com.jm
Japan Asahi Net	+81 3 3666 2811 info@asahi-net.or.jp
Japan Global OnLine	+81 3 5330 9380 info@gol.org
Japan HA Telecom Corp.	+81 58 253 7641 info@hatelecom.or.jp
Japan Internet Initiative Japan	+81 3 3580 3781 info@iij.ad.jp
Japan M.R.T., Inc.	+81 3 3255 8880 sysop@janis-tok.com
Japan TWICS	+81 3 3351 5977 info@twics.com
Japan Typhoon, Inc.	+81 3 3757 2118 info@typhoon.co.jp
Kazakhstan Bogas Soft Laboratory Co.	+7 322 262 4990 pasha@sl.semsk.su

Kuwait Gulfnet Kuwait	+965 242 6728 info@kw.us.com
Latvia LvNet-Teleport	+371 2 551133 vit@riga.lv
Latvia Versia, Ltd.	+371 2 417000 postmaster@vernet.lv
Lisboa Esoterica	716 2395 info@esoterica.com
Luxemburg EUnet Luxemburg	+352 47 02 61 361 info@luxemburg.eu.net
Mexico Datanet S.A. de C.V.	+52 5 1075400 info@data.net.mx
Mexico Internet de Mexico S.A.	+52 5 3602931 info@mail.internet.com.mx
Netherlands The Delft Connection	+31 15560079 info@void.tdcnet.nl
Netherlands Hobbynet	+31 365361683 henk@hgatenl.hobby.nl
Netherlands Holland Online	+31 71 40 16943 Sales@hol.nl
Netherlands Internet Access Foundation	+31 5982 2720 mail-server@iafnl.iaf.nl
Netherlands NEST	+31 206265566 info@nest.nl
Netherlands NetLand	+31 206943664 info@netland.nl
Netherlands NLnet (EUnet)	+31 206639366 info@nl.net
Netherlands Psyline	+31 80445801 postmaster@psyline.nl
Netherlands Simplex Networking	+31 206932433 skelmir@simplex.nl
Netherlands Stichting XS4ALL	+31 206225222 helpdesk@xs4all.nl
New Zealand Actrix Networks Limited	+64 4 389 6356 john@actrix.gen.nz
New Zealand Efficient Software Limited	+64 3 4738274 bart@dunedin.es.co.nz
Norway Oslonett A/S	+47 22 46 10 99 oslonett@oslonett.no
Poland ATM	+48 22 6106073 szeloch@ikp.atm.com.pl
Poland PDi Ltd. - Public Internet	+48 42 30 21 94 info@pdi.lodz.pl
Romania EUnet Romania SRL	+40 1 312 6886 info@romania.eu.net
Russia ELCOM	+7 092 223 2208 root@centre.elcom.ru
Russia GlasNet	+7 95 262 7079 support@glas.apc.org
Russia InterCommunications, Ltd.	+7 8632 620562 postmaster@icomm.rnd.su
Russia NEVAlink, Ltd.	+7 812 592 3737 serg@arcom.spb.su
Russia Relcom CO	+7 95 194 25 40 postmaster@ussr.eu.net

Russia SvjazInform	+7 351 265 3600 pol@rich.chel.su
Singapore Singapore Telecom Limited	+65 7308079 admin@singnet.com.sg
Slovakia EUnet Slovakia s.r.o.	+42 7 839 404 info@Slovakia.EU.net
Slovenia NIL, System Integration	+386 61 1405 183 info@slovenia.eu.net
South Africa Aztec	+27 21 419 2690 info@aztec.co.za
South Africa Internet Africa	+27 0800 020003 info@iaccess.za
South Africa The Internet Solution	+27 11 447 5566 info@is.co.za
Spain INTERCOM S.T.A.	+34 3 5802846 info@intercom.es
Spain OFFCAMPUS SL	+34 1 577 3026 infonet@offcampus.es
Spain Servicom	+34 93 580 9396 info@servicom.es
Sri Lanka Information Laboratories	+94 1 61 1061 info@infolabs.is.lk
Sweden NetGuide	+46 31 28 03 73 info@netg.se
Switzerland EUnet AG, Zurich	+41 1 291 45 80 info@eunet.ch
Switzerland EUnet SA, Geneva	+41 22 348 80 45 deffer@eunet.ch
Switzerland Internet ProLink SA	+41 22 788 8555 info@iprolink.ch
Switzerland SWITCH	+41 1 268 1515 postmaster@switch.ch
Tataretan KAMAZ, Inc.	+7 8439 53 03 34 postmaster@kamaz.kazan.su
Ukraine ConCom, Ltd.	+7 0572 27 69 13 igor@ktts.kharkov.ua
Ukraine Crimea Communication Centre	+380 0652 257214 sem@snail.crimea.ua
Ukraine Electronni Visti	+7 44 2713457 info%elvisti.kiev.ua@kiae.su
Ukraine PACO Links Int'l, Ltd.	+7 48 2200057 info@vista.odessa.ua
Ukraine UkrCom-Kherson, Ltd.	+7 5522 64098 postmaster@ukrcom.kherson.ua
United Kingdom Compulink (CIX Ltd)	+44 181 390 8446 cixadmin@cix.compulink.co.uk
United Kingdom CONNECT - PC User Group	+44 181 863 1191 info@ibmpcug.co.uk
United Kingdom Demon Internet Limited	+44 181 371 1000 internet@demon.net
United Kingdom The Direct Connection	+44 81 313 0100 helpdesk@dircon.co.uk
United Kingdom EUnet GB	+44 1227 266466 sales@britain.eu.net

United Kingdom ExNet Systems, Ltd.	+44 81 244 0077 info@exnet.com
United Kingdom Frontier Internet Services	+44 171 242 3383 info@ftech.net
United Kingdom GreenNet	+44 71 713 1941 support@gn.apc.org
United Kingdom Lunatech Research	+44 1734 791900 info@luna.co.uk
United Kingdom Pavilion Internet plc	+44 1273 606072 info@pavilion.co.uk
United Kingdom Planet Online, Ltd.	+44 113 234 5566 info@theplanet.net
United Kingdom Sound & Visions BBS	+44 1932 253131 info@span.com
United Kingdom Utopia! Internet, Ltd.	+44 121 5614621 sales@utopia.co.uk
United Kingdom WinNET (UK)	+44 181 863 1191 info@win-uk.ne
Venezuela Internet Comunicaciones c.a.	+58 2 959 9550 info@ccs.internet.ve

Appendix C—URL List

1-800-MUSIC-NOW
   http://www.1800musicnow.mci.com

1 Mall
   http://www.1mall.com/

1st Shopping Planet
   http://www.shoppingplanet.com/

1 World Plaza
   http://www2.clever.net/1world/plaza/shop.htm

Adobe
   http://www.adobe.com
   http://www.adobe.com/Amber/Index.html
   http://w1000.mv.us.adobe.com/Amber/Index.html
   http://w1000.mv.us.adobe.com/Amber/makepdf.html
   http://w1000.mv.us.adobe.com/Acrobat/Exch.html

Aereal Serch
   http://www.virtpark.com/theme/cgi-bin/serch.html

Aladdin Systems:
    http://www.aladdinsys.com/ under Shareware/Freeware products

All-In-One Search Site
    http://www.albany.net/allinone/

AlterDial/UUNet
    info@uu.net   www.uu.net   www.alter.net

America Online, Inc.
    info@aol.com
    www.aol.com
    ftp://mirror.aol.com/

American Internet Mall
    http://www.ammall.com/

Apple
    http://www.apple.com/
    QuickTime VR: http://qtvr.quicktime.apple.com/
    QuickTime Player: http://quicktime.apple.com/

Beyond our Borders
    http://www.freenet.hamilton.on.ca/Beyond.html

Canadian Free-Nets
    http://www.synapse.net/~radio/freenet.htm

CBS Eye on the Net
    http://www.cbs.com/

Center for Disease Control, Morbidity and Mortality Weekly Report
    http://www.cdc.gov/epo/mmwr/mmwr_wk.html

Chaco
    VR Scout VRML: http://www.chaco.com
    VR Scout plugin: http://www.chaco.com/vrscout/
    Jack O' Lantern: http://www.chaco.com/~glenn/jack/

Cheap & Easy
    http://www.cheapandeasy.com

City.Net
    http://www.city.net

C l Net Radio
    http://www.cnet.com
    http://www.cnet.com/Content/Radio/index.html
    http://www.shareware.com/

C l Net Vendor Rolodex
    http://www.cnet.com/Resources/Info/Vendor/index.html

Cleveland Free-Net Telnet
    freenet-in-a.cwru.edu
    freenet-in-b.cwru.edu
    freenet-in-c.cwru.edu

CMP Tech Web
    http://techweb.cmp.com/

Community Network guide
    http://http2.sils.umich.edu/~ckummer/community.html

Compaq Computer Corp.
    http://www.compaq.com/

CompuServe Information Service
    70006.101@ compuserve.com
    www.compuserve.com

Connectix QuickCam
    http://www.connectix.com/

ConnectSoft
    http://www.connectsoft.com/
    ftp.connectsoft.com in the directory /pub/emc25/.nd Windows 95

Cool Site of the Day
    http://www.infi.net/cool.html

CUSeeMe
    http://cu-seeme.cornell.edu/

Cyberian Outpost
http://cybout. com

Dallas Market Center
http://www.the-center.com/

David Singer's OS/2 Page of Pointers
http://index.almaden.ibm.com/

Dell Computer Corp.
http://www.us.dell.com

Dial-A-Book
http://dab.psi.net/DialABook/

Digital Equipment Corp.
http://www.digital.com/

DreamShop
http://www.dreamshop.com

Epicurious
http://www.epicurious.com/

ESPN
http://espnet.sportszone.com/index.text.html

Excite!
http://www.excite.com

Firehorse
http://www.peg.apc.org/~firehorse/welcome.html

Forte FreeAgent
http://www.forteinc.com/forte/
FTP at papa.indstate.edu in the directory /winsock-l/news/

FREEnet INF-0001 General Information
http://www.free.net/FREEnet/INF/INF-0001.en.html

FreeNet Newsflash
http://www.freenet.vancouver.bc.ca/vrfa/newsflash/

Front Page, The
   http://www.thefrontpage.com/

Galaxy
   http://galaxy.tradewave.com

Georgia Tech Research Corporation
   http://www.cc.gatech.edu/gvu/user_surveys/User_Survey_Home.html

GNN
   http://gnn.com

Hewlett-Packard Co.
   http://www.hp.com

Hot Wired
   http://www.hotwired.com

IBM Corp.
   http://www.ibm.com

IBM Personal Software Co.
   http://www.austin.ibm.com/pspinfo/

InfoSeek
   http://www.infoseek.com/

Integrated Data Systems VRealm plugin
   http://www.ids-net.com/

Intel Corp.
   http://www.intel.com

InterArt
   http://www.interart.net/

Internal Revenue Service
   http:// www.irs.ustreas.gov/prod/cover.html
   http://www.irs.ustreas.gov/

Internet Mailing Lists Guides and Resources
   http://www.nlc-bnc.ca/ifla/I/training/listserv/lists.htm

Internet Service Providers worldwide
>   http://www.celestin.com/pocia/index.html
>   http://thelist.com

Internet Telephony Page, The
>   http://rpcp.mit.edu/~asears/main.html
>   http://www.northcoast.com/savetz/voice-faq.html

Internet Underground Music Archive
>   http://www.iuma.com

InterRamp/PSI
>   interramp-info@psi.com
>   www.psi.net

Liszt
>   http://www.liszt.com/

Live3D plugin
>   http://home.netscape.com/comprod/products/navigator/live3d/index.html

Lotus Development Corp.
>   http://www.lotus.com

Lycos
>   http://www.lycos.com

Macromedia
>   http://www.macromedia.com

Macromedia Director
>   http://www.macromedia.com/Tools/Shockwave/sdc/Plugin/index.htm

Macromedia Shockwave
>   http://www.macromedia.com/Tools/Shockwave/sdc/Plugin/index.htm

MakeMusic.com
>   http://www.makemusic.com

McAffee
>   http://www. mcafee.com/

Michigan PC Archives
http://www.umich.edu/~archive/msdos/

Microsoft Corp.
http://www.microsoft.com

Microsoft Internet Explorer
http://www.microsoft.com/windows/ie/iexplorer.htm
http://www. microsoft.com/windows/ie/ieinfo.htm
ftp.microsoft.com in directory /Softlib/MSLFILES/

mIRC Web
http://sunsite.nijenrode.nl/software/mirc/index.html
ftp://ftp.demon.co.uk/pub/ibmpc/win3/winsock/apps/mirc/mirc392.zip

MIT FAQ FTP archive
ftp://rtfm.mit.edu/pub/usenet/news.answers/

MTV, Music Television
http://www.mtv.com/

National Public Telecomputing Network (NPTN)s
http://www.nptn.org/

NCSA Mosaic
http://www.ncsa.uiuc.edu/SDG/Software/WinMosaic/HomePage.html
ftp.ncsa.uiuc.edu in the directory /Mosaic/Windows/ Win95/
http://www.ncsa.uiuc.edu /SDG/Software/WinMosaic/Features.htm
http://www.nptn.org/

NEC Corp.
http://www.nec.com

NetCom Internet Services
info@netcom.com
www.netcom.com

Netcom On-Line Communication Services
http://www.netcom.com

NetManatge
http://www.netmanage.com

Net.Radio
http://www.netradio.net

Netscape Comunications Corp.
http://home.netscape.com
http://www.netscape.com

Netscape plug-in page
http://home.netscape.com/comprod/products/navigator/version_2.0/
plugins/index.html

Netscape Web browser
http://home.netscape. com/comprod/mirror/index. html
ftp.netscape.com

New York Times Fax
http://nytimesfax.com/

Novell, Inc.
http://www.novell.com

OAK Software Depository
http://www.acs.oakland.edu/oak.html

OpenText
http://www.opentext.com

Oracle
http://www.oracle.com/

Oracle PowerBrowser
http://www.oracle.com/PowerBrowser/

O'Reilly & Associates and Trish Information Services
http://www.ora.com/survey/

Oxford's USENET Newsgroup
http://www.lib.ox.ac.uk/internet/news/

Paper, Inc.
http://www.paperinc.com/

Pathfinder
  http://www.pathfinder.com

Performance Systems International Inc.
  http://www.psi.net

Plugins and addons
  http://home.netscape.com/comprod/products/navigator/version_2.0/
          plugins/index.html
  http://www2.netscape.com/assist/helper_apps/windowhelper.html
  http://charlotte.acns.nwu.edu/internet/helper/
  http://wwwhost.cc.utexas.edu/learn/use/helper.html
  http://www.ncsa.uiuc.edu/SDG/Software/WinMosaic/viewers.htm

Power Computing Corporation
  http://www.powercc.com

Prodigy
  freetrial@ prodigy.com
  www.prodigy. com

Publically Accessible Mailing Lists
  http://www.neosoft.com/internet/paml/index.html

Qualcomm
  http://www.qualcomm. com/ ProdTech/quest/
  ftp.qualcomm.com in the directory /Eudora/windows/light/
  http://www.qualcomm.com/ ProdTech /quest/eudora.html
  http://www.qualcomm.com/quest/

Quarterdeck
  http://www.qdeck.com

QuickRes
  http://www.windows.microsoft.com/windows/software/powertoy.htm

RealAudio
  http://www.realaudio.com/
  2.0 Sites: http://www.realaudio.com/products/ra2.0/sites

SBI List
  http//dkeep.com/sbi.htm

Search The List of Lists
   http://catalog.com/vivian/interest-group-search.html

Shockwave Gallery
   http://www.macromedia.com/Tools/Shockwave/Gallery/index.html.
   http://www.shocker.com/shocker/

Shop-The-Net
   http://www.shop-the-net.com/

Silicon Graphics, Inc.
   http://www.sgi.com

Speek Freely Web
   http://www.fourmilab.ch/netfone/windows/speak_freely.html

Spry, Inc.
   http://www.spry.com

Storm Chaser Page
   http://taiga.geog.niu.edu/chaser/chaser.html

Suck
   http://suck.com

Sun Microsystems, Inc.
   http://www.sun.com
   HotJava: http://java.sun.com/
   FTP: java.sun.com in directory /pub
   http://www.gamelan.com/

Symantec's Anti-Virus Research Center
   http://www.symantec.com/avcenter/avcenter.html

Telnet
   http://www.shareware.com or http://vsl.cnet.com

TimesFax
   http://nytimesfax.com/cgi-bin/tmp/login

Todd Rundgren's Freedom Fighters Home Base
   http://www.iglou.com/scm/cgi-bin/todd.pl

UMass-Lowell PC Game Archives
ftp://ftp.ulowell.edu/msdos/Games

USENET
http://www.indirect.com/user/steiners/usenet.html

USENET Graphics FAQs
http://www.cis.ohio-state.edu/hypertext/faq/usenet/graphics/top.html

Usenet Newsgroups Resources
http://scwww.ucs.indiana.edu/NetRsc/usenet.html

UUNET Technologies
http://www.uu.net

Vancouver Regional FreeNet Association
http://freenet.vancouver.bc.ca/vrfa/

Virtual Tourist
http://www.vtourist.com/webmap/

VREAM
http://www.vream.com

VREAM WIRL
http://www.vream.com/3dl1.html

VRML
http://www.vrml.org/

VRML Review
http://www.imaginative.com/Chuck/vrml/

VRML Site of the Week
http://www.virtus.com/modmonth.html

VR Scout
http://www.chaco.com/vrscout/

Washington U. PC Archives
ftp://ftp.wustl.edu/systems/ibmpc

WeatherNet
   http://cirrus.sprl.umich.edu/wxnet/

WebCrawler
   http://www.webcrawler.com

WebFX
   http://www.paperinc.com

WinVN
   http://www.ksc.nasa.gov/software/winvn/winvn.html
   ftp.coast.net in directory /SimTel/win3/winsock for Windows 3.1/3.11
   /SimTel/win95/winsock for Windows 95

WinZip
   http://www.winzip.com/

WIRL Virtual Reality Browser
   http://www.vream.com

Xing Technology Corporation
   http:// www.xingtech.com/

Yahoo!
   http://www.yahoo.com.
   http://www. yahoo.com/Computers_and_Internet/Internet/

ZD Net: http://www.zdnet.com

Ziff-Davis/ZD Net
   http://www.zdnet.com

Appendix D—
Internet BBS's

There are some great Internet BBS's you may want to check out. There are even spots to nab lists of Internet BBS's. Probably the best one is "The Guide to Select BBS's on the Internet. You can find it at http://dkeep.com/sbi.htm. The current listing contains over 400 private Internet accessible BBS systems from around the world, and is the touted as the most complete list of its kind available anywhere.

We're partial to FirstClass BBS's. We've included SoftArc's FirstClass Client software on the CD-ROM that comes with Cheap & Easy. Be sure to check out some of the FirstClass BBS's listed below. There are some good ones. This list—like everything else on the Net—is subject to change. Big time. So bear with it if you can't access some.

Thanks to Dan Broberg for letting us include the list and for posting it regularly on the Net!

Have fun—hanging out on BBSs was how we both got interested in the Net in the first place!

BBS NAME	DOMAIN NAME	IP NUMBER	PORT	LOCATION
AMDA	allinz.uni-linz.ac.at	140.78.5.56	3000	Austria
AMUG (Atlanta)	fc.atlmug.org	none posted	3004	Atlanta, GA
BEST Online	ml.celcorp.com	198.161.97.63	3004	Alberta, Canada
Bitstream	bitstream.mpls.mn.us	204.73.77.17	3004	Minneapolis, MN
BlackBoard	bboard.blackbox.or.at	193.170.155.5	3000	Vienna, Austria
California Lip Service	lips.com	204.31.61.42	3000	CA
Calpark	calpark.crai.it	138.41.202.243	3004	
CyberDen	cyberden.com	204.182.11.180	3000	San Rafael, CA
DesignOnline	fcserver.dol.com	204.95.49.2	3000	Chicago, IL
DigitalNation	dn.csgi.com	204.91.31.64	3004	
Dimensions Online	fc.nilenet.com	204.227.31.4	3000	
E Street Mail	fc.estreet.com	204.30.121.20	3000	Denver, Colorado
Emigre		204.86.239.2	3004	
Eureka	fc.eureka.qc.ca	205.151.56.28		
Faludi Mail		204.182.40.1	3000	
The Familar Spirit	tfs.necronomi.com	198.6.114.252	3000	
Finder BBS of Orlando		132.170.21.101	3000	Orlando, Fl
GameNet		204.254.224.50	3004	
Gay BBSemerald.	route66.net	198.145.80.4	3000	
GNJ Spectrum	gnj.gnj.or.jp	202.243.53.3	3004	Tokyo
Great Lakes Free-Net	fc2.glfn.org	198.108.144.81	3004	
Infinet	shakti.txinfinet.com	204.96.111.157	3000	Austin, TX
LiveWire		204.162.28.80	3004	San Jose, CA
MacChoicel	t4.lasertone.com	204.57.240.4	3000	
MacEAST	fc.maceast.com		3000	New England
MacLairma	clair.computize.com	199.1.198.31	3000	Austin, TX
Magic Online Services	gandalf.magic.mb.ca	204.112.14.6	3000	
MagicVillage	fc.hh.magicvillage.de	194.120.171.64	3004	Hamburg, Germany

Magnet	magnet.at1	93.80.248.21	3000	
Manhattan Online	mhtonline.com	205.160.44.120	3004	
Metnet	stevem.opi.mt.gov	161.7.104.96	3000	
Metronet		204.112.14.6	3000	
Mt. Parnassus	fc.delphic.com	204.30.14.3	3000	
N.E.T.	firstclass.northcoast.com	199.4.102.21	3000	California
NitELiƒE	nite.intermac.com		3004	
NP1.COM	np1.com	204.139.8.2	3000	
nyforestsONLINE		149.119.1.25	3004	Syracuse, NY
OUTline	fc.out.org	206.86.61.123	3000	
Paradigm Online	paradigmonline.or.jp	202.33.54.66	3000	
Paradise	blkbox.com	198.64.53.173	3000	
Productivity Online		198.30.22.11	3000	Cincinnati, Ohio
Rete Civica	ghost.dsi.unimi.it	149.132.120.68	3004	
Skios BBS		194.30.20.5	3004	
SKYlink		194.96.2.67	3000	Vienna, Austria
SoftArc Online		198.133.37.10	3004	Canada
StarNet Online		204.178.185.2	3000	
T»l»Graphique LC	utlglc.upc.qc.ca	204.19.34.22	3004	
Terminus	terminus.interworks-inc.com	204.57.346.11	3000	
TerraX	terrax.spk.wa.us	199.79.239.40	3000	
TogetherNet/TGF Tech		204.97.123.70	3000	
TunaNet	tunanet.com	204.235.81.14	3004	New York, New York
TVO Online	fc.tvo.org	204.41.126.10	3004	
Tyrell BBS	tyrellco.com	199.1.22.171	3000	
UDLA-Puebla (RIA)	ria.pue.udlap.mx	140.148.1.9	3004	Mexico
Ultimate Mac Source	umsedm.afternet.com		3867	Edmonton, Alberta
Versacom	shakti.versa.com	204.96.111.93	3000	
Virtual Valley		204.162.28.81	3004	San Jose, CA
WCA Academy	marathon.wca95.org	193.45.142.40	3000	

Index

A

access provider
    questions to ask, 23
    choosing, 21

addons, 160

Adobe's Acrobat, 162, 240, 242

AfterDial, 56

AltaVista, 62, 177

AlterDial, 13–14

AlterNet, 13–14

Amber, 162, 240–242

America Online (AOL), 2, 6, 8, 14–15, 18
    AOL's browser, 7

American Internet Mall, 210–211

animation, 164

applets, 101, 164, 247, 249

Archie, 6, 156

Austin Free-Net, 189–190

B

BBSs, 19–20, 220

betas and demos, 169–170

bindings, 48, 51

bookmarks, 85–86, 93, 100–102, 105

bottom line, 19

busy signals, 21, 25

C

CBS Eye on the Net, 198

Chameleon, 13–14, 54, 56, 58

chat rooms, 7, 19

cheesy.html, 2

choosing an access provider, 21

City.Net, 192–193

classical, 161, 247

clock rate, 34–35

color depth, 38

color monitor, 38

commercial online service, 5–6, 14, 17, 19–20
    comparison charts for, 14

CompuServe Information Service, 8

computer-related resources, 217–218

About the CD-ROM

The enclosed CD has all the software you'll need to get yourself up and running on the Net! Versions of shareware and freeware applications include:

NETSCAPE NAVIGATOR 2.0 FOR WINDOWS AND WINDOWS 95 (Commercial)
Netscape's famous World Wide Web browser lets you surf the Net! Only available if you subscribe to EarthLink Network TotalAccess. See below.

EUDORA LIGHT BY QUALCOMM (Freeware)
Eudora Light is the freeware version of Eudora Pro—the Net's most popular e-mail client software.

ACROBAT AMBER READER BY ADOBE (Freeware)
The "Amber" version of the Acrobat Reader lets you view, navigate, and print Portable Document Format (PDF) files right in your Navigator window.

ASTOUND WEB PLAYER BY GOLD DISK (Freeware)
The Astound Web Player is a Netscape plug-in that plays dynamic multimedia files created with Gold Disk's Astound or Studio M software.

CARBON COPY/NET BY MICROCOM (Freeware)
Carbon Copy/Net is a Netscape plug-in that lets you remotely control another PC over the Internet.

DWG/DXF PLUG-IN BY SOFTSOURCE (Shareware)
SoftSource's DWG/DXF plug-in for Netscape Navigator 2.0 lets you dynamically view AutoCAD (DWG) and DXF drawings over the Web.

EARTHLINK NETWORK TOTALACCESS (Commercial)
The cornerstone of the CD disc is a full installation of EarthLink Network TotalAccess. If you choose to load this software, you can use EarthLink Network as your Internet provider; if so, it will load Netscape Navigator for you.

ENVOY PLUG-IN BY TUMBLEWEED SOFTWARE (Freeware)
The Envoy plug-in lets users view embedded or entire Envoy documents from within Netscape Navigator.

FIGLEAF INLINE BY CARBERRY TECHNOLOGY/EBT (Freeware)
FIGleaf Inline extends your graphical support for the Netscape 2.0 browser by offering you several more formats including: CGM (first Vector MIME standard), GIF, JPEG, PNG, TIFF, CCITT GP4, BMP, WMF, EPSF, Sun Raster, and RGB.

FORMULA ONE/NET BY VISUAL COMPONENTS (Freeware)
Formula One/NET is an Excel-compatible spreadsheet with built-in Internet functionality that brings the power of spreadsheets to Netscape Navigator 2.0.

FRACTAL VIEWER BY ITERATED SYSTEMS (Freeware)
Fractal Viewer enables the in-line use of fractal images on the Web.

INTERCAP INLINE BY INTERCAP GRAPHICS SYSTEMS (Freeware)
InterCAP's well-known MetaLink RunTime CGM viewer for Netscape gives you in-line viewing, zooming, dynamic panning and magnification, and animation of intelligent, hyperlinked Computer Graphics Metafiles (CGM) vector graphics.

KEYVIEW FOR WINDOWS BY FTP SOFTWARE (Freeware)
Keyview lets you view, print, convert, and manage nearly 200 different file formats from inside Netscape Navigator 2.0.

LIGHTNING STRIKE BY INFINET OP (Freeware)
Lightning Strike is an optimized wavelet image codec plug-in for Netscape 2.0. It provides higher compression ratios, smaller image files, faster transmissions, and improved image quality.

LIVE3D BY NETSCAPE (Freeware)
Live3D is a high-performance 3D VRML platform that lets you fly through VRML worlds on the Web and run interactive, multiuser VRML applications written in Java.

LOOK@ME BY FARALLON (Shareware)
The Look@Me plug-in gives you the ability to view another Look@Me user's screen anywhere in the world in real time from within Netscape Navigator 2.0.

QUICKSILVER BY MICROGRAFX (Freeware)
Micrografx introduces QuickSilver, a software plug-in for Netscape Navigator 2.0 that extends the Micrografx ABC Graphics Suite, allowing users to place, view, and interact with object graphics inside Web pages.

REALAUDIO BY PROGRESSIVE NETWORKS (Freeware)
RealAudio provides live and on-demand real-time audio over 14.4Kbps or faster connections to the Internet.

SHOCKWAVE FOR DIRECTOR BY MACROMEDIA (Freeware)
The Shockwave plug-in lets users interact with Director presentations right in a Netscape Navigator window.

SIZZLER BY TOTALLY HIP (Freeware)
Totally Hip's Sizzler plug-in allows simultaneous viewing and interaction with Web pages while streaming animation is delivered over the Web. Let's you view a Quicktime animation before completely downloading it.

SVF PLUG-IN BY SOFTSOURCE (Shareware)
SoftSource's SVF plug-in for Netscape Navigator 2.0 brings new power to viewing CAD drawings and other complex graphics over the Web.

VR SCOUT VRML PLUG-IN BY CHACO COMMUNICATIONS (Freeware)
Chaco's VR Scout VRML plug-in lets you cruise through 3D graphical scenes.

VREALM BY INTEGRATED DATA SYSTEMS (Shareware)
VRealm, the VRML plug-in for Netscape 2.0 from Integrated Data Systems, fully supports 3D VRML and adds features such as object behaviors, gravity, collision detection, autopilot, and multimedia.

WAVELET IMAGE VIEWER BY SUMMUS (Freeware)
The Wavelet Image viewer plug-in provides superior image quality, compression ratios, and speed. Lets you quickly get to the content of an image without having to wait for all the details.

WIRL VIRTUAL REALITY BROWSER BY VREAM (Freeware)
WIRL is a VRML browser that lets you play virtual slot machines, fly helicopters, see cybergymnasts flip, throw virtual TVs, watch business logos spin, visit exotic islands in cyberspace, and much more.

WORD VIEWER PLUG-IN BY INSO CORPORATION (Freeware)
Word Viewer lets you view any Microsoft Word 6.0 or Microsoft Word 7.0 document from inside Netscape Navigator 2.0.